Primary Language Impact on Second Language and Literacy Learning

Primary Language Impact on Second Language and Literacy Learning

Linguistically Responsive Strategies for Classroom Teachers

Edited by
Bogum Yoon and Kristen L. Pratt

LEXINGTON BOOKS
Lanham • Boulder • New York • London

Published by Lexington Books
An imprint of The Rowman & Littlefield Publishing Group, Inc.
4501 Forbes Boulevard, Suite 200, Lanham, Maryland 20706
www.rowman.com

86-90 Paul Street, London EC2A 4NE

British Library Cataloguing in Publication Information Available

Library of Congress Cataloging-in-Publication Data Available

ISBN: 978-1-66690-711-7 (cloth : alk. paper)
ISBN: 978-1-66690-713-1 (pbk. : alk. paper)
ISBN: 978-1-66690-712-4 (electronic)

♾™ The paper used in this publication meets the minimum requirements of American National Standard for Information Sciences—Permanence of Paper for Printed Library Materials, ANSI/NISO Z39.48-1992.

Contents

Preface

As editors of this book, we started the project with a clear goal: to support educators who seek ideas on how to better serve English language learners (ELLs), those who learn English as their new and additional language, in the classroom. Both of us are in the field of language and literacy education who have worked with pre-service and in-service teachers in teacher education programs for decades. We are thrilled to see the labors of this project coming to fruition and are humbly grateful for the contribution of the chapter authors.

The premise of this book project is grounded in the knowledge that providing equitable learning opportunities to ELLs is the responsibility of all educators. All educators play an important role in meeting the needs of linguistically and culturally diverse groups of students in the United States. Our motivation in creating this book was to address the pressing need to support general education and monolingual teachers/teacher candidates as they prepare to effectively teach and support linguistically diverse students from around the world. We intended to provide linguistically responsive strategies using students' primary languages to support their acquisition of English as a new/additional language. We also offer needed resources for teacher education programs to help teacher candidates build their general linguistic and cross-linguistic knowledge, so they can effectively support ELLs' language and literacy learning. This book focuses on the principled elements of ELLs' 12 home languages including Arabic, Chinese, and Spanish.

The need for this book is evident through educational scholars' continuous calls over decades. For instance, Cochran-Smith (2011) posed a question in her work: "what do teachers really need to know?" (p. 11). In her work later, she (2020) continuously posed a question for educators to consider for justice and equity-based teacher preparation: "What kinds of knowledge are needed to teach well?" (p. 49). In relation to ELLs, Fillmore and Snow (2000) note that "teachers need access to a wide range of information to function well in the classroom" (p. 3) and "need to know more about language" (p. 4). We echo these scholars' sentiments and offer this scholarly and accessible book to address these queries, which can be used in teacher education programs as a course text as well as a resource for professional development workshops.

Specifically, educators will understand the impact of ELLs' primary languages (L1) and culture on learning English (L2) by learning basic elements of L1. Throughout the following chapters, readers will learn basic linguistic and cultural elements of ELLs' L1. These linguistic and cultural elements, which may have been previously unknown, can serve as foundational frameworks from which to build. For example, readers will understand through the Arabic language chapter that Arabic does not have capital letters, so the students from an Arabic language background may not capitalize words in English in written form. Through the chapter on the Bengali language, readers will also learn that Bengali does not have gender specifics, so the students from a Bengali language background might use *he* for *she* and *she* for *he* as pronouns, which may affect students' reading comprehension and writing. Understanding these principled elements of students' L1 is important to better serve ELLs by understanding how ELLs' L1 impacts their learning of English. The chapter authors, whose expertise is in both English and ELLs' particular home languages such as Filipino and Russian, invite general educators to learn the fundamental elements through tangible classroom and students' examples. Considering general educators, they wrote the chapters to be as accessible as possible.

Although the contributing chapter authors have varied foci across each section, they include the following common elements: a brief history of the primary language, principled elements of the first language, concrete examples of L1's impact on L2, and instructional implications for educators. The chapters in the text are not organized in alphabetical order and are written to be read independently according to the educator's needs. For example, when educators have students from Pakistan, reading the chapter on the Urdu language will enable educators to purposefully support their students effectively. Although this book is situated in the United States that consists of diverse language groups of students, it might be useful to educators who are situated in other countries due to the applicable characteristics of the chapters.

As educators read the chapters, they might see our consistent position: critical plural-lingualism. We take the stance that our students should sustain bi- and multilingual abilities and capacities. Although we focus on what challenges ELLs might have while acquiring English as an additional language, we resist positioning English as a hegemonic power. Learning English does not mean that ELLs' primary languages need to be forgotten or ignored. We advocate that educators provide opportunities for ELLs to utilize diverse linguistic repertoires, to continue to develop their L1 as they acquire their L2, and to empower the students during the process of engaging in language and literacy practices. In sum, this collected volume of cross-linguistic strategies that are language-specific within each chapter will serve as an overview of ELLs' L1, their general and typical language transfer patterns of like-language groups, and implications for instruction.

Bogum Yoon and Kristen L. Pratt
Summer, 2022

REFERENCES

Cochran-Smith, M. (2011). Teaching in new times: What do teachers really need to know? *Kappa Delta Pi Record, 47*(1), 11–12.

Cochran-Smith, M. (2020). Teacher education for justice and equity: 40 years of advocacy. *Action in Teacher Education, 42*(1), 49–59.

Fillmore, L. W., & Snow, C. E. (2000). *What teachers need to know about language.* Office of Educational Research and Improvement.

Acknowledgments

This edited book is the result of the collective efforts of the contributing authors. The authors' linguistic expertise as well as their cultural backgrounds contributed to making each chapter authentic with specific student examples and instructional implications. We appreciate that the authors embraced the book's goals and purpose and that they worked with us throughout the revision process. We learned a great deal from the authors and appreciate their collaborative partnership in this work. Their expertise and time are invaluable.

Our gratitude also goes to our publisher, Lexington, who contacted us first, listened to our initial ideas on the topic, and proceeded with the project effectively and efficiently. Lexington's proactive initiative and the professional staffs' continued support made the publication process pleasant. We particularly thank Holly Buchanan, the senior acquisition editor, for her support and professionalism.

We also appreciate Diana Murtaugh, who was an English language arts teacher and currently is a doctoral candidate for an education program, for her comments and edits on the chapters. Her perspectives as a general education teacher helped us to see what our classroom teachers needed and reminded us to keep our focus on meeting their needs. We would also like to thank our treasured friend and colleague Maria Dantas-Whitney for her support in reading early drafts and offering her expert feedback to hone the connection of this work to the greater body of literature. The generosity of her time and expertise is deeply appreciated.

I (Kristen) would like to thank my dear friend and colleague Bogum for taking a chance on this project with me, for her patient mentorship, and for her continued advocacy for equity. Her brilliant mind and commitment to excellence in her work inspire me to do and be better. I would also like to extend humble gratitude and admiration to Kelley and Isaiah for their persistent encouragement, their enduring understanding, and their steadfast commitment to creating space for me to do this work.

Last, but not least, I (Bogum) would like to thank Kristen, my esteemed friend and colleague, who worked with me as co-editor for this book project. She might be the scholar that anyone wishes to collaborate with for their research projects. Kristen's genuine and heartfelt words during the communication with me and the fellow authors are contagious. Her commitment to this book project and insights are greatly appreciated.

Bogum and Kristen

Introduction

Bogum Yoon and Kristen L. Pratt

"I never worked with English language learners (ELLs) before."

"I truly had no idea what it takes to teach these students."

"What would I do if I had a child in my classroom who didn't know the English language? I am not multi-lingual . . . how would I communicate with them in any meaningful way, let alone be able to teach them?"

"I only speak English. I don't know what to do with the students who speak other languages."

"My undergraduate program did not teach me how to work with English language learners."

"Do I need to know all of ELLs' home languages?"

As teacher educators who work with pre- and in-service teachers (e.g., mostly monolingual teachers) in the teacher education program, we often hear their concerns about working with linguistically diverse students. The statements and questions above capture common sentiments we have heard from teachers over the decades (see Yoon, 2021b; Yoon et al., 2015). These teachers' voices reflect the concerns that they might not serve English language learners (ELLs) well because they do not speak the students' languages and have had few opportunities to learn about how to support ELLs' language and literacy learning in their teacher education programs.

The idea for this book started from the following questions to address the needs of educators. What are the ways that we, as teacher educators, can support the needs of current and future teachers in our teacher education programs? How can we provide monolingual teachers with the foundational knowledge of ELLs' first languages (L1) that affect the students' learning in English (L2)? There is a dearth of resource books and materials that teacher educators can utilize to deepen teachers' understanding of ELLs' primary languages as a means to better support their English language instruction in

1

schools. This lack of primary language-centered resource books and materials prompted our motivation to proceed with this collaborative book project so that educators could have readily accessible materials to engage in linguistically responsive instruction for ELLs in their classrooms. This book serves as a resource guide to contribute to the field of teacher education.

To move this initial idea to the next step, we sent out a call to scholars who are multilingual teacher educators to address the key elements of diverse ELLs' first languages. Among the proposals that we received, we included 12 languages out of the 15 most common home languages of ELLs in U.S. schools, including Spanish, Arabic, and Chinese, where linguistically and culturally diverse students increasingly populate the English-dominant classroom. These most common home languages were identified from the data of the National Center for Education Statistics (NCES, 2019). The main purpose of this collected work is to provide key elements of ELLs' first languages (e.g., a total of 12 languages) to help educators understand how the unique features of each primary language influence and intersect with the learning of the English language and engaging in literacy practices.

This book is intended to help general education teachers feel empowered to work with ELLs in their classroom with basic principles of ELLs' primary languages by offering more opportunities for the students to utilize their L1 to engage in meaningful L2 learning and activities. With knowledge of ELLs' home languages, teachers might be able to predict students' oral and written language patterns and use that knowledge to plan lessons and evaluate students' work based on the perspectives of language difference instead of language deficit. Educators, who have knowledge of ELLs' native language, are in a better position to develop ELLs' English language and literacy by scaffolding ELLs' learning. Indeed, a clear understanding of the major principles related to ELLs' primary languages will deepen teachers' understanding of the cross-linguistic transfer strategies that are possible, of the potential miscues and what they may mean, and of the pattern of ELLs' developmental use of English.

To provide more context for this book, in the following section, we first discuss the definition of ELLs, as well as the role of educators in relation to ELLs in the present educational context. Next, we draw on the current research related to ELLs' L1 impact when learning English. Then, we provide the organization of the book for the reader.

DEFINITION OF ENGLISH LANGUAGE LEARNERS

In this book, we refer to linguistically diverse students as ELLs. ELLs are defined as *learners who are in the process of acquiring English as an additional language* (Yoon, 2021a, 2022a, 2022b). We choose the term, ELLs, as it aligns with the Teaching English to Speakers of Other Languages (TESOL) International Association and the majority of PreK-12 education policies. There are alternative terms for ELLs such as emergent bilingual learners and multilingual learners. These terms are desirable since they are asset-based labels (García et al., 2008; Martinez, 2018). However, these terms do not necessarily singularly define students who learn *English* as a new language, which is the focus of this book, so for clarity and consistency, we have chosen to use the term ELLs. Emergent bilinguals and multilingual learners can refer to students who acquire multiple languages in a non-dominant English context (e.g., Arabic and French). To avoid confusion, we elected to use the term ELLs to emphasize the learners who bring their primary language and literacy knowledge to English as their new, additional language.

EDUCATORS' ROLES FOR DIVERSE ELLS

The need for this book is grounded in the reality of present-day classrooms. Classrooms are enriched with cultural and linguistic diversity in the United States, where students and families are from all around the world. Immigrant, refugee, international, and transnational students are an increasing population in U.S. public schools. Specifically, the population of ELLs in public schools in 2010 was 4.5 million, but it increased to 5.1 million by 2019 (NCES, 2021). In 2019, ELLs "constituted an average of 14.8 percent of total public-school enrollment in cities, 10.0 percent in suburban areas, 7.0 percent in towns, and 4.4 percent in rural areas" (NCES, 2021, para. 4.). This means that ELLs are relatively evenly dispersed throughout the country dispelling the myth of being isolated to urban areas. In addition, the U.S. Department of Education data (2021) indicated that ELLs' home languages were also extremely diverse. There are more than 400 languages that account for ELLs' native languages in U.S. public schools. Among them, the 15 most common languages are Spanish, Arabic, Chinese, Vietnamese, Somali, Russian, Portuguese, Haitian, Hmong, Korean, Urdu, Tagalog, French, Japanese, and Bengali.

Among these languages, Spanish, Arabic, and Chinese are the top three native languages for ELLs. More specifically, Spanish was the first language of 3.8 million ELLs, constituting almost 80 percent of all ELLs and 7.7 percent of all public-school students in K-12. Arabic (i.e., 135,900 ELLs) and Chinese (i.e., 102,800 ELLs) were the next most reported home languages (NCES, 2021). The population trend also shows that Asian ELLs are increasing in U.S. classrooms, and they are the next largest group (i.e., 528,700 Asian ELLs), constituting about 11 percent of all ELLs.

As shown in the data of NCES and U.S. Department of Education, the students' population reflects diversity; however, the teachers' population does not (Simmons, 2019; U.S. Department of Education, 2016). According to the recent data from the NCES (2020), "about 79 percent of public-school teachers were white, 9 percent were Hispanic, 7 percent were Black, 2 percent were Asian, 2 percent were of two or more races, and 1 percent were American Indian/Alaska Native" (para. 3). The overwhelming majority of the teaching profession consists of white monolingual teachers in the United States (Cochran-Smith & Lytle, 2009; NCES, 2020; Yoon, 2021b).

These current data imply that many monolingual teachers work with linguistically diverse students. ELLs deserve the same educational opportunities as native English-speaking peers. Yet, over decades, research has shown (Coady et al., 2016; de Jong, 2013; de Oliveira, 2011; Mohr, 2004; Pritchard, 2012; Yoon, 2008, 2022a) that ELLs have not been receiving equitable access to the language and content in the U.S. classroom. There is a persisting opportunity gap between ELLs and non-ELLs and "teachers' lack of professional knowledge and credentials for teaching ELLs is especially concerning" (Coady et al., 2016, p. 340).

How do we as teacher educators prepare teachers to serve these diverse students to ensure equity? Many teachers view American monolingualism as the norm. Research (Holdway & Hitchcock, 2018; Osborn, 2007; Yoon, 2007, 2021b; Yoon et al., 2015) suggests that the vast majority of monolingual teachers tend to teach multilingual learners through an assimilative pedagogy. They often insist that ELLs use only English in the classroom without utilizing the students' primary language and culture as resources. ELLs' first language has been treated as the one that needs to be "eliminated" to achieve English proficiency (Yoon, 2015). Under this inequitable educational context, ELLs are often positioned as disempowered and excluded from fully participating in learning activities (Miller, 2000; Yoon, 2008).

These situations call for action from teacher education programs. Teacher education programs are tasked to provide ample opportunities for teachers to value ELLs' primary language and to learn focused linguistically responsive strategies to draw in ELLs' language and cultural ways of knowing as assets to their learning. Numerous scholars suggest that ELLs' literacy knowledge developed in their home language can transfer to the learning of an additional language (Brown, 2014; Cummins, 2000; Lucas et al., 2008). It is important for teacher educators to prepare all pre-service teachers to hold space for ELLs to actualize their own power in English-dominant contexts by valuing ELLs' home language before entering the teaching profession in their own classrooms. It is the teacher educators' responsibility to prepare general education teachers who have the necessary tools to afford equitable access to the language and content of school for ELLs in the classroom regardless of where they work. This book intends to support teacher educators and educators alike who commit to the success of ELLs and who will continuously seek out new ideas to effectively work with *all* students.

GUIDING THEORETICAL PERSPECTIVES

The need for this book is also theoretically and conceptually grounded in current research. The research we draw upon will serve as an overarching framework for the subsequent chapters on ELLs' native languages including Spanish, Arabic, and Chinese. Given that chapter 1 will provide a more extended discussion of the research looking at L1 impact on L2 learning, we provide a brief overview of the topic in this section.

Research on ELLs' L1 Impact on L2

Second language acquisition theories (e.g., Brown, 2014; Cummins & Swain, 2014; Krashen, 1981; Lightbown & Spada, 2013) posit that ELLs' L1 influences their L2 positively or negatively. It is a positive transfer when L1 facilitates L2 learning (e.g., when there is the same concept between L1 and L2), and it is a negative transfer when the primary language interferes with L2 learning (e.g., when there is a different sentence structure between L1 and L2). According to Wang (2014), there are four different areas of transfer that ELLs make during the process of L2 learning. These areas include: (1) *sounds* (e.g., phonological awareness), (2) *words* (e.g., borrowing words), (3) *syntax* (e.g., word order), and (4) *culture* (e.g., habit).

For instance, ELLs who have phonological awareness skills developed in their native language can transfer to and facilitate English language and literacy development (Ford, 2005; Gotardo, 2002; Helman, 2004). This means that ELLs' L1 plays a positive role in acquiring their L2. For instance, the word *animal*, in Spanish, is written using the same graphemes and sounds similar to English. Spanish-speaking ELLs' understanding of the word animal might play a positive role in understanding its concept in English. On the other hand, ELLs might overgeneralize their L1 rules and apply them inaccurately to English language learning, which is called a negative transfer. For example, ELLs from Bengali backgrounds might use the pronoun *he* for *she* and *she* for *he*. This could be perhaps because in Bengali the third person pronoun is gender neutral (see the examples from chapter 7 on Bengali). Indeed, the linguistic features of an ELL's L1 is "one of the greatest factors" (Wang, 2014, p. 57) impacting their learning of English language and literacy.

ELLs' positive and negative transfer patterns demonstrate the complexities of ELLs' learning. These complexities call for educators' attention. Educators' understanding of these patterns influenced by ELLs' primary languages is critical to scaffolding learning for their academic success. When teachers are aware of these transfer patterns, they might approach the students' reading and writing patterns from the point of L1 influence and can support students' acquisition of an additional language. When teachers understand the principles of ELLs' L1, they will be able to view students in the stage of interlanguage, "a system that has a structurally intermediate status between the native and target languages" (Brown, 2014, p. 243), and be able to offer more meaningful supports.

Furthermore, through knowledge of ELLs' languages, teachers will understand that ELLs' silence (e.g., interlanguage stage of the silent period) in the classroom and their use of non-standard English forms do not mean that they are not attending to what is expected but rather are drawing on their resources to make sense of what is before them. Teachers with language knowledge will recognize these patterns as ELLs' language acquisition processes. With knowledge of ELLs' languages, teachers are also better able to understand plausible reasons that lead to ELLs' difficulty and modify their instruction accordingly. Indeed, it is important for teacher educators to use resources as a way to promote pre- and in-service teachers' understanding of how "structural differences among languages and contrasting cultural patterns for language use" (Adger et al., 2018, p. 2) actually affect ELLs' learning.

Despite the importance of L1 knowledge, however, research (e.g., Atkinson, 1987; Yoon, 2015, 2021b) shows that many general education teachers are unprepared to utilize ELLs' primary languages to support their learning of English. One of the major reasons is that teacher education programs often do not offer a TESOL or English as an additional language course as a requirement. Many pre- and in-service teachers graduate from their teacher education programs without understanding how they can meet the needs of ELLs from diverse language backgrounds. Additionally, given that nearly 80 percent of teachers in the United States are monolingual, it might be daunting to understand the complex process of second/additional language and literacy acquisition. According to Cook (2001), teachers who do not speak and understand ELLs' native languages rarely invite the students to use their native language in their classroom, which can and should be used as a learning tool.

As shown in the study by Pappamihiel and Lynn (2014), ELLs, who are invited to use their L1 in literacy activities, are able to build schema for new concepts in English. Understanding primary language norms, positive and negative transfer, and culturally sustaining resources, all contribute to helping teachers understand how ELLs utilize primary language as an asset when engaging in second language and literacy learning experiences. In short, research shows that ELLs' L2 learning is connected to L1 knowledge.

Examples of ELLs' L1 Impact on L2

Concrete examples are useful for teacher educators to discuss with monolingual pre- and in-service teachers in order to show tangible evidence of the complex concepts of language transfer. Therefore, we invited all of the chapter authors to provide examples for the reader, beyond the description of key characteristics of ELLs' native language. As shown below, the specific examples of L1 impact on L2 take a central position in each chapter. In this section, we provide two sample examples for the reader to obtain a sense of chapter structure, drawn from the chapters on Arabic (chapter 8) and Korean (chapter 3) languages, respectively.

For instance, a sentence order in Arabic is verb + subject + object while in English it is subject + verb + object (see chapter 8 on the Arabic language). ELLs from Arabic language backgrounds might write in English in the v/s/o order (e.g., "love I apples," instead of "I love apples"). The Arabic language chapter discusses that, when teachers understand the basic elements of the Arabic language, they might view the students' writing patterns from the perspective of L1 impact on L2 learning, rather than viewing them from a deficit perspective and evaluating the language pattern as "poor" English. By inviting ELLs from Arabic language backgrounds to compare Arabic sentences (e.g., "love I apples") and English sentences (e.g., "I love apples"), teachers can help students identify the contrasting patterns as they become more conscientious about language in use. The authors of the chapter emphasize that, instead of simply correcting ELLs' errors, it is important for the students to be engaged in a meaningful learning process by having them compare the differences between the two languages. This will help ELLs promote their monitoring process.

Another chapter on the Korean language (see chapter 3 on the Korean language) also provides rich examples of ELLs' L1 impact on L2. The authors explain that when teachers work with ELLs from Korean linguistic backgrounds, they might observe that Korean speakers often miss the definite and indefinite articles (e.g., a, an, the) in their reading and writing because definite and indefinite articles do not exist in the Korean language (e.g., "I have pen" instead of "I have a pen"). Native English speakers acquire and use articles naturally with minimal explicit instruction (e.g., first language), but Korean ELLs need to explicitly learn articles as part of the process of learning English.

These two sample language patterns from Arabic and Korean serve as an overview of the subsequent chapters on diverse ELLs' languages. Through the specific examples of ELLs' language patterns, teacher educators will help teachers understand that there are different processes of learning between the first and second languages. Once monolingual teachers are aware of these differences, they might assist the students more effectively by understanding where the differences come from and by focusing on particular areas to grow.

In short, we believe educators who have basic linguistic knowledge on ELLs' first languages can better serve their students by valuing their linguistic and cultural identities, which are central to ELLs' academic success. Through building upon the fundamental knowledge, they might learn that ELLs' native languages can be used as a resource and, accordingly, might provide ELLs with more opportunities to use their primary languages to utilize their "entire linguistic repertoire[s]" (Flores & Beardsmore, 2015, p. 216). We hope teacher educators who work with pre-service and in-service teachers use this book as a way to promote the teachers' understanding of ELLs' first language as a learning tool for success.

ORGANIZATION OF THE BOOK

The organization of the book consists of introduction, theoretical perspectives, and 12 language chapters. As shown in this chapter, the Introduction provides a background and an overview of this book. It discusses the need for educators' understanding of ELLs' L1 impact on L2 learning. We situate our book project in the current educational contexts of an ever increasingly diverse student population of ELLs in U.S. schools. In chapter 1, we present theoretical perspectives of L1 impact on L2 learning through an extensive literature review. This chapter will serve as a condensed version of current research on the topic.

Additionally, we include 12 chapters out of the most common ELLs' home languages in the U.S context. The contributing authors present foundational elements of ELLs' first languages. All of the authors are experts in both the identified primary languages (e.g., Vietnamese) and the English language. The reader will see the brief history of each language (e.g., Urdu is influenced by Arabic, Persian, and Turkish), followed by key units of ELLs' home languages and students' examples that show their L1 impact on English language and literacy learning. In short, the chapters provide educators with foundational linguistic knowledge related to each language. Although we focus on 12 different languages, based on the availability of the relevant scholars and the available space for this book, we hope to include more languages in a future edition.

In summary, we planned and organized this book to help teacher educators in teacher education programs to guide teachers who work with ELLs in diverse classroom settings, PreK-12, across the curriculum. As linguistically diverse students populate U.S. classrooms, the field of teacher education is obliged to purposefully attend to the preparation of teachers to meet the needs of these students. The responsibility in working with culturally and linguistically diverse students no longer relies on the English for Speakers of Other Languages or bilingual teachers. It is the responsibility of all teachers to know and understand how to deliver linguistically responsive instruction to support all students.

REFERENCES

Adger, C. T., Snow, C. E., & Christian, D. (Eds.). (2018). *What teachers need to know about language*. Multilingual Matters.

Atkinson, D. (1987). The mother tongue in the classroom: A neglected resource. *ELT Journal, 41*(4), 241–247.

Brown, H. D. (2014). *Principles of language learning and teaching* (6th ed.). Pearson.

Coady, M. R., Harper, C. A., & de Jong. E. J. (2016). Aiming for equity: Preparing mainstream teachers for inclusion or inclusive classrooms? *TESOL Quarterly, 50*(2), 340–368.

Cochran-Smith, M., & Lytle, S. L. (2009). *Inquiry as stance: Practitioner research for the next generation*. Teachers College Press.

Cook, V. (2001). Using the first language in the classroom. *Canadian Modern Language Review, 57*(3), 402–423.

Cummins, J. (2000). *Language, power, and pedagogy: Bilingual children in the crossfire*. Multilingual Matters.

Cummins, J. (2007). Rethinking monolingual instructional strategies in multilingual classrooms. *Canadian Journal of Applied Linguistics, 10*(2), 221–240.

Cummins, J., & Swain, M. (2014). *Bilingualism in education: Aspects of theory, research and practice*. Routledge.

de Jong, E. (2013). Preparing mainstream teachers for multilingual classrooms. *Association of Mexican-American Educators, 7*(2), 40–49.

de Oliveira, L. C. (2011). *In their shoes*: Teachers experience the needs of English language learners through a math simulation. *Multicultural Education, 19*(1), 59–62.

Flores, N., & Beardsmore, H. (2015). Programs and structures in bilingual and multilingual education. In W. Wright, S. Boun, & O. Garcia (Eds.), *The handbook of bilingual and multilingual education* (pp. 205–225). Wiley Blackwell.

Ford, K. (2005, July). Fostering literacy development in English language learners. Paper presented at the American Federation of Teacher's QuEST Conference. https://www.colorincolorado.org/article/fostering-literacy-development-english -language-learners.

García, O., Kleifgen, J. A., & Falchi, L. (2008). *From English language learners to emergent bilinguals*. Equity Matters.

Genesee, F., & Lindholm-Leary, K. (2015). The education of English language learners. In K. Harris, S. Graham, & T. Urdan (Eds.), *APA handbook of educational psychology* (pp. 499–526). APA Books.

Gottardo, A. (2002). The relationship between language and reading skills in bilingual Spanish-English speakers. *Topics in Language Disorders, 22*(5), 46–70.

Helman, L. A. (2004). Building on the sound system of Spanish: Insights from the alphabetic spellings of English-language learners. *The Reading Teacher, 57*(5), 452–460.

Holdway, J., & Hitchcock, C. H. (2018). Exploring ideological becoming in professional development for teachers of multilingual learners: Perspectives on translanguaging in the classroom. *Teaching and Teacher Education, 75*, 60–70.

Krashen, S. (1981). *Second language acquisition and second language learning*. New York.

Lightbown, P. M., & Spada, N. (2013). *How languages are learned* (4th ed.). Oxford University Press.

Lucas, T., Villegas, A., & Freedson-Gonzalez, M. (2008). Linguistically responsive teacher education: Preparing classroom teachers to teach English language learners. *Journal of Teacher Education, 59*, 361–373.

Martinez, R. A. (2018). Beyond the English learner label: Recognizing the richness of bi/multilingual students' linguistic repertoires. *Reading Teacher, 71*(5), 515–522.

Miller, J. M. (2000). Language use, identity, and social interaction: Migrant students in Australia. *Research on Language and Social Interaction, 33*(1), 69–100.

Mohr, K. A. J. (2004). English as an accelerated language: A call to action for reading teachers. *Reading Teacher, 58*(1), 18–26.

National Center for Education Statistics. (2019). *English language learners in public schools*. https://nces.ed. gov/programs/coe/indicatorcgf.asp.

National Center for Education Statistics. (2020). *Characteristics of public school teachers*. https://nces.ed.gov/programs/coe/indicator_clr.asp.

National Center for Education Statistics. (2021). *English language learners in public schools*. https://nces.ed.gov/programs/coe/indicator/cgf.

Osborn, T. A. (Ed.). (2007). *Language and cultural diversity in U.S. schools: Democratic principles in action*. Rowman & Littlefield Education.

Pappamihiel, E., & Lynn, C. A. (2014). How can monolingual teachers take advantage of learners' native language in class? *Childhood Education, 90*(4), 291–297.

Ponzio, C. M. (2020). (Re)Imagining a translingual self: Shifting one monolingual teacher candidate's language lens. *Linguistics and Education, 60*, 1–11.

Pritchard, R. (2012). Monolingual teachers in multilingual settings: Changing attitudes and practices. *The CATESOL Journal, 23*(1), 194–204. https://files.eric.ed.gov/fulltext/EJ1112020.pdf.

Simmons, D. (2019). How to be an antiracist educator. *ASCD Education Update, 61*(10). http://www.ascd.org/publications/newsletters/education-update/oct19/vol61/num10/How-to-Be-an-Antiracist-Educator.aspx.

U.S. Department of Education. (2016). *The state of racial diversity in the educator workforce.* https://www2.ed.gov/rschstat/eval/highered/racial-diversity/state-racial -diversity-workforce.pdf.

U.S Department of Education. (2021). *Our nation's English learners.* https://www2 .ed.gov/datastory/el-characteristics/index.html.

Wang, Z. M. (2014). Review of the influence of L1 in L2 acquisition. *Studies in Literature and Language, 9*(2), 57–60. http://www.cscanada.net/index.php/sll/article/ view/5721; http://dx.doi.org/10.3968/5721.

Yoon, B. (2007). Offering or limiting opportunities: Teachers' roles and approaches to English language learners' participation in literacy activities. *The Reading Teacher, 61*(3), 216–225. https://ila.onlinelibrary.wiley.com/doi/10.1598/RT.61.3.2.

Yoon, B. (2008). Uninvited guests: The influence of teachers' roles and pedagogies on the positioning of English language learners in regular classrooms. *American Educational Research Journal, 45*(2), 495–522. https://journals.sagepub.com/doi/ full/10.3102/0002831208316200.

Yoon, B. (2015). Complexities of critical practice: The conflict between the teacher's ideological stance and the students' critical stance. In B. Yoon & R. Sharif (Eds.), *Critical literacy practice: Applications of critical theory in diverse settings* (pp. 79–93). Springer.

Yoon, B. (2021a). English language learners' language and literacy development: A brief synopsis of theoretical orientations for middle school teachers. *Middle School Journal, 52*(1), 23–29.

Yoon, B. (2021b). Toward equity-based pedagogy: Monolingual teachers' transformative thinking process. *Beijing International Review of Education, 3*(3), 387–406.

Yoon, B. (Ed.). (2022a). *Effective teacher collaboration for English language learners: Cross-curricular insights from K-12 settings.* Routledge.

Yoon, B. (2022b). Critical literacy for English language learners. In *Oxford research encyclopedia of education.* Oxford University Press. https://doi.org/10.1093/acre-fore/9780190264093.013.1740.

Yoon, B., Sharif, R., Czumak, L., Miller, M., & Pierce, A. (2015). Teachers' narratives: Learning from professional experiences with English language learners. In M. T. Cowart & G. Anderson (Eds.), *Professional practice in diverse settings: Attitudes and dispositions that facilitate success* (pp. 87–112). Canh Nam Publishers.

Chapter 1

Theoretical Perspectives

English Language Learners' L1 Impact on L2 Development

Kristen L. Pratt and Bogum Yoon

There is an ever-pressing need for educators to be well equipped with the knowledge and skills necessary to facilitate equitable access to the language and content of school for English language learners (ELLs). Equitable access to the language and content of school supports students' academic opportunities both within preK-12 contexts and beyond as they enter into additional educational and economic opportunities (August & Shanahan, 2006). The increasing reality of linguistically diverse classrooms compels educators, educator programs, as well as policy and funding entities, to cultivate more culturally and linguistically sustaining practices through asset-based pedagogies. Thoroughly understanding how languages are learned and the role played by students' primary languages (L1) in acquiring additional languages (L2) while simultaneously attempting to learn the academic content required in schools is an essential skill for all pre-service and in-service educators.

Rooted in an extensive review of current literature, we aim to cultivate awareness of language processes and pedagogical practices supporting ELLs' language and literacy development. Specifically, we review first and second language acquisition (SLA) theory and the role of students' primary language(s) in second or additional language learning. We provide an overview of how languages are learned, the role of oral language, the importance of explicitly teaching language forms and functions, and a brief review of L1 and L2 language subsystems.

SITUATING EQUITY FOR ELLS

Addressing individual differences in second language learning equips educators in K-12 contexts to better differentiate support as they create spaces for more equitable access to the language and content of school (Fairbairn & Jones-Vo, 2010). Developing a critical awareness (Alim, 2010; Alim et al., 2020) within a deeper understanding of the key principles related to ELLs' primary languages will help educators better understand the science behind students' use of English in particular ways, as noted in the "Introduction" chapter (e.g., Brown, 2014; Cummins & Swain, 2014; Krashen, 1981; Lightbown & Spada, 2013). Recognizing the ways in which students engage in English as an additional language allows educators to adjust instruction and provides more intentional scaffolding through explicit differentiation to better meet students' needs. Offering equitable access to the language and content of school is central to being linguistically (Gort et al., 2011; Lucas & Villegas, 2013) and culturally responsive (Au, 2011; Ladson-Billings, 1995; Paris, 2012; Puzio et al., 2018) educators.

The official mandate for reasonable and fair access stems from the Lau v Nichols Supreme Court Decision (1974). In this decision, the definition of effective instruction was expanded to include the creation of spaces for equitable access to both the language and content of school. Effective instruction for ELLs incorporates rightful access which builds on students' background knowledge (Gonzalez et al., 2005; Moll et al., 1992); offers explicit instruction and modeling (Linan-Thompson & Vaughn, 2007); provides guided practice, peer practice, and independent practice (Frey & Fisher, 2008a; Pearson & Gallagher, 1983); and offers regular formative assessments of the content and language learned (Abedi, 2011; Alvarez et al., 2014; Sadler, 1989). English language development and content instruction are essential to ensure meaningful, sustainable, and successful learning (Baker et al., 2014; Heritage et al., 2015). Successful learning is made possible through scaffolded instruction. This scaffolded instruction builds upon and leverages ELLs' funds of knowledge (Daniel et al., 2018; Moje et al., 2004). Scaffolded instruction is also standards-driven (Herman et al., 2015; Kachru, 1985) to develop discipline-specific academic language (Ernst-Slavit & Mason, 2011; Lemke, 1990; Zwiers, 2008) while simultaneously developing content area knowledge (Lee et al., 2013; Snow, 2010). Ultimately, scaffolded instruction includes making the content comprehensible across multiple entry points (Deussen et al., 2008) embracing the deliberate view of students' L1 as an asset to support their L2.

THE ROLE OF THE PRIMARY LANGUAGE
IN SECOND LANGUAGE LEARNING

The need for educators' understanding of students' language learning process has been discussed over decades in the education field. What we as educators do

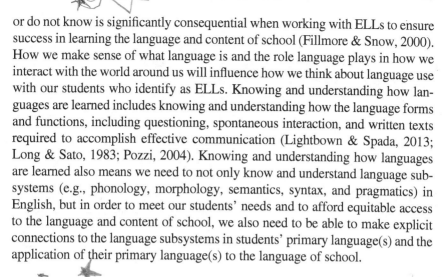

or do not know is significantly consequential when working with ELLs to ensure success in learning the language and content of school (Fillmore & Snow, 2000). How we make sense of what language is and the role language plays in how we interact with the world around us will influence how we think about language use with our students who identify as ELLs. Knowing and understanding how languages are learned includes knowing and understanding how the language forms and functions, including questioning, spontaneous interaction, and written texts required to accomplish effective communication (Lightbown & Spada, 2013; Long & Sato, 1983; Pozzi, 2004). Knowing and understanding how languages are learned also means we need to not only know and understand language sub-systems (e.g., phonology, morphology, semantics, syntax, and pragmatics) in English, but in order to meet our students' needs and to afford equitable access to the language and content of school, we also need to be able to make explicit connections to the language subsystems in students' primary language(s) and the application of their primary language(s) to the language of school.

How Languages Are Learned

Scholars in the field of language education stress that language choice, use, the words, language variety, and language forms are central pillars shaping teaching and learning experiences for students. Language choice and use (Ochs & Schieffelin, 1984; Reyes & Ervin-Tripp, 2010) are demonstrative aspects of social alliance (Street & Leung, 2010; Wei & Hua, 2013). In other words, the words, language variety, and language forms we use align with how we see ourselves positioned within different social groups. Language choice and use reveal how individuals and cultural groups position themselves and are positioned by others in society (Bloome et al., 2005; Halliday, 1978; Zavala, 2015) which are influenced by the sociocultural and sociopolitical contexts impacting their experiences.

Understanding the nuanced layers of how languages are learned within embedded sociocultural (Gort & Sembiante, 2015; Pennycook, 2000) and socio-political (García & Leiva, 2014; Pratt & Ernst-Slavit, 2019) contexts invites educators to have a more thorough awareness of typical and atypical developmental patterns. Understanding the differences between language variety choice and representative language use versus a developmental language learning challenge or uncharacteristic development along a continuum (Meisel et al., 1981) is grounded in understanding how languages are learned. Knowing and understanding how languages are learned also allows educators to integrate language subsystems more meaningfully from students' L1 as intentional and purposed bridges to support the development of language and literacy in students' L2.

First language acquisition. Linguists have sought to explain and understand the connection between the communication we experience as infants and small children to the utterances we are able to produce as we grow. In trying to understand how young children develop their first language, patterns across languages, environments, and multiple contexts have been identified. One such pattern is the developmental sequence of early first language acquisition, which is interestingly similar across languages (Lightbown & Spada, 2013). These developmental patterns include such markers as recognizing and being able to differentiate the sound of one's caretaker and one's ability to distinguish unique sounds, for example, between minimal pairs. The fact that small children are able to differentiate the subtle nuances of language has fascinated and inspired the field of linguistics

First language acquisition theories initially explored language development through imitation and reinforcement, also known as behaviorist theory (Skinner, 1957). Skinner (1957) proposed that young children learn language through a "three-term relation between a stimulus, a response, and a reinforcement" (p. 57). In his argument, utterances that were pleasing to the interlocutor, a person who participates in the communication act, were given positive praise and as such encouraged additional utterances. This behaviorist framework for understanding first language acquisition was later contested by Noam Chomsky (1965), who views language learning from innatist perspectives. Chomsky cited evidence of unique utterances beyond what children heard and experienced, for example, the production of the word *goed*, when what the child heard was *went*. Chomsky called for a new framework of understanding that supported the idea of Universal Grammar. The idea of Universal Grammar assumes typical developmental and ideal environmental conditions and argues for the notion that we are all born with the ability (e.g., Language Acquisition Device) to learn any language, but which language and how is dependent on our community. Lev Vygotsky (1978) builds on the idea of Universal Grammar calling forward the argument that social interaction shapes not only our language but the way we think about language and form our thoughts as we age and engage across language-rich experiences (Heath, 1983; Sachs et al., 1981; Snow, 1995) within a nurturing environment.

Second language acquisition. SLA theories explore language socialization, interaction (Long, 2018), processing (Pienemann, 2015), comprehensible input (VanPatten, 2010), and comprehensible output (Swain, 2005). Similar to first language acquisition, SLA follows a comparable developmental pattern (Lightbown & Spada, 2013; Meisel et al., 1981). SLA theory has also been influenced by behaviorist and innatist theories. Stephen Krashen (1982) suggested five hypotheses that build on the cognitive theory of language learning. Those hypotheses include: the monitor hypothesis, the natural order hypothesis, the acquisitional learning hypothesis, the comprehensible input hypothesis, and the affective filter hypothesis. The influence of these hypotheses in second language learning contexts gave way to the development of sociocultural theory (Lantolf & Thorne, 2007; Lewis et al., 2007). Sociocultural theory considers the role context and environment play in one's ability to receive comprehensible input and feel safe enough to explore output within conversational interactions as speakers try out new language forms.

Implications from understanding SLA theories significantly impact educators who work with ELLs. The fundamental principles of language acquisition theories inform how educators design meaningful lessons that maximize cross-linguistic transfer in what Cummins (2017) calls *teaching for transfer*. Teaching for transfer presses on the importance of asset-based frameworks that purposefully engage students' L1 to support their L2 acquisition. Wright (2019) describes that all teachers are language teachers and, as such, we all share the responsibility to build on the foundational knowledge that students bring with them to school. Educators are charged to tap into students' existing language and ways of knowing (Esteban-Guitart & Moll, 2014; Gonzalez, 2005; Moje et al., 2004), engaging with how our students understand and experience the world in order to hold space for students to *add* to what they already know and understand, not to *assimilate* (Macedo et al., 2003; Zwiers, 2008). To maximize teaching effectiveness and successful academic outcomes for ELLs, educators are tasked to support the development of core L2 language skills through the use of students' L1. The foundational knowledge students bring with them to our classes should be used as a tool to help students transfer what they know about language, including the language forms and functions of their L1, in order to constructively do what we are asking them to do in their L2.

Language Functions and Forms

Research suggests that educators understand and explicitly teach both language functions and forms when they work with ELLs (Zwiers, 2008). Language functions refer to the purpose(s) for which individuals use language in oral, sign, or written communication. In linguistically diverse classrooms, these functions need to be explicitly taught along with their accompanying form(s) prior to being expected to implement them. For example, ELLs use language to make predictions, compare and contrast, and draw conclusions. As educators, the question then is, how do we explicitly teach students the language required to be able to make predictions, articulate compare and contrast statements, or explain how they drew their conclusion. The possible answer is by teaching the associated language forms. Language forms refer to the types of language required to perform these language functions. For example, to be able to make predictions, ELLs would already need to know how to form the future and conditional tenses of verbs. To perform the language function of comparing and contrasting, ELLs would need to be explicitly taught about adjectives, conjunctions, superlatives, and adverbs (Pozzi, 2004).

Learning integrates grammatically encoded lexical and discursive elements. For ELLs, this includes the use of the functions and forms in students' L1 to make sense of L2 functions and forms (Pons, 2017). Students use their previously known languages to carry out the organization and completion of tasks, co-construct meaning, and facilitate language understanding (Martínez-Adrián & Arratibel-Irazusta, 2020). It is important for educators to understand language functions, forms, and subsystems in order to then teach explicitly said functions and forms. One way educators are better able to explicitly teach the necessary forms to carry out the required language functions is through a deep and thorough understanding of the language subsystems.

Language Subsystems

Along with language forms and functions, literature also suggests that educators understand language subsystems. Language subsystems include phonology, morphology, semantics, syntax, and pragmatics. Explicit instruction of subsystems has evidenced benefits for ELLs' language and literacy development (August & Shanahan, 2006). Some of the subsequent chapters in this book are guided by these concepts, and the reader can consult them for specific examples of how to meaningfully integrate the language subsystems of students' L1 with English subsystems during instruction.

Phonology. Phonology, or the study of the sound systems of language, explores phonemes (the smallest unit of sound) and intonation and stress. Phonology also looks at the syllable structure and sequence of sounds, both the perception and production. For example, if we think about the letter *a* in English, the sound this letter makes depends if the letter is positioned between consonants, as in *cat*, or if the letter is neighbored by a vowel, such as *gait*. Phonology studies how these sounds change and what those changes mean which helps us identify patterns of anticipation. Understanding the fundamental sound systems of ELLs' primary languages and of English will support instruction as it relates to pronunciation, predicting, and establishing patterns of understanding. Conducting error analyses of the pronunciation like L1 language groups helps to identify common causes of those errors and solutions for teachers to develop effective strategies for supporting students' learning (Uribe-Enciso et al., 2019).

Morphology. Morphology examines the structure and meaning of words. This is accomplished through understanding the ways morphemes (the smallest unit that holds meaning) combine to create new meaning, for example, geology. Geo comes from the Latin root meaning relating to earth and ology means the study of, thus, geology means the study of matter relating to earth.

Morphology is important because once a student learns geo as Latin for earth, they can make sense of new words such as geography and geophysics. Once students learn *ology* means the study of, they can then infer the meaning of words like biology, criminology, and the like. However, it is important to keep in mind that morphemes must be a smallest unit of meaning so, for instance, *work* in English is the smallest unit, which cannot be separated as "wo" and "rk" to hold meaning.

Identifying morphological patterns supports ELLs' ability to read and understand beyond the explicit instruction and allows the necessary space for students to be inventive and creative. A cross-linguistic example of where understanding morphology in the student's L1 might support the student's acquisition of their L2 (Osborn, 2007) can be seen through the use of Chinese pinyin (the romanization system of standard Mandarin, see chapter 5 on Mandarin Chinese). Chinese pinyin supports morphological development and word formation when students are learning English, contributing to positive L1 to L2 transfer (Li, 2017). While L1 (regardless of language—that is, Spanish, Mandarin, or Japanese) phonology is likely a factor in the development of L2 English morphology, it alone does not fully explain morphological miscues in English (Cabrelli-Amaro et al., 2018).

Creating opportunities for positive L1 transfer as students develop both language and literacy skills in English are made possible by understanding the morphological structures of students' L1. Reading processes, lexical decision making specifically, in students' L2 are modified and influenced by students' L1 morphological background as it relates to the presence or absence of familiar root and word-pattern morphemes (Norman et al., 2016). Thus, understanding ELLs' morphological background in their L1 will guide instruction to build literacy skills in their L2.

Semantics. Semantics explores the meaning of and between words, phrases, and sentences. For example, the differences between elder, senior citizen, and aged or teachers, educators, professors, instructors. While technically, these words are synonymous, the subtle differences in meaning matter. The teaching of and familiarity with semantics supports appraising students of the subtle and nuanced differences between semantically related words. Extended instruction and modeling, developing, and sustaining a broad lexical tool kit allow ELLs to effectively communicate for both social and academic purposes (August et al., 2018; Nagy & Townsend, 2012). With semantic familiarity in ELLs' L1 and L2, teachers and teacher educators are able to build integrated units that draw forward cognates (words that look, sound, and mean similar things across languages) as well as false cognates (words that look and sound similar but mean different things) bridging for students across similarities. When semantic instruction is embedded in a meaningful context, it is more effective than in isolated forms.

Syntax. The rules that influence the way words are combined to form sentences and the ways sentences are combined in particular sequences to convey an intended meaning is called syntax. For example, "John read the sign" carries a significantly different meaning than "The sign read John." The rules of subject, verb, and object (s/v/o) in English dictate the ways we are allowed to interpret meaning. Syntactic structures are unique to each language and often convey value and priority. It is essential for educators to be familiar with general syntax comparatives between ELLs' L1 and their L2 as a means of helping them name syntactic differences across languages (e.g., s/o/v in Korean) to make sense of L2 structures (e.g., s/v/o in English) more readily. Predictive skills to improve reading comprehension change over time, but ELLs use the correspondence between L1 and L2 syntax to learn L2 (Siu & Ho, 2015). Articulating these different skills in each language will help educators develop effective strategies to meet learner needs.

Pragmatics. One of the last language subsystems to learn about is pragmatics. Pragmatics deals with language in use from a particular point of view that considers context, interlocutors, and inferred meaning couched in a shared understanding, conversational nuance, implied meaning, for example, I am *hot*, as in I am gorgeous versus, I am *hot*, as in I feel warm in English. Another example, in response to a question the interlocutor replies, *sure*. Without pragmatic feedback, it would be unclear if the speaker meant, I guess so (insert sigh), whatever (insert eye roll), okay (insert head nod), or no problem (insert thumbs up). Instruction should attend to cross-linguistic contrasts as well as integration of the linguistic and pragmatic demands of the L2 (Pons et al., 2017). Understanding the pragmatics of a particular speech community allows the participant to adhere to social perceptions of civility and the expected order of spontaneous or unpredictable conversations. The objective in deconstructing the pragmatics of language for and with ELLs aims to address making visible often invisible norms of communication.

Oral Language Proficiency and Literacy Development

While explicit instruction of language subsystems is key to supporting students' language and literacy development, this type of instruction alone is not sufficient (August & Shanahan, 2006). In addition to explicit instruction of language subsystems, there is also a need to intentionally build on students' L1 oral language proficiency and literacy skills when developing oral language proficiency and literacy skills in students' L2. Students' oral language skills in both their L1 and L2 are of paramount importance to supporting their L2 literacy development and have historically been under-taught. The correlation between L2 oral language development and their L2 literacy development is evidenced in the research (Lervåg & Lervåg, 2011) where the authors complete a thorough review of the research which supports the need for educators to create spaces in classrooms where students have opportunities to intentionally cultivate oral language development in their L2.

Recently, research on ELLs has particularly focused on oral language and its impact on their learning in literacy. Oral language, or one's ability to recognize and produce sequences of sounds that encompass all of the language subsystems noted above, develops first in children. Because oral language is invisible, and because once an utterance has been spoken it is gone forever (Wright, 2019), the development of communicative competence (Hymes, 1971) for ELLs in diverse classrooms is top priority in supporting their equitable access to the language and content of school. Oral language has been shown to influence reading comprehension and, as such, supports the argument for integrating syntactic and semantic knowledge in order to build comprehension (Foorman et al., 2015).

As noted in the introduction, in a study by Pappamihiel and Lynn (2014), ELLs, who are invited to use their L1 in classroom literacy activities, are able to build schema for new concepts in English. There is consistent evidence for cross-linguistic transfer as it relates to elements of language, including: lexical (phonological and morphological) development, syntactic development, language functions, and discourse expectations (Siu & Ho, 2015). According to Siu and Ho (2015), "L1 syntactic skills cross-linguistically predicted L2 reading comprehension" (p. 335). The syntactic skills were evident across age and language variations but were involved differently. This scaffolded involvement of students' syntactic skills proposes that students would benefit from L1 to L2 transfer of these skills such as word order and morphosyntactic skills in order to support literacy development in students' L2.

As the reader will see in the subsequent chapters of this book, understanding the language subsystems of ELLs' L1 supports a positive transfer of skills, which in turn supports ELLs' L2 literacy development. Students' L1 literacy and L1 working memory and L2 aptitude mirror L2 achievement and supply evidence to support cross-linguistic transfer (Sparks et al., 2019). Research consistently emphasizes the importance of developing core language skills as students' L1 impacts their L2 and their L2 oral language literacy development. Providing intensive instruction across the curriculum while integrating the teaching of both the language and content of school offers students the opportunity to effectively acquire English (Lightbown & Spada, 2020).

CONCLUSION

In this chapter, specifically, we reviewed and discussed first and second language acquisition theory, the role of students' first language in influencing the development of their additional languages, the role of forms and functions in language learning, and current understandings of L1 and L2 language subsystems. Additionally, we explored oral language and its impact on ELLs' literacy skills as well as applications of these theoretical understandings in K-12 contexts. The theoretical perspectives briefly overviewed in this chapter evidenced how ELLs use their previously known language(s) to carry out the oral language and literacy tasks, co-construct meaning, and facilitate language in their L2 (Martínez-Adrián & Arratibel-Irazusta, 2020).

As editors of this book, we hope the summarized overview of current literature helps educators to deepen their understanding of ELLs' complex learning process. The theoretical perspectives presented in this chapter will serve as overarching frameworks for the subsequent chapters. The subsequent chapters will focus on the most common languages identified in U.S. schools and how students' primary language(s) transact with the language and literacy learning taking place in the classroom. The authors in the chapters will offer educators, who work with ELLs in diverse classroom settings, language-specific examples that they can draw from to support students' English language and content development.

REFERENCES

Abedi, J. (2011). Assessing English language learners: Critical issues. In M. Basterra, E. Trumbull, & G. Solano-Flores (Eds.), *Cultural validity in assessment: Addressing linguistic and cultural diversity* (pp. 49–71). Routledge.

Alim, H. S. (2010). Critical language awareness. In N. Hornberger & S. L. McKay (Eds.), *Sociolinguistics and language education* (pp. 205–231). Multilingual Matters.

Alim, H. S., Rickford, J. R., & Ball, A. F. (2020). *Raciolinguistics: How language shapes our ideas about race.* Oxford University Press.

Alvarez, L., Ananda, S., Walqui, A., Sato, E., & Rabinowitz, S. (2014). *Focusing formative assessment on the needs of English language learners.* WestEd.

Andrews, D. J. C., Castro, E., Cho, C. L., Petchauer, E., Richmond, G., & Floden, R. (2019). Changing the narrative on diversifying the teaching workforce: A look at historical and contemporary factors that inform recruitment and retention of teachers of color. *Journal of Teacher Education, 70*(1), 6–12. https://doi.org/10.1177/0022487118812418.

Antonova Unlu, E. (2019). Pinpointing the role of the native language in L2 learning: Acquisition of spatial prepositions in English by Russian and Turkish native speakers. *Applied Linguistics Review, 10*(2), 241–258. https://doi.org/10.1515/applirev-2016-1009.

Au, K. H. (2011). *Literacy achievement and diversity: Keys to success for teachers, students, and schools.* Teachers College Press.

August, D., Artzi, L., Barr, C., & Francis, D. (2018). The moderating influence of instructional intensity and word type on the acquisition of academic vocabulary in young English language learners. *Reading and Writing: An Interdisciplinary Journal, 31,* 965–989. https://doi.org/10.1007/s11145-018-9821-1.

Baker, S., Lesaux, N., Jayanthi, M., Dimino, J., Proctor, C. P., Morris, J., Gersten, R., Haymond, K., Kieffer, M. J., Linan-Thompson, S., & Newman-Gonchar, R. (2014). *Teaching academic content and literacy to English learners in elementary and middle school* (NCEE 2014-4012). National Center for Education Evaluation and Regional Assistance (NCEE), Institute of Education Sciences, U.S. Department of Education. The NCEE Website: http://ies.ed.gov/ncee/wwc/publications_reviews.aspx.

Billings, E., & Walquí, A. (n/d). *Topic brief 5: Dispelling the myth of "English only": Understanding the importance of first language in second language learning.* http://www.nysed.gov/bilingual-ed/topic-brief-5-dispelling-myth-english-only -understanding-importance-first-language.

Bloome, D., Carter, S. P., Christian, B. M., Otto, S., & Shuart-Faris, N. (2005). *Discourse analysis and the study of classroom language and literacy events: A microethnographic perspective.* Lawrence ErlBaum Associates.

Cabrelli-Amaro, C., Campos-Dintrans, G., & Rothman, J. (2018). The role of L1 phonology in L2 morphological production. *Studies in Second Language Acquisition, 40*(3), 503–527. https://doi.org/10.1017/S0272263117000122.

Chomsky, N. (1965). *Aspects of the theory of syntax.* MIT Press.

Cummins, J. (2017). Teaching for transfer in multilingual school contexts. In O. García, A. Lin, & S. May (Eds.), *Bilingual and multilingual education: Encyclopedia of language and education* (3rd ed., pp. 103–115). Springer.

Daniel, S. M., Jiménez, R. T., Pray, L., & Pacheco, M. B. (2018). Scaffolding to make translanguaging a classroom norm. *TESOL Journal, 10*(1), e00361.

Deussen, T., Autio, E., Miller, B., Lockwood, A. T., & Stewart, V. (2008). *What teachers should know about instruction for English language learners.* Center for Research, Evaluation, and Assessment, Education Northwest.

Ernst-Slavit, G., & Mason, M. (2011). "Words that hold us up": Teacher talk and academic language in five upper elementary classrooms. *Linguistics and Education, 22,* 430–440.

Fairbain, S., & Jones-Vo, S. (2010). *Differentiating instruction and Assessment for English language learners: A guide for K-12 teachers.* Caslon.

Foorman, B., Koon, S., Petscher, Y., Mitchell, A., & Truckenmiller, A. (2015). Examining general and specific factors in the dimensionality of oral language and reading in 4th-10th grades. *Journal of Educational Psychology, 107*(3), 884–899.

Frey, N., & Fisher, D. (2008). *Gradual release of responsibility instructional framework.* Association for Supervision and Curriculum Development (ASCD). https://pdo.ascd.org/lmscourses/pd13oc005/media/formativeassessmentandccswithelaliteracymod_3-reading3.pdf.

García, O., & Leiva, C. (2014). Theorizing and enacting translanguaging for social justice. In A. Blackledge & A. Creese (Eds.), *Heteroglossia as practice and pedagogy* (pp. 199–218). Springer. https://doi.org/10.1007/978-94-007-7856-6.

Gonzalez, N., Moll, L. C., & Amanti, C. (Eds.). (2005). *Funds of knowledge: Theorizing practices in household, communities and classrooms*. Routledge.

Gort, M., Glenn, W. J., & Settlage, J. (2011). Toward culturally and linguistically responsive teacher education: The impact of a faculty learning community on two teacher educators. In T. Lucas (Ed.), *Teacher preparation for linguistically diverse class-rooms: A resource for teacher educators* (pp. 178–194). Routledge.

Gort, M., & Sembiante, S. F. (2015). Navigating hybridized language learning spaces through translanguaging pedagogy: Dual language preschool teachers' languaging in practices in support of emergent bilingual children's performance of academic discourse. *International Multilingual Research Journal, 9*(1), 7–25.

Halliday, M. A. K. (1978). *Language as social semiotic*. Edward Arnold.

Heath, S. B. (1983). *Words at work and play: Three decades in family and community life*. Cambridge University Press.

Heritage, M., Walqui, A., & Linquanti, R. (2015). *English language learners and the new standards: Developing language content knowledge and analytical practices in the classroom*. Harvard Education Press.

Herman, J. L., Epstein, S., Leon, S., Dai, Y., La Torre Matrundola, D., Reber, S., & Choi, K. (2015). *The implementation and effects of the Literacy Design Collaborative (LDC): Early findings in eighth-grade history/social studies and science courses* (CRESST Report 848). National Center for Research on Evaluation, Standards, and Student Testing (CRESST), University of California.

Hymes, D. (1971). *On communicative competence*. University of Pennsylvania Press.

Kachru, B. (1985). Standards, codification, and sociolinguistic realism: The English language in the outer circle. In R. Quirk & H. G. Widdowson (Eds.), *English in the world: Teaching and learning the language and literature* (pp. 11–30). Cambridge University Press.

Ladson-Billings, G. (1995). But that's just good teaching! *Theory Into Practice, 34*(3), 159–165.

Lantolf, J., & Thorne, S. L. (2007). Sociocultural theory and second language learning. In B. vanPatten & J. Williams (Eds.), *Theories in second language acquisition* (pp. 201–224). Lawrence Erlbaum.

Larvåg, M. M., & Lervåg, A. (2011). Cross-linguistic transfer of oral language, decoding, phonological awareness and reading comprehension: A meta-analysis of correlational evidence. *Journal of Research in Reading, 34*(1), 114–135.

Lau v. Nichols et al., No. 72-6520. Supreme Court of the United States 414. U.S. 563 (1974). https://www2.ed.gov/about/offices/list/ocr/ell/lau.html.

Lee, O., Quinn, H., & Valdés, G. (2013). Science and language for English language learners in relation to next generation science standards and with implications for Common Core State Standards for English language arts and mathematics. *Educational Researcher, 42*(4), 223–233.

Lemke, J. L. (1990). *Talking science: Language, learning, and values*. Ablex.

Lewis, C., Enciso, P. E., & Moje, E. B. (2007). *Reframing sociocultural research on literacy: Identity, agency, and power*. Lawrence Erlbaum Associates.

Li, M. (2017). The effect of L1 Chinese transfer on L2 English learning: A brief review of the research. *Theory and Practice in Language Studies, 7*(5), 350–355. https://doi.org/10.17507/tpls.0705.04.

Li, M., & Dekeyser, R. (2019). Distribution of practice effects in the acquisition and retention of L2 Mandarin tonal word production. *The Modern Language Journal, 103*(3), 607–628. https://doi.org/10.1111/modl.12580-0026-7902/19/607–628.

Lightbown, P. M., & Spada, N. (2013). *How languages are learned* (4th ed.). Oxford University Press.

Lightbown, P. M., & Spada, N. (2020). Teaching and learning in the L2 classroom: It's about time. *Language Teaching, 53*, 422–432.

Linan-Thompson, S., & Vaughn, S. (2007). *Research-based methods of reading instruction for English language learners.* Association for Supervision and Curriculum Development (ASCD).

Long, M. H. (2018). Interaction in L2 classrooms. In J. I. Liontas & M. DelliCarpini (Eds.), *The TESOL encyclopedia of English language teaching.* John Wiley & Sons. https://doi.org/10.1002/9781118784235.eelt0233.

Long, M. H., & Sato, C. J. (1983). Classroom foreigner talk discourse: Forms and functions of teachers' questions. In H. W. Seliger & M. H. Long (Eds.), *Classroom oriented research in second language acquisition* (pp. 268–285). Newbury House.

Lucas, T., & Villegas, A. M. (2013). Preparing linguistically responsive teachers: Laying the foundation in preservice teacher education. *Theory Into Practice, 52*(2), 98–109. http://dx.doi.org/10.1080/00405841.2013.770327.

Martínez-Adrián, M., & Arratibel-Irazusta, I. (2020). The interface between task-modality and the use of previously known languages in young CLIL English learners. *Studies in Second Language Learning and Teaching, 10*(3), 473–500. https://doi.org/10.14746/ssllt.2020.10.3.4.

Meisel, J. M., Clahsen, H., & Pienemann, M. (1981). On determining developmental stages in natural second language acquisition. *Studies in Second Language Acquisition, 3*(2), 109–135.

Moje, E. B., Ciechanowski, K. M., Kramer, K., Ellis, L., Carrillo, R., & Collazo, T. (2004). Working toward third space in content area literacy: An examination of everyday funds of knowledge and discourse. *Reading Research Quarterly, 39*(1), 38–70.

Moll, L. C., Amanti, C., Neff, D., & Gonzalez, N. (1992). Funds of knowledge for teaching: Using a qualitative approach to connect homes and classrooms. *Theory into Practice, 31*(2), 132–141.

National Center for Education Statistics. (2021). *English language learners in public schools.* https://nces.ed.gov/programs/coe/indicator/cgf.

Norman, T., Degani, T., & Peleg, O. (2016). Transfer of L1 visual word recognition strategies during early stages of L2 learning. *Second Language Research, 32*(1), 109–122. https://doi.org/10.1177/0267658315608913.

Ochs, E., & Schieffelin, B. (1984). Language acquisition and socialization: Three developmental stories and their implications. In R. Schweder & R. LeVine (Eds.), *Culture theory: Essays in mind, self, and emotion.* Cambridge University Press.

Osborn, T. A. (Ed.). (2007). *Language and cultural diversity in U.S. schools: Democratic principles in action*. Rowman and Littlefield Education.

Pearson, P. D., & Gallagher, M. C. (1983). The instruction of reading comprehension. *Contemporary Educational Psychology, 8*, 317–344.

Pennycook, A. (2000). The social politics and the cultural politics of language classrooms. In J. K. Hall & W. G. Eggington (Eds.), *The sociopolitics of English language teaching* (pp. 89–103). Multilingual Matters.

Pienemann, M. (2015). An outline of processability theory and its relationship to other approaches in SLA. *Language Learning, 65*(1), 123–151.

Pons, J. A., Ahern, A., & Fuentes, P. G. (2017). L1 French learning of L2 Spanish past tenses: L1 transfer versus aspect and interface issues. *Studies in Second Language Learning and Teaching, 7*(3), 489–515. https://doi.org/10.14746/ssllt.2017.7.3.7.

Pozzi, D. C. (2004). *Forms and functions in language morphology, syntax*. College of Education, University of Houston. https://woucentral.weebly.com/uploads/7/4/6/9/7469707/langfunc.pdf.

Pratt, K. L., & Ernst-Slavit, G. (2019). Equity perspectives and restrictionist policies: Tensions in dual language bilingual education. *Bilingual Education Research Journal, 42*(3), 356–374. https://doi.org/10.1080/15235882.2019.1647900.

Puzio, K., Newcomer, S., Pratt, K. L., Burkes, K., Jacobs, M., & Hooker, S. (2017). Creative failures in culturally sustaining pedagogy. *Language Arts, 94*(4), 223–233.

Reyes, I., & Ervin-Tripp, S. (2010). Language choice and competence: Code switching and issues of social identity in young bilingual children. In M. Shatz & L. C. Wilkinson (Eds.), *The education of English language learners: Research to practice* (pp. 67–86). The Guilford Press.

Sachs, J., Bard, B., & Johnson, M. (1981). Language learning with restricted input: Case studies of two hearing children of deaf parents. *Applied Psycholinguistics, 2*(1), 33–54. https://doi.org/10.1017/S0142716400000643.

Sadler, D. R. (1989). Formative assessment and the design of instructional strategies. *Instructional Science, 18*, 119–144.

Siu, C., & Ho, C. (2015). Cross-language transfer of syntactic skills and reading comprehension among young Cantonese-English bilingual students. *Reading Research Quarterly, 50*(3), 313–336. https://doi.org/10.1002/rrq.101.

Skinner, B. F. (1957). *Verbal behavior*. Martino Fine Books.

Snow, C. (1995). Issues in the study of input: Fine-tuning, universality, individual and developmental differences, and necessary causes. In P. Fletcher & B. MacWhinney (Eds.), *The handbook of child language* (pp. 180–193). Blackwell.

Snow, C. (2010). Academic language and the challenge of reading for learning about science. *Science, 328*, 450–452.

Sparks, R. L., Patton, J., & Luebbers, J. (2019). Individual differences in L2 achievement mirror individual differences in L1 skills and L2 aptitude: Crosslinguistic transfer of L1 to L2 skills. *Foreign Language Annals, 52*(2), 255–283. https://doi.org/10.1111/flan.12390.

Street, B., & Leung, C. (2010). Sociolinguistics, language teaching and new literacy studies. In N. Hornberger & S. L. McKay (Eds.), *Sociolinguistics and language education* (pp. 290–316). Multilingual Matters.

Swain, M. (2005). The output hypothesis: Theory and research. In E. Hinkel (Ed.), *Handbook of research in second language teaching and learning*. Routledge.

Uribe Enciso, O. L., Fuentes Hernandez, S. S., Vargas Pita, K. L., & Rey Pabón, A. S. (2019). Problematic phonemes for Spanish-speakers' learners of English. *GIST Education and Learning Research Journal*, *19*, 215–238. https://doi.org/10.26817/16925777.701.

VanPatten, B. (2003). *From input to output: A teacher's guide to second language acquisition*. McGraw Hill.

Vygotsky, L. S. (1978). *Mind in society: The development of higher psychological processes*. Harvard University Press.

Wei, L., & Hua, Z. (2013). Translanguaging identities: Creating transnational space through flexible multilingual practices amongst Chinese university students in the UK. *Applied Linguistics*, *34*(5), 516–535.

Wright, W. (2015). *Foundation for teaching English language learners: Research, theory, policy, and practice* (3rd ed.). Caslon Publishing.

Yosso, T. (2005). Whose culture has capital? A critical race theory discussion of community cultural wealth. *Race Ethnicity and Education*, *8*(1), 69–91.

Zavala, V. (2015). "It will emerge if they grow fond of it": Translanguaging and power in Quechua teaching. *Linguistics and Education*, *32*, 16–26.

Zwiers, J. (2008). *Building academic language: Essential practices for content classrooms*. Jossey-Bass.

Chapter 2

Spanish Support within Linguistically Responsive Instruction for Latina/o/x English Language Learners

Kristen L. Pratt, Gabriela Tellez-Osorno, and Maria José Solis

There are currently 59.8 million people in the United States who identify as Latina/o/x, 67 percent of whom are native-born (Batalova et al., 2021). Latina/o/x students enrolled in K-12 U.S. schools comprise 22.7 percent of all students (Bauman, 2017), or 3.9 million students. Latina/o/x English language learners (ELLs) represent just over 75 percent of all ELLs and 7.9 percent of public-school students in the U.S. schools (National Center for Educational Statistics [NCES], 2022). While there is a significant, 66 percent, increase in Latina/o/x high school completers since 1996 (Bauman, 2017), Latina/o/x students in the United States continue to encounter persisting systemic threats both within and outside of school.

The deficit dominant frames (Caldas et al., 2019) that regularly prevail within classrooms ignore students' linguistic resources as capital, equitable esteeming of diverse cultural norms, and inclusive practices of community values (Potowski, 2004; Valenzuela, 1999). Deficit frames are magnified in the current political times where the "contrasts between additive and subtractive practices reveal the root of schools' and teachers' [ideologies] and why many schools are ineffective in adequately meeting the linguistic needs of [the Latina/o/x student] population" (Randolph, 2017, p. 275). Asking students to acquire the necessary content and to demonstrate sufficient understanding of learning through the medium of English without adequate access to academic English is not reasonable (Egbert & Ernst-Slavit, 2010), especially given that the gap between the percentage of Latina/o/x teachers and students is larger than for any other racial or ethnic group (Carver-Thomas, 2018). Below we discuss a brief history of the Spanish language in the United States and then move through key principles of the Spanish language that are helpful for educators to be aware of when working with Latina/o/x ELLs.

A BRIEF HISTORY OF THE SPANISH
LANGUAGE IN THE UNITED STATES

Spanish has significant similarities to English from the early church's influence and the Norman conquest in the eleventh century. Spanish originated following the fall of the Roman Empire as Arab Moors began to take over what is now modern-day Spain posturing the Mozarabic language. Spoken Latin, which had usurped Proto-Indo-European indigenous languages, began to change. The first documented variety of Spanish, that is, Castilian Spanish, evolved. King Alfonso X officially adopted Castilian Spanish in the thirteenth century and eventually the monarchy reconquested the land, forcing the dissolution of the Mozarabic language and Moorish peoples in 1492 (Posner et al., 2022). Castilian Spanish developed into a writing system derived from the Roman alphabet, and both spoken and written Spanish began to spread. In addition to eradicating other language varieties and cultures in Spain, the Spanish kingdom sent forth conquistadors intended to conquer indigenous civilizations abroad. Where the conquistadors landed, every effort was taken to destroy the languages and cultural traditions encountered and Spanish Christian traditions and language practices were imposed.

The territory wars across the Americas between the colonizing countries of France, Britain, and Spain left destruction, cruelty, and harm in their wake. The Spanish conquistadors migrated northward from current-day Mexico, and European colonizers were filing from the East into the Southwestern territories. Mexico declared independence from Spain in 1821, and Spanish became the lingua franca of the territory. Spanish has been a part of the land occupied within the colonized borders of what is currently the United States for hundreds of years and is firmly situated at the intersection of colonial politics, language rights, and identity (Fritz, n/d; Lozano, 2018).

The confluence of Spanish and European settlers in the American Southwest created Spanish-English bilingual communities where governments, policies, and agreements moved between Spanish and English with fluidity (Lozano, 2018). However, following the Mexican American War in 1846–1848 with the signing of the Treaty of Guadalupe Hidalgo in 1848, this bilingual way of being was under direct threat. As part of the treaty, Mexico ceded territory that is now known as California, Arizona, New Mexico, Texas, Colorado, and Utah (Treaty of Guadalupe Hidalgo, 1848, Article V). Following the signing of this treaty, English-only language regulatory efforts were almost immediately pushed forward influencing the role of the Spanish language in official documents, public spaces, and government proceedings. To further impress English-only regulatory efforts, in 1917, congress superseded a veto by President Wilson passing the Immigration Act of 1917, institutionalizing limitations to immigration. These political repressions of laws and English-only efforts repeatedly demonstrated violations of four first amendment rights, which included: (1) the right to free speech for government employees, (2) the right to free speech for elected government officials, (3) the right to free speech for constituents, and (4) the right for all citizens, including citizens who speak languages other than English, to petition the government to redress their grievances (Vile, 2009). The usurpation of these rights has influenced the role of Spanish in schools and in places of government.

As we position the realities of implementing equitable education in schools, we are dared to wrestle with the impact of students' first amendment rights and the ways Spanish is racialized in schools, specifically for Latina/o/x ELLs. Educators are challenged to navigate the tension of honestly engaging with history while understanding how to use the linguistic resources students bring within linguistically responsive instruction grounded in the principled elements of Spanish.

PRINCIPLED ELEMENTS OF SPANISH

Spanish in the United States is regularly in contact with English. Through such contact, both significantly influence the other. It is important to understand the most influential elements of Spanish to support students' content knowledge and their academic English language acquisition of vocabulary and language forms and functions (Gottlieb & Ernst-Slavit, 2014; Zwiers, 2014). Affording access to the vocabulary and language forms and functions of the lesson is key to being able to deliver equity-centered linguistically responsive instruction.

Vocabulary

The Spanish alphabet consists of 29 letters—27 single letters or graphemes and 2 double letters (e.g., ch, 2). There are 5 vowel sounds, or phonemes, and less than 20 consonant sounds, depending on the Spanish language variety. The majority of the graphemes have a one-to-one correlation with the subsequent phoneme, or letter sound correlation. For a few brief examples, in table 2.1, we show how the vowels and some of the consonants demonstrate this correlation.

Table 2.1   Grapheme and Phoneme Single Sound

Grapheme and Phoneme 1-to-1 Correlation in Spanish Examples			
	Vowels		*Consonants*
a	/a/	b	/b/
e	/e/	d	/d/
o	/o/	t	/t/

This one-to-one correlation is relative to the majority of letters and sounds in Spanish making the transfer from spoken Spanish to written Spanish comparatively accessible. In general, the orthography, or spelling of Spanish words, tends to be much more direct than their corresponding counterparts in English.

In English, also derived from the Roman alphabet, we see 26 graphemes make a combination of 44 different sounds depending on how they are written. The vowels alone in English consist of at least 14 different phonemes depending on the language variety. For students, this means when learning to read in Spanish, the strategy of sounding out the word is a reasonably effective tool, whereas in English, it is only a useful tool less than 15 percent of the time. What this also means is that when heritage Spanish-speaking students are learning to read and write in English, as they draw from their linguistic capital in Spanish, the initial spelling, or orthography, will appear phonetic in nature and should be drawn on as a strong foundation from which to build additional word-attack skills. In Spanish, one grapheme, h, when written at the beginning of a word, holds a silent letter in words like *hablar*, /ab/lar/, and *hola*, /o/la/. Four graphemes represent two or more sounds, as seen in table 2.2.

Table 2.2 Graphemes with Multiple Sounds

Graphemes with Multiple Sounds in Spanish		
Grapheme	Sound Combinations	Examples
c	/k/; /s/	cuello; cine
g	/g/; /x/	gato; gente
r	/r/; /-r/	hora; arroz
x	/ks/; /gs/; /s/; /j/	exacto; exhibir; texto; laxitud

Where to exert sound emphasis when pronouncing Spanish words, unless indicated otherwise by a written demarcation, often called a diacritic or accent mark, tends to be placed on the second to last vowel of the word. For example, *gato* (cat) is pronounced with an emphasis on the /a/. However, with words like *alacrán* (scorpion), the emphasis goes on the last /a/ because of the written indication. There are, of course, other more nuanced rules with strong and weak vowels, consonant combinations, and the like, but for the purposes of positive cross-linguistic transfer for Latina/o/x ELLs, an awareness of potential points of negative transfer, understanding that when reading in Spanish, conventionally pronouncing words in texts is much more overt than it is in English. In English, written signals for pronunciation emphasis do not exist, and context is heavily relied upon for knowing the meaning of a word and how to pronounce it.

For example in English, homographs, or words that are written the same but have different meanings, can create challenges for Latina/o/x ELLs. An example of a homograph in English is the word content. Pronouncing the word content (the noun that means what is contained inside something) with the emphasis on the /o/ and the word content (the adjective meaning peaceful or satisfied) where the emphasis is on the /e/. Another example is tear (the noun meaning liquid drops out of the eye), where the emphasis is on the /e/, and tear (meaning to rip something) where the emphasis is on the /a/.

Acknowledging for Latina/o/x ELLs that context is key when knowing how to pronounce words in English should lead educators to emphasize word-attack skills that rely on context, whereas in Spanish, phonemic awareness is a central tenet to successfully pronouncing words. These typical language patterns serve as useful tools when supporting ELLs language and literacy development in English (Helman, 2004).

Cognates

There are many similar root words between English and Spanish, which are called "cognates." Nearly 30 percent of the words in Spanish have similar root words and somewhat similar meanings in English (Colorín Colorado, n. d). Cognates can be used to support positive language transfer. For example, with the cognate, *hora* | | hour, we can have explicit conversations about how the initial "h" in both Spanish and English are silent, which in English creates a homophone with our, and should serve as a caution when reading and writing in English. In English and Spanish, there are a significant number of cognates, a small example of which is shown in table 2.3. For a thorough list of cognates, see Colorado (2007).

Table 2.3   Spanish–English Cognates

Cognate Examples in Spanish and English	
Spanish	*English*
animal	animal
cafetería	cafeteria
práctica	practice
restaurante	restaurant

Cognates of this nature occur across the Romance languages so if students in the class speak a Romance language other than Spanish with Latin or Greek roots, cognate identification will serve as a linguistically responsive practice.

A caution, however, is to be aware of false cognates. False cognates are words that appear similar in writing and sound but that do not have the same meaning. Below, in table 2.4, are examples of some common false cognates to be mindful of when helping Latina/o/x ELLs make connections across their linguistic resources.

Table 2.4   False Cognates

False Cognate Examples in Spanish and English			
Spanish	English Meaning	English	Spanish
actual	current	actual	exacto, real
pie	foot	pie	la tarta, el 'pie'
lectura	reading	lecture	conferencia, dar una clase
asistir	to attend	assist	ayudar, apoyar
embarazado	pregnant	embarrassed	avergonzado
carpeta	folder	carpet	la alfombra

With false cognates, it is important to seek understanding from your students and their families, and their linguistic experiences. For example, with the word pie (as in apple, cherry, chocolate) in English, students who speak the variety of Spanish that is often referred to by speakers of this variety as, Spanglish, the phrase typically is spoken, *el "pie" de manzana*, meaning apple pie with the word "pie" pronounced using English phonemes. If educators do not know the norms and typical language patterns within this variety of Spanish, they might misinterpret the student's language use in a pejorative manner.

Understanding and explicitly teaching cognates and false cognates are an important tool when supporting the language and literacy development of Latina/o/x ELLs in K-12 U.S. schools. To avoid linguistic bias, educators are urged to inform themselves of the language varieties their students speak to build on students' and families' linguistic capital as a strength for English language acquisition (Sayer, 2008). False cognates can easily be misinterpreted so it is important to make sure to build on the linguistic resources students and families bring into the space to confirm lexical understandings prior to posting on a word wall or explicitly instructing students. Having authentic and caring relationships with students and families is key to building reliable support to corroborate language variety norms. It is also essential to couch the instruction of linguistic features within the context of meaningful and rich text where the nuance of meaning and pronunciation is understood within contextualized discussion and negotiation.

Specific Examples for Vocabulary

In a third grade, dual language bilingual Spanish-English classroom, the classroom teacher served as both the content teacher and the English language development (ELD) teacher. The literacy content in third grade in the dual language program was taught in Spanish, but during the literacy block, students participated in a *Daily Five* model, where students rotated between stations and various literacy activities. One of the stations ELLs rotated through was an ELD station. At this ELD station, the students had weekly stories they read that varied in content across both fiction and non-fiction, wherein, students would partake in weekly word study. This word study consisted and grounded in asset-based instruction supported students by helping them identify prefixes, suffixes, cognates, false cognates, and word-attack skills.

During one week, students were reading a story about Cesar Chavez, a Mexican American civil rights activist and labor leader devoted to improving the working and living conditions for farm workers. Within the story, students were focused on the literacy skill of sequencing events, using the strategy of visualizing. Students were working on the word-attack skill of using sentence clues to build the meaning of words they did not yet know. The focal words were celebrate | | *celebrar*, courage | | *el valor*, disappointment | | *la decepción*, precious | | *precioso*, remind | | *recordar*, symbol | | *el símbolo*, and tradition | | *la tradición*. During the students' small group instruction, the teacher focused on teaching cognates, false cognates, and pronunciation comparisons. The students had to draw special attention to the false cognates in English, deception and record, which can be used by novice language learners when what they mean is *decepción* | | disappointment or *recorder* | | remind. To support this instruction, the teacher used picture clues to show the word's meaning in both English and Spanish and then had students use a jigsaw four-square vocabulary activity, explained below, with the words. The teacher was also able to discuss diacritics in Spanish and how the written symbol in the Spanish word, for cognates in English, can sometimes support cognate pronunciation in words like symbol, when trying to decide where to place the emphasis in English.

Application in the Classroom for Vocabulary Development

There are multiple ways to support students' academic vocabulary development. For example, creating a word wall with the cognates color coded with Spanish in one color and English in another and include images to represent the meaning. Explicitly discussing the phonematic difference is advantageous

See if I can modify this for Darwin

in cultivating linguistic awareness. Students can also use highlight tape to identify the possible cognates in their text and then pose their queries to the class during class discussion, after which, if decided by the class to indeed be a cognate, can be placed on the cognate word wall.

An additional, words-in-context, activity that supports students' development of new vocabulary includes word sorts, where students arrange words based on patterns they see across the words following a mini-lesson on prefixes and/or suffixes and/or word-family words. There is also the use of Total Physical Response as proposed by Asher (1972) and advanced by Krashen (1982) where students use their bodies to connect movements to words. Lastly, students can engage in a jigsaw four-square vocabulary activity. In small groups of four, students write the vocabulary word in the middle of the paper, then in each corner write one of the following: conventional definition, word in context of the text, their own use of the word in words or images, and one to two synonyms along with one antonym. Getting students to make explicit cross-linguistic connections supports not only their ELD but their Spanish language development too (Beeman & Urow, 2012; Escamilla et al., 2013).

Language Forms and Functions

Language forms and functions are essential tools to deconstruct understanding and to build cross-linguistic transfer for Latino/a/x ELLs. Language form refers to a set of conventions for organizing symbols, words, and phrases, and their relative order through a given set of rules or norms. For example, the norm that subject pronouns are in agreement with the subject and verb. Language function, on the other hand, refers to what someone does with the language form to communicate a specific purpose. For example, asking questions, giving commands, or making inferences. Language forms, or syntax, are used to support the various types of language functions an interlocutor, or speaker/communicator is trying to accomplish. Students bring a rich set of linguistic resources from their first language(s) related to how language forms support language function in oral and written communication. For Latina/o/x ELLs, being explicit about the compare and contrast of language forms will help students to able to successfully accomplish their desired language function through the use of diagramming sentences, graphic organizers, tables, sorting games, figures, and diagrams.

One of the most poignant language forms to be conscious of when teaching Latina/o/x ELLs is the language form that, typically, adjectives in Spanish appear after their noun, whereas in English they appear before. For example, *el libro azul* || the blue book. This is significant to understand to be able to use students' linguistic capital as a resource when there appears to be a miscue in students' language output. When students write the sentence, the book blue, educators know this isn't a random mistake or inattentiveness, but rather a language form that students are drawing on from their first language. Educators can use that linguistic capital as an opportunity to provide explicit compare and contrast activities during instruction to draw students' awareness to the form differences and use.

Another important consideration related to language form and function resides within the role of the subject pronoun and verb. In non-pro-drop "non-pronoun-dropping" languages such as English, a subject, verb, object language form, the verb itself typically only differentiates between the third person and all others, predicating the identification and use of the subject pronoun as an established practice. However, in pro-drop languages such as Spanish, pronouns can be omitted when they are inferable in other ways. In Spanish, almost every verb form, tense, and mood, with the exception of a few first- and third-person similarities, have a unique marker within the verb itself indicating the number and subject. In table 2.5, the English and Spanish examples offer a glimpse into this distinction across regular and irregular verbs alike.

Table 2.5   Subject Pronoun

Subject Pronoun Use in Spanish and English Present Tense Verb "To Do"	
Spanish — HACER	English — TO DO
(yo) hago	I do
(tú) haces	you do
(él, ella) hace	he, she, it does
(nosotros) hacemos	we do
(vosotros) [forma de España] hacéis	y'all/you all do
(ellos, ellas) hacen	they do

Understanding the linguistic capital Latina/o/x ELLs bring with them to the context of language learning and use, specifically related to subject pronoun and verb use can be drawn on as a strength. Latina/o/x ELLs have already learned at least five different verb forms/words of every verb in each tense, creating a large linguistic repertoire from which to draw. When applying this knowledge to learning English as an additional language, students can feel encouraged that there are generally only two forms of each verb in each tense to learn, but they may need explicit instruction regarding the importance of inserting the subject pronoun to clarify about whom one is speaking.

In addition to adjectives and subject pronouns, it is beneficial for educators of Latina/o/x ELLs to be aware of object, both direct and indirect, pronoun use, and placement. A typical placement of the object pronoun in Spanish is before the conjugated verb. For example, *ella la escribe* || she writes it. A common exception to this rule is when using commands or infinitives. When using a command in Spanish, the object pronoun is attached to the end of the verb creating a new single word. For example, *escríbala* || write it. When using an infinitive such as ella quiere *escribirla* || she wants to write it, the object pronoun is flexible; it can either go before the conjugated verb or be attached to the end of the verb creating a new word. In English, these object pronouns typically appear after the verb. To encourage positive cross-linguistic transfer, educators can build on the command and infinitive rules of Spanish, where the object pronoun is at the end of the word, to help students connect to where those object pronouns are typically found when using English through sentence building activities, described in table 2.6.

Lastly, an important language form to note for Latina/o/x ELLs includes a discussion of the interrogative, or question, formation. In both Spanish and English, interrogative words such as *cómo* || how, *quién* || who, *qué* || what, and *por qué* || why typically function in a similar way, placed at the beginning of the interrogative statement followed by the verb. The exception to this rule is the auxiliary verb do or does in English, not to be confused with the verb to do || *hacer*. The auxiliary verb does or do does not exist in Spanish. As such, supporting students learning of this auxiliary requirement in English necessitates explicit instruction that this auxiliary verb is only used in simple tense questions and negated declarative statements, or negated replies. For example, *Do* you like to eat ice cream? *No*, I *do not* like to eat ice cream. Versus, Yes, I like to eat ice cream. In order to assimilate this auxiliary verb into typical language output when developing English as an additional language, Latina/o/x ELLs need authentic opportunities to practice through activities such as concentric circles, sentence frames, sentence strip sorts, or sentence scrambles, described in the application section below.

Specific Example for Language Form and Function

With an emphasis on adjectives, subject pronouns, prepositions, and direct objects, students were tasked with authoring a short story. This third grade, dual language Spanish-English classroom used a helpful example of teaching language form to support language function through an activity called *oraciones niveladas* || leveled sentences. Following students' initial attempt to author their short story, the teacher observed that students repetitively wrote simple subject verb sentences, sometimes omitting the subject and rarely including additional details. As a result, she planned a mini-lesson during the students ELD station to help them learn how to build more complex sentences for their short stories with language forms in mind.

Within this activity, shown in table 2.6, the classroom teacher showed students how to use different elements of language to build more complex sentences in order to communicate more intricate ideas within an engaging narrative. The teacher modeled the activity below on large chart paper for the students.

Following her modeling, the small group collectively brainstormed adjectives, verbs, and details such as location ideas, what they would do there, and similes. Students had been exposed to these isolated concepts in previous lessons but had not yet assimilated the ideas in such a way as to interlace them into their short stories. The brainstormed ideas were written on chart paper and posted on the bulletin board behind the table where the small group station took place. On the chart, the verbs were color coded green, the adjectives were color coded orange, the additional details were color coded red, the why was color coded blue, and the simile/metaphor purple. Table 2.6 shows the teacher model of this activity.

Table 2.6   Leveled Sentences

Leveled Sentence Building Activity		
Level	*Syntax Feature(s)*	*Sentence*
Level 1	Subject, verb	I went.
Level 2	Subject, verb, object	I went to the store.
Level 3	Subject, verb, object, adjective	I went to the large store.
Level 4	Subject, verb, object, adjective, and one additional detail about how, who, what, when, or where	I walked to the large store near my house.
Level 5	Subject, verb, object, adjective, one additional detail (how, who, what, when, or where), and why	I walked to the large store near my house to buy a chocolate cake.
BONUS Level	Subject, verb, object, adjective, one additional detail (how, who, what, when, or where), why, and a simile or metaphor	I walked like an elephant to the large store near my house to buy a chocolate cake.

The students, while in small group, then began to build practice sentences with partners to share using whiteboards and colored markers. Following this collaborative supported practice, students began to build their own stories sentence by sentence. These stories were eventually published on the "*Somos Escritores*" (We Are Writers) bulletin board for the entire *comunidad de aprendizaje* (community of learning) to see.

Application in the Classroom for Language Form and Function

When teaching Latina/o/x ELLs language forms and functions, there are several linguistically responsive strategies that have proven to be effective. One strategy includes the scaffolded use of sentence frames. Sentence frames are sentences that have strategically missing words to support student use of a particular form. For example, if newcomer students are learning about adjectives, a possible sentence frame could be: I like the _____ (choose an adjective) cat. For newcomers, inserting a single word or phrase in response to a predictable question is linguistically responsive and supportive. This same sentence frame could then be scaffolded for early intermediate students who are learning the verb, to like, with the corresponding subject and adjective with a possible sentence frame such as: She ___ (correct form of to like) the ____ (choose an adjective) cat. This sentence can then be further expanded for intermediate and advanced ELLs with varied sentence structures, demonstrative endings, and conjunctions. An important consideration when using sentence frames is intentionality. It is vital to be intentional about which words or phrases are missing to align with the language form goals and students' ELD levels.

Another linguistically responsive instructional strategy that supports students' acquisition of English language forms is called a sentence strip sort or sentence scramble. For this activity, students are working on the development of a particular language form, for example, using subject pronouns with simple present tense verbs in English. Students are organized into small groups of three with an envelope that has three sentences cut up into individual words inside. Each sentence contains a subject pronoun—ideally one first person, one second person, and one third person—a present tense verb, and an object. For example, *I eat cake, you eat cake*, and *she eats cake*. Each student from the group takes one word at a time, and they read it aloud to the group. The students then, in collaboration, puts the sentences in order matching the subject pronouns and the verbs. This strategy can of course become more advanced, using forms such as verb tense endings, present and past with different singular and plural subjects, object pronouns, adjectives, and the like, depending on the language form goal. Students can also engage as language detectives, a metacognitive compare/contrast exercise to think through how languages are the same and different through discussion (Escamilla et al., 2013).

As Latina/o/x ELLs are supported with sentence starters, purposed graphic organizers, and targeted language form instruction, they are better able to use poignant language directed toward their desired purpose. With repeated and intentional scaffolds in place to practice and develop the necessary language forms to perform the desired language function, students develop linguistic competence and targeted language function awareness.

DISCUSSION OF EQUITABLE ACCESS TO THE LANGUAGE AND CONTENT OF SCHOOL

Understanding first and second language acquisition theories (Chomsky, 1959; Krashen, 1985; Long, 2018; Pienemann, 2015; Swain, 2005) along with being able to recognize the ways learners make sense of input (VanPatten, 2003) during guided instruction (Lightbown & Spada, 2013) in light of the sociolinguistic (Hymes, 1971) and sociocultural (Vygotsky, 1978) impact of language socialization (Ochs & Schieffelin, 1984) provides the foundation to build a framework that foregrounds the importance of equitable education. Languages and literacies of multilingual learners are interdependently woven together (Riches & Genesee, 2006). Developing language and literacy through linguistically responsive instructional strategies provides Latina/o/x ELLs opportunities to use language to make meaning along a continuum (Hornberger, 1989). With targeted attention toward making meaning through intensively teaching academic vocabulary and language forms and functions (August & Shanahan, 2006; Nagy & Townsend, 2012), educators are better able to cultivate students' academic language (Beeman & Urow, 2013) and conduct assessments that measure what is intended in order to inform decisions for next-step instruction (Abedi, 2004; Basterra et al., 2011; Valdés & Figueroa, 1996). Using Latina/o/x ELLs' primary language to support ELD is critical for English literacy development. As such, classroom literacy instruction combined with small group and individualized interventions can have a positive impact in promoting students' academic literacy outcomes (Burns & Gibbons, 2008).

SIGNIFICANCE FOR EDUCATORS IN U.S. K-12 CONTEXTS

Although there persists an adage that the United States is a monolingual country, the reality of the history of Spanish in the United States would dispute this claim and instead reveal that the United States has always been a land of multiculturalism and multilingualism (Wright, 2019). Spanish has been and continues to be a language of emigration, migration, and immigration. Spanish is a language deeply embedded in the history, the present, and the future of the United States, and the challenges to equitable access to the language and content of school for Latina/o/x ELLs that persists in K-12 schools are tied to the ways we racialize language use and the users of said language (Alim et al., 2020). To change the persisting opportunity gaps for Latina/o/x ELLs, acknowledging the historical-structural frames that shape repressive contexts in education and engaging linguistically responsive instructional strategies to effectively teach vocabulary, and language forms and functions in English is of the utmost importance. Our hope within this chapter is for educators to learn meaningful ways to center equity within linguistically responsive instruction through purposed instructional strategies that support Latina/o/x ELLs' acquisition and use of both Spanish and English. Students' first language resources can and should be used as valuable assets to support instruction of both content and language so that all students are able to equitably participate and engage in meaningful ways. Academic language, the oral and written language used for academic purposes, and the way students express content understandings need to be made explicit to expand students' control over their own language use and to support students' language choices according to the language function and audience.

The reality of education, specifically for Latina/o/x ELLs and families, is that schooling experiences, from curriculum to gentrified dual language programs (Valdez et al., 2016), are firmly situated at the intersection of colonial politics, first amendment rights, and identity politics. Educators are challenged during these current political times to approach their instruction not only from a critical content and language lens but also from a critical sociocultural and critical sociopolitical lens that acknowledges the differences between additive and subtractive practices in order to employ linguistically responsive instruction that affords equitable educational opportunities for Latina/o/x ELLs.

REFERENCES

Abedi, J. (2004). The no child left behind act and English language learners: Assessment and accountability issues. *Educational Research, 33*(1), 4–14.

Alim, H. S., Rickford, J. R., & Ball, A. F. (2020). *Raciolinguistics: How language shapes our ideas about race.* Oxford University Press.

Asher, J. (1972). Children's first language as a model for second language learning. *Modern Language Journal, 56*, 133–139.

August, D., & Shanahan, T. (2006). *Developing literacy in second-language learners: Report of the national literacy panel on language minority children and youth.* Lawrence Erlbaum Associates.

Basterra, M. R., Trumbull, E., & Solano-Flores, G. (2011). *Cultural validity in assessment: Addressing linguistic and cultural diversity.* Routledge.

Batalova, J., Hanna, M., & Levesque, C. (2021). *Frequently requested statistics on immigrants and immigration in the United States.* Migration Information Source, February 11. https://www.migrationpolicy.org/article/frequently-requested-statistics-immigrants-and-immigration-united-states-2020.

Bauman, K. (2017). School enrollment of the Hispanic population: Two decades of growth. *United States Census Bureau.* https://www.census.gov/newsroom/blogs/random-samplings/2017/08/school_enrollmentof.html.

Beeman, K., & Urow, C. (2013). *Teaching for biliteracy: Strengthening bridges between languages.* Caslon Publishing.

Burns, M. K., & Gibbons, K. A. (2008). *Implementing response-to-intervention in elementary and secondary schools: Procedures to assure scientific-based practices.* Routledge.

Caldas, B., Palmer, D., & Schwedhelm, M. (2019). Speaking educación in Spanish: Linguistic and professional development in a bilingual teacher education program in the US-Mexico borderlands. *International Journal of Bilingual Education and Bilingualism, 22*(1), 49–63.

Calderón, M., August, D., Slavin, R., Duran, D., Madden, N., & Cheung, A. (2005). Bringing words to life in classrooms with English-language learners. In *Teaching and learning vocabulary: Bringing research to practice* (pp. 115–136). Lawrence Erlbaum Associates Publishers.

Carver-Thomas, D. (2018). *Diversifying the teaching profession: How to recruit and retain teachers of color.* Learning Policy Institute. https://learningpolicyinstitute .org/product/diversifying-teaching-profession-report.

Chomsky, N. (1959). A review of B. F. Skinner's verbal behavior. *Language, 35,* 26–57. DOI: 10.2307/411334.

Colorado, C. (2007). *Using cognates to develop comprehension in English.* https://www.luc.edu/media/lucedu/education/pdfs/languagematters/Sp16_Strauts &Seidler_Article_Using-Cognates.pdf.

Colorado, C. (n/d). *Academic language.* https://www.colorincolorado.org/academic -language.

Egbert, J., & Ernst-Slavit, G. (2010). *Access to academics: Planning for instruction for K-12 classrooms with ELLs.* Pearson.

Escamilla, K., Hopewell, S., & Butvilofsky, S. (2013). *Biliteracy from the start: Literacy squared in action.* Caslon.

Fritz, C. (n/d). 1989: *400 Years later, Acoma protests Spanish cruelty.* National Institutes of Health, Health and Human Services Freedom of Information Act, NLM. https://www.nlm.nih.gov/nativevoices/timeline/630.html.

Gee, J. P., & Green, J. L. (1998). Discourse analysis, learning, and social practice: A methodological study. *Review of Research in Education, 23,* 119–169.

Gottlieb, M., & Ernst-Slavit, G. (2014). *Academic language in diverse classrooms: Definitions and contexts.* Corwin Press.

Helman, L. (2004). *Building on the sound system of Spanish: Insights from the alphabetic spellings of English-language learners* (pp. 452–460). International Reading Association.

Hornberger, N. H. (1989). Continua of biliteracy. *Review of Educational Research, 59,* 271–296.

Hymes, D. (1971). *On communicative competence.* University of Pennsylvania Press.

Krashen, S. (1982). *Principles and practices in second language acquisition.* New York.

Krashen, S. (1985). *The input hypothesis: Issues and implications.* Longman. Lemke, J. L. (1990). *Talking science: Language, learning, and values.* Ablex.

Lightbown, P. M., & Spada, N. (2013). *How languages are learned* (4th ed.). Oxford.

Long, M. H. (2018). Interaction in L2 classrooms. In J. I. Liontas & M. DelliCarpini (Eds.), *The TESOL encyclopedia of English language teaching.* John Wiley & Sons. https://onlinelibrary.wiley.com/doi/epdf/10.1002/9781118784235.eelt0233.

Lozano, R. (2018). *An American language: The history of Spanish in the United States* (1st ed.). University of California Press. http://www.jstor.org/stable/10.1525 /j.ctt21668qw.

Mortimer, E. F., & Scott, P. H. (2003). *Meaning making in secondary science classrooms.* Open University Press.

Nagy, W., & Townsend, D. (2012). Words as tools: Learning academic vocabulary as language acquisition. *Reading? Research Quarterly, 47*(1), 91–108.

National Center for Education Statistics (NCES). (2022). *English learners in public schools: Condition of education.* U.S. Department of Education, Institute of Education Sciences. https://nces.ed.gov/programs/coe/indicator/cgf/english-learners.

Ochs, E., & Schieffelin, B. (1984). Language acquisition and socialization: Three developmental stories and their implications. In R. Schweder & R. LeVine (Eds.), *Culture theory: Essays in mind, self, and emotion* (pp. 276–320). Cambridge University Press.

Pienemann, M. (2015). An outline of processability theory and its relationship to other approaches in SLA. *Language Learning, 65*(1), 123–151.

Posner, R., & Sala, M. (2022, February 14). Spanish language. *Encyclopedia Britannica.* https://www.britannica.com/topic/Spanish-language.

Potowski, K. (2004). Student Spanish use and investment in a dual immersion classroom: Implications for second language acquisition and heritage language maintenance. *Modern Language Journal, 88*, 75–101.

Randolph, L. J. (2017). Heritage language learners in mixed Spanish classes: Subtractive practices and perceptions of high school Spanish teachers. *Hispania, 100*(2), 274–288.

Riches, C., & Genesee, F. (2006). Literacy: Crosslinguistic and crossmodal issues. In F. Genesee, K. Lindholm-Leary, W. M. Saunders, & D. Christian (Eds.), *Educating English language learners: A synthesis of research evidence* (pp. 64–108). Cambridge University Press.

Sayer, P. (2008). Demystifying language mixing: Spanglish in school. *Journal of Latinos and Education, 7*(2), 94–112. DOI: 10.1080/15348430701827030.

Swain, M. (2005). The output hypothesis: Theory and research. In E. Hinkel (Ed.), *Handbook of research in second language teaching and learning* (pp. 495–508). Routledge.

Treaty of Guadalupe Hidalgo. (1984). *National archives.* https://www.archives.gov/education/lessons/guadalupe-hidalgo.

Valdés, G., & Figueroa, R. A. (1996). *Bilingualism and testing: A special case of bias* (3rd ed.). Ablex Publishing Corporation.

Valdez, V. E., Freire, J. A., & Delavan, M. G. (2016). The gentrification of dual language education. *Urban Review, 48*, 601–627.

Valenzuela, A. (1999). *Subtractive schooling: U.S.-Mexican youth and the politics of caring.* State University of New York Press.

VanPatten, B. (2003). *From input to output: A teacher's guide to second language acquisition.* McGraw Hill.

Vile, J. (2009). English only laws. *The First Amendment Encyclopedia.* https://www.mtsu.edu/first-amendment/article/1209/english-only-laws.

Vygotsky, L. S. (1978). *Mind in society: The development of higher psychological processes.* Harvard University Press.

Wright, W. (2019). *Foundations for teaching English language learners: Research, theory, policy, and practice* (3rd ed.). Caslon.

Zong, J., & Batalova, J. (2015). The limited English proficient population in the United States. *Migration Policy Institute.* http://www.migrationpolicy.org/article/limited-english-proficient-population-united-states#Age,%20Race,%20and%20Ethnicity.

Zwiers, J. (2014). *Building academic language: Meeting common core standards across disciplines, grades 5–12* (2nd ed.). John Wiley & Sons.

Chapter 3

Korean Students' First Language Impact on English Language and Literacy Learning

Kwangok Song and Jieun Kiaer

The number of K-12 English learners from the Korean language background is increasing worldwide, including in the United States. Each year from 2016 to 2021, approximately 8,000–9,000 South Korean K-12 students stayed in other countries, mostly English-speaking countries (e.g., The United States, Australia, United Kingdom, New Zealand, Philippines) (Korean Educational Statistics Service [KESS], 2021). The United States alone hosted 5,500 South Korean K-12 students in 2020, according to the U.S. Immigration and Custom Enforcement (2020). This figure does not include the total number of Korean immigrant descendants, who were either born in the United States or moved to the United States at an early age. K-12 students from Korea have learned English to some degree because English-as-a-foreign language is taught officially in the school system and private education markets.

As English holds *linguistic capital* status for academic and professional success in South Korea, learning English is promoted at all grade levels (Park, 2011). Since 2008, students in South Korea have been learning English-as-a-foreign language from first grade onward. English education markets were expanding long before then and still are now, allowing students to learn English outside the school system. Since the early 2000s, when the interest in English language education became heightened, Korean early-study-abroad students have increased dramatically (Abelmann et al., 2015; Jahng, 2011; Park, 2009). After reaching its peak in 2006, the number of students studying abroad has decreased slowly over the past 15 years (KESS, 2021).

Differences between English and Korean can cause difficulties as Korean-speaking English learners develop their skills in the English language. To create equitable learning opportunities for Korean-speaking English learners, it is important for teachers to understand unique characteristics that the students may demonstrate in the process of learning English due to the influence of their first language and the ways English is used in Korea. Such an understanding can help teachers offer appropriate instructional support for Korean-speaking English learners.

This chapter first introduces the historical background of the Korean language and *Hangeul,* the Korean writing system. Then, we discuss the patterns that characterize Korean-speaking English learners' oral and written communication in English. And we conclude with instructional implications for educators.

AN INTRODUCTION TO THE KOREAN LANGUAGE

History of the Korean Language

The periods of the Korean language are marked primarily by social and political changes in East Asia and are typically understood as the following: Old Korean (0–935), Middle Korean (935–1592), Modern Korean (1592–1900), and Contemporary Korean (1900–present). The study of the Korean language in times before modernist empirical approaches using video and audio recordings relied on the interpretation of historical texts. This feat was rendered even more difficult by the lack of a native Korean writing system before the mid-fifteenth century because most publications before this time were written in Classical Chinese. There have been multiple attempts to establish a genetic relationship between Korean and Altaic languages such as Turkish since Gustaf Joh Ramstedt, a well-known Altaic linguist in the mid-twentieth century (see Vovin, 2010). Due to the lack of reliable evidence, Korean is generally considered a "language isolate," which means that it has no provable historical connection to any other language. According to Ethnologue (2013), there are approximately 79 million speakers of Korean across the globe (48.6 million in South Korea, 23.8 million in North Korea, and 7 million globally), including speakers of Korean-as-a-native-language and Korean-as-an-additional-language. Korean is now the 13th most widely spoken language globally (National Institute of Korean Language, 2021). With the immense international success of Korean pop culture, or *Hallyu* (한류, "Korean wave") in the recent decade, the interest in studying the Korean language has increased substantially (Wang & Pyun, 2020). Fans of Korean pop culture want to learn the Korean language and *Hangeul* to understand lyrics and lines in dramas or movies and to participate in affinity groups.

Hangeul, the Korean Writing System

Hangeul [한글], the Korean writing system, was invented by King Sejong the Great and was publicized in 1443 during the Chosŏn Dynasty (1392–1910), the last imperial dynasty of Korea. *Hangeul* is the official romanization of 한글 since 2000. Although King Sejong and his successors took great pains to encourage the use of *Hangeul*, it took more than 400 years before *Hangeul* started gaining prominence as the official orthography of the Korean peninsula. *Hangeul* is written as a syllable block in which letters and phonemes mostly have a one-to-one correspondence. Some of the original letters are no longer used in contemporary Korean because the sounds represented by those letters are also no longer present. The designs of the 14 basic consonant letters and 10 basic vowel letters in *Hangeul* are based on linguistic principles such as the places of articulation, or the locations within the mouth where sounds are made, and the shapes of the mouth, tongue, and vocal cords when the sounds are produced. Some of these basic letters are combined to form 16 consonant clusters and 11 additional vowels. Table 3.1 shows consonant and vowel letters in *Hangeul.* Now we will turn to characteristics that define the English that is spoken by Korean-speaking learners of English.

Table 3.1   Consonant and Vowel Letters in Hangeul in Order

Classification		Letters
Basic letters (N=24)	Consonants (n=14)	ㄱ, ㄴ, ㄷ, ㄹ, ㅁ, ㅂ, ㅅ, ㅇ, ㅈ, ㅊ, ㅋ, ㅌ, ㅍ, ㅎ
	Vowels (n=10)	ㅏ, ㅑ, ㅓ, ㅕ, ㅗ, ㅛ, ㅜ, ㅠ, ㅡ, ㅣ
Complex letters (N=16)	Complex letters for consonants (n=5)	ㄲ, ㄸ, ㅃ, ㅆ, ㅉ
	Complex letters for vowels (n=11)	ㅐ, ㅒ, ㅔ, ㅖ, ㅘ, ㅙ, ㅚ, ㅝ, ㅞ, ㅟ, ㅢ

CHARACTERISTICS OF KOREAN-SPEAKING ENGLISH LEARNERS' USE OF ENGLISH

Certain linguistic features of the Korean language may change the ways native Korean speakers use English. Additionally, as English has been taught in the Korean educational system and has been used in various social contexts in Korea for decades, unique ways to use English have emerged (Kiaer & Ahn, 2021). Therefore, English learners from Korean language backgrounds may exhibit unique features in their speech or writing influenced by their first language and *Konglish* or Korean English. The influence of the first language and Korean English is likely to appear mostly in adult learners' English use due to their reliance on the first language and familiarization with Korean English in limited second language entries (e.g., Hadikin, 2014; Rüdiger, 2019). However, K-12 English learners may also show some of these patterns as they acquire and develop skills in the use of English.

In the following sections, therefore, we discuss some of these distinctive characteristics to help educators understand the ways in which Korean-speaking English learners make sense of complexities in English by integrating linguistic resources from their first language and their prior knowledge of the English language.

Challenges in Producing Some Phonemes

Korean-speaking English learners may experience challenges in identifying and producing certain phonemes (the smallest sound units of a spoken word) in English because the Korean language's phonetic and articulatory properties, or ways to articulate sounds and phonemic inventory, are different from those of the English language (Cho & Jeong, 2013; Jang, 2014). Certain English phonemes do not exist in the Korean language. These include [f], [l], [r], [v], [z], [θ] as in _thorn_, and [ð] as in _thus_. Korean-speaking English learners who have difficulties in perceiving these phonemes also have difficulties in articulating them (Lee, 2011). Korean-speaking English learners may replace them with familiar phonemes available in the Korean language (Kiaer & Ahn, 2021) as shown in table 3.2.

Table 3.2   **English Sounds that Korean-speaking English Learners May Have Difficulties Perceiving and Producing and How They May Sound**

English Sounds and Examples	Possible Alternative Sounds	English Sounds and Examples	Possible Alternative Sounds
[θ] as in _three_	With [s] sree	[f] as in _fox_	[p] as in pox
[ð] as in _this_	With [t] _t_is	[v] as in _valley_	[b] belly
[ð] as in lea_th_er	With [d] le_d_er		
[z] as in _z_ebra and	[tɕ] similar to [ch]:	[r] as in rain and [l]	[l/r] Both words may
[ʒ] as in _j_am	_ch_ebra and _ch_am	as in lane	sound the same

Additional difficulties in articulating some phonemes in the English language may arise because the ways to articulate those sounds in English differ from the method of articulation of the same sounds in the Korean language. Unlike the phonemes presented above, some phonemes in English have shared qualities with those in Korean. For example, some phonemes such as [b] as in _bed_, [d] as in _desk_, and [g] as in _gate_ can create difficulties in articulation despite their similarities with corresponding phonemes in the Korean language. When these phonemes appear at the onset of the first syllable in a word, Korean-speaking English learners may articulate them differently

(Kim, 2012). This is because in English, [b], [d], [g], and [j] as initial sounds are voiced (vibrating vocal cords), whereas the corresponding phonemes in the Korean language are voiceless (no vibrating vocal cords) (Hong et al., 2014). Therefore, [b], [d], [g], and [j] can be replaced with voiceless sounds that may sound similar to [p], [t], [k], and [ch], respectively (Ha et al., 2009).

Quite a few studies have shown that learners who started learning English as children can achieve so-called native-like performance in articulating sounds in English (Flege et al., 1995; Munro et al., 1996). Therefore, the first language influence on the articulation of English sounds in young English learners' performance may not be as great as that in older or adult learners (Yeni-Komshian et al., 2000). Tsukada et al.'s (2005) comparative study on Korean-speaking English learners clearly showed such a difference in children's and adults' production and perception of English vowel sounds. As Korean-speaking English learners become socialized in the English-speaking environment, they gradually develop skills to articulate the sounds of the English language with increased comprehensibility. Nevertheless, teachers can be keenly aware of new English learners' potential difficulties in perceiving and articulating specific English sounds caused by the first language influence. Teachers can make concerted efforts to pay close attention to speech contexts and English learners' intention to encourage their meaning-making.

Challenges in Making Plurals and Tenses

The omission or misinterpretation of inflectional endings for plurals and tenses (i.e., -(e)s, -(e)d) can also be another characteristic of Korean-speaking English learners' production of English (Rüdiger, 2019). Korean does not have an obligatory plural marker (e.g., (e)s in English), and singular and plural forms of nouns are often identical (Song, 2005). When one tries to emphasize the plurality of a noun, the suffix -들 (plural inflectional ending) can be used. However, this is uncommon and typically only used for human animate nouns (e.g., 사람들 [people], 학생들 [students]). When a counting number is used in Korean, such as "사과 다섯 개 [five apples]," the plural marker -들 is seen as redundant because the numeral classifier (i.e., 다섯 개) already expresses plurality. Additionally, plural markings for English loan words are trimmed when used in the Korean language (e.g., 선글라스 [sunglass*] for *sunglasses*; 진 [jean*] for *jeans*). Beginning Korean-speaking English learners may transfer this tendency of omitting plural markers. Textbox 3.1 shows the oral reading miscues produced by Hyunmin (all names are pseudonyms), a fifth-grade English learner receiving education in the United States for one year. Please note that "—" in the transcript indicates omission; italics indicate substitution; and the underlines indicate words read without an inflectional ending (e.g., -(e)s, (e)d).

HYUNMIN'S ORAL READING MISCUES

Original Text	Hyunmin's Oral Reading
First, the beaver must build a dam. It uses sticks, leaves, and mud to block a stream. The beaver uses its two front teeth to get the sticks. The animal uses its large flat tail to pack mud into place. A pond forms behind the dam. The beaver spends most of its life near this pond. . . .	First, the beaver must *make* a dam. It **use stick, leave,** and mud to block—stream. The beaver, **use** its two front teeth to get the **stick.** The animal use its large flat tail to pack mud into place. *The* pond **form** behind the dam. The beaver **spend** most of its life near this pond. . . .
All this work changes the land. As trees are cut down, birds, squirrels, and other animals may have to find new homes.	All this work **change** the land. As trees are cut down, **bird, squirrel**, and other **animal** may have to find new **home.**
Animals that feed on trees lose their food supply. The pond behind the dam floods part of the ground. Animals that used to live there have to move. However, the new environment becomes a home for different kinds of birds, fish, and plants. All this happens because of the very busy beaver. (Leslie & Caldwell, 2011)	Animals that feed on trees lose their food **supplies**. The pond behind the dam **flood** part of the ground. **Animal** that used to live there have to move. However, the new environment *because* a home for different **kind** of **bird**, fish, and **plant**. All this **happen** because of the very busy beaver.

As shown in the excerpt of Hyunmin's oral reading, he skipped the plural inflectional ending (-(e)s) in most of the plural words in the text. Such omission may indicate that he needs instructional support in understanding the role of plural endings in the English language. Additionally, beginning Korean-speaking English learners may overgeneralize the use of plural markings by using them rather generously (e.g., "more *informations**" instead of "more information"; "many helpful *advices**" instead of "many helpful advice").

Challenges in Following English Sentence Structures

The basic sentence structure of Korean differs greatly from that of English. Simply put, Korean is a Subject-Object-Verb (SOV) language, whereas English is a Subject-Verb-Object (SVO) language. In English, the verb comes early in a sentence and sets the expectation for the rest of a sentence. In Korean, the verb comes at the end, which means that the meaning of a sentence is constructed in other ways, predominantly with case particles. A case particle, mostly a single-syllable morpheme (the smallest unit of meaning) directly attached to a preceding noun, determines the role of a noun (e.g., subject, noun, possessive). Therefore, syntactic structures can be flexible, and the meaning of a sentence does not change despite the basic structure being varied. Additionally, the total omission of a subject can be acceptable in Korean.

Due to the syntactic differences between English and Korean, beginning Korean-speaking English learners may find forming sentences in English challenging. For example, because Korean-speaking English learners may use syntactic features in the Korean language to produce English sentences, they may not always follow basic syntactic features of English by presenting a series of words and omitting a subject (Kil, 2003). These syntactic errors decrease as Korean-speaking English learners develop their understanding of sentence structures in English. However, even if Korean-speaking English learners understand the basic word order in English, some syntactic errors may continue to appear due to the transfer from Korean (Seong & Lee, 2008). Particularly, when the input from English is not enough, Korean-speaking English learners tend to use their knowledge of Korean phrases and expressions and directly transfer certain syntactic features into English. These syntactic features caused by first language influence may appear randomly as learners transfer familiar ways to express ideas from their first language.

Challenges in Using Articles

Beginning Korean-speaking English learners may frequently omit or misuse articles (e.g., the, a(n)) (Rüdiger, 2019). Although the lack of articles in the first language does not directly impact English learners' misuse of articles (Ko et al., 2009; Zdorenko & Paradis, 2008), it is possible that the absence of articles in the Korean language may be related to beginning Korean-speaking English learners' confusion about articles to some extent. Because the Korean language does not have articles, definiteness and indefiniteness can be expressed in context without an article (Kang, 2021). Bare noun phrases, or nouns without an article or plural markers (i.e., -(e)s), have multiple meanings. For example, "동물 [animal]" means "an animal," "the animal," "the animals," and "animals." As English learners develop proficiency, the accuracy in using articles would increase (Park, 2006).

Challenges in Using Prepositions

Another common characteristic that Korean-speaking English learners may show is the misuse of prepositions (Back, 2011). In English, prepositions indicate locations and time, and they are also a part of phrasal verbs (e.g., bring up, graduate from, drop out of, fill out). Unlike English, the Korean language does not have prepositions. Instead, it has case particles and postpositions, which have morphemes (the smallest meaning unit) attached to a noun to grant grammatical functions (e.g., subject, object, locative adverb, time adverb) in a sentence. These morphemes that indicate a space (i.e., 에, 에서, 안에, 뒤에, 앞에, 옆에, 위에) or a time (i.e., -에) are located after a noun (e.g., 건물에 [in a building] 안에 [inside]; 책상에 [on a desk] 위에 [on]). Additionally, because phrasal verbs are a unique linguistic feature of English, Korean-speaking English learners may omit or misuse prepositions in phrasal verbs (Ryoo, 2013).

Korean-speaking English learners may transfer semantic aspects of postpositions in Korean to their use of prepositions in English (Yoon, 2012). For example, differentiating prepositions such as *on, in,* and *at* to indicate a time (e.g., on Tuesday, in December, at 1 pm) and location (e.g., in the park, at the lake, at school, on the playground) can be confusing to beginning Korean-speaking English learners because the ways to use postpositions in the Korean language are not always the same as those to use prepositions in English. The following example further shows how Jinhee's (an eighth-grade English learner from Korea) use of prepositions in her speech is influenced by her first language, Korean:

> If you get closer with* the person who got Ebola, you can get Ebola in your body*. I think those who got Ebola under the body* cannot think they got like serious virus on their body*.

In the above excerpt, Jinhee used several prepositional phrases to explain how one can be infected by Ebola virus, and these uses of prepositional phrases show the first language influence. First, the phrase "get closer with the person" is likely to be influenced by Korean. In the corresponding Korean phrase, "에볼라에 걸린 사람과 가까이 있으면" [if you are exposed to a person with Ebola], the Korean postposition used in this phrase is ~과, which carries the meaning *with* in English. Additionally, the use of prepositional phrases such as "in the body" may be unnecessary in English to mean "to contract a disease or to get a virus." However, in the Korean language, it is acceptable to include "in the body" as in "몸에 [in the body] 바이러스가 걸리다 [to get a virus]." Interestingly, as shown in the examples above, Jinhee switched prepositions from "in" to "under" again to "on" in one speech event to mean "몸에." Such changes in prepositions seem to indicate how she might have assumed that more than one preposition could be used to mean "몸에," and how she was not yet sure about which one should be used.

Using *Konglish,* or Korean English (Korean-Style English)

Konglish, or Korean English, encompasses a wide range of syntactic and semantic features appearing in Korean-speaking English learners' oral and written communication, which may be influenced by the features of the Korean language and specific ways that English is used in Korea. This chapter focuses only on lexical items called loan words and unusual lexical choices made by Korean-speaking English learners.

Fabricated English Loan Words

A vast inventory of English loan words has been adopted into the everyday Korean vernacular. English words of various themes such as technology, science, sports, economics, and fashion have entered the Korean language (Lee, 2020). These English words have become Koreanized and transliterated with *Hangeul* by following the phonological and orthographic rules of the Korean language. Many of them are semantically the same as original English words with phonetic modifications such as 컴퓨터 [*keompyuteo*] to refer to "computer" with modifications by using sounds available in the Korean language.

Quite a few loan words are used differently from their original English words or have different meanings. Some of them do not exist in English. They include truncated words with shortened forms of original words and fabricated loan words that are semantically modified English words (Kiaer, 2014). For example, 오피스텔 [*opiseutel*] is a fabricated loan word that comprises two words from *office* and *motel* to mean "a studio apartment." These semantically and morphologically modified loan words are one of the distinctive features of *Konglish* or Korean English (Kiaer & Ahn, 2021). Table 3.3 shows examples of the truncated and fabricated loan words commonly used in Korean.

Table 3.3 Fabricated Loan Words in Korean and Corresponding English Words

Fabricated Loan Words (Direct Translation in English)	Corresponding English Words Used in the United States
핸드폰 [Hand phone]	Mobile phone or cell phone
매니큐어 [Manicure]	Nail polish
리본 [Ribbon]	Bow
센스 [Sense]	Wit
핫도그 [Hot dog]	Corn dog
사인 [Sign]	Signature
탤런트 [talent]	Actors/actresses
리모컨 [remotecon]	Remote control
핸들 [handle]	Steering Wheel/ handlebar
아파트 [apart]	Apartment
화이팅 [fighting]	Come on! Let's go! Go, XXX!
서비스 [service]	Free of charge
컨닝 [cunning]	Cheating

Beginning Korean-speaking English learners may use *Konglish* words when speaking and writing in English because these words are commonly considered English words in Korea. As English learners may access meanings through their first language entries, they are likely to assume that the meanings of these modified loan words can be transferable to English. Therefore, using *Konglish* words may demonstrate learners' active and creative engagement in making meaning in English by using resources from Korean.

Unusual Word Choices

Korean-speaking English learners may make a semantically unusual lexical choice even if their sentences are syntactically appropriate. This is because they may retrieve lexical items or phrases from Korean and translate them into English (Wang, 2003; Woodall, 2002). Consequently, such sentences or phrases may sound unusual to U.S. native English speakers. Baratta (2013) analyzed sixth-grade Korean children's writing samples to discuss how students (e.g., Paul, Jane, and Adam) constructed semantically unusual phrases. Here, we focus on three examples shared in Baratta's study.

> *Example 1. When me and my sister were born, we got divided love.* (Paul, as cited in Baratta, 2013, p. 12)

Example 1 could be interpreted to express Paul's frustration with *divided love*. "나누어" in Korean has three different meanings: "to share," "to divide," and "to distribute." Thus, Paul might not be able to come up with the word "share" at the moment but had considered the word "divide" to indicate how his parents loved him and his sister equally.

Example 2. but if we meet with other countries' people, we usually speak English. (Jane, as cited in Baratta, 2013, p. 12)

In Example 2, Jane used the phrase "other countries' people" instead of "people from other countries." Because the corresponding Korean phrase is "다른 나라 [other countries] 사람 [people]," it is likely that Jane directly translated the Korean phrase into English. Because the order of a modifier (e.g., adjectives, numerals, possessives) in a noun phrase can be the same both in English and Korean in certain cases, Jane might overgeneralize her knowledge about a modifier by keeping the same order in English by using a possessive ('s) instead of a prepositional phrase (i.e., from other countries).

Example 3. the food chain will be wrong. (Adam, as cited in Baratta, 2013, p. 14)

Adam's intended meaning in Example 3 is unclear because the word "wrong" is an unusual choice to describe the food chain. In this case, "imbalanced" seems to make the meaning clearer than "wrong." Adam seemed to translate the way he would express it in Korean directly into English. The corresponding Korean phrase for "will become wrong" is "잘못될 것이다." "잘못된" in Korean carries several meanings, including "not correct or true," "messed up," or "damaged."

As shown in the above examples, the direct translation of Korean words or phrases can make meanings unclear. Nevertheless, such direct translation also shows how Korean-speaking English learners creatively transfer their linguistic and cultural resources to construct meaning in English when they do not know alternative ways to construct meanings in English.

INSTRUCTIONAL IMPLICATIONS FOR EDUCATORS

The features in Korean-speaking English learners' oral and written production in English as discussed in this chapter provide a few instructional implications for all teachers to consider in their instruction.

First, Korean-speaking English learners could benefit from opportunities to examine distinctive phonological features of English, different from their first language (Derwing, & Munro, 2005). Explicit attention to phonological features in English can encompass both how to pronounce the sounds of words (e.g., vowels, consonants) and how to use prosodic features (e.g., tone, rise and fall, stress, rhythm) of words and phrases (Zielinski, 2015). The importance of supporting English learners in developing their awareness of phonological features is both in increasing comprehensibility in speech or the quality of making oneself understood, and in improving their comprehension of others' speech in social interactions (Derwing, & Munro, 2005).

The production of pronunciation is closely interrelated to the perception of sounds in oral language. As discussed earlier in this chapter, Korean-speaking English learners may be confused about some English phonemes (e.g., [f], [r], [v], [z]) not existing in the Korean language. Therefore, Korean-speaking English learners' understanding of phonological features in English could support their identification of sound segments and the production of those sounds (Nelson & Kang, 2015). Teachers could encourage students to explore how the changes in sound segments impact the meaning of certain words (e.g., *very* vs. *berry, fetch* vs. *patch, valley* vs. *belly, rain* vs. *lane*) and how such changes could cause incomprehensibility. Additionally, teachers can enunciate new words so that their students can identify the sounds of words clearly and practice pronouncing them with teacher scaffolding.

Because pronouncing words takes place within connected speech rather than in isolation, fluency instruction can further support Korean-speaking English learners in practicing oral reading with meaingful, coherent texts. Fluency instruction should not just support accuracy and automatic recognition of words, but it can also address using prosodic features (e.g., rise and fall, changes in tone, rhythm) in the English language. Teachers can model reading a text to students first. After that, teachers can use echo and choral reading, through which students can hear how a text can be read and practice reading the text with teachers' guided support (Kuhn et al., 2019). Students can also practice oral reading with a partner or in a small group through alternate or choral reading. Such fluency instruction can further be enhanced by discussing the meanings and prosodic features. Fluency instruction can be used across grade levels and content areas.

In supporting English learners' attention to pronunciations, teachers can be mindful of English learners' transfer of their first language in their production of sounds in English, or so-called foreign-accented speech. Instruction on pronunciation and fluency should not aim to "fix" English learners' pronunciation. However, it can be intended to provide meaningful support to increase English learners' ability to identify and manipulate distinctive phonological features in English. Overtly correcting English learners' pronunciation and overemphasizing individual sounds can be counterproductive. Such a practice impinges on their meaning-making efforts and willingness to speak while problematically shifting learners' attention from meaning-making to isolated linguistic forms and correctness (Lasagabaster & Sierra, 2005; Lyster et al., 2013). Therefore, pronunciation and fluency instruction goals should be focused on supporting English learners' attention to contextualized meaning-making in their speech to enhance their comprehensibility and comprehension in their interaction with others.

Next, explicit instruction on inflectional endings (e.g., plurals, tense), as well as the use of articles (e.g., a(n), the), may help Korean-speaking English learners become aware of such features in reading and how to use them in writing. Concomitantly, teachers can understand how missing inflectional endings could impact English learners' overall meaning-making in communication. Students may comprehend the overall ideas even if they do not pay close attention to inflectional endings in their reading. This is because missing inflectional endings in reading may not impact the overall meaning of a text. However, missing these elements in writing or speaking may create confusion in communication. Students can explore how inflectional endings and articles can change meanings and how using these elements in the English language is different from that in their first language.

Third, beginning Korean-speaking English learners can benefit from understanding that the basic pattern of an English sentence has SVO, and a sentence always requires a subject. Sentences in the Korean language are structured differently, and a subject can frequently be omitted particularly in oral language. The knowledge and awareness of syntactic structures can support comprehension as it can enhance an awareness of functions and associated meanings of words within a sentence. It also leads to an increased understanding of how words can be organized in a sentence to create meaning (Brimo et al., 2017; Thompson & Mohktari, 2012). Subsequently, Korean-speaking English learners could learn how to formulate complete sentences and differentiate sentences, clauses, and phrases. They can further explore different types of sentences and ways to combine simple sentences by using conjunctions and relative clauses. Additionally, the English language has numerous phrasal verbs (e.g., give in, carry over) that consist of the combination of a verb and one or more prepositions to create a semantic unit different from original verbs' meanings. As the Korean language does not have such a concept, Korean learners can benefit from explicit instruction on phrasal verbs, through which they can examine the meaning and explore ways to use them in different contexts.

Finally, Korean-speaking English learners' unique formation of expressions may be based on their direct translation of Korean expressions and *Konglish*, or Korean English. Notably, older Korean-speaking English learners with extensive literacy experience in their native language are more likely to transfer their use of loan words and direct translation in a second language (L2) production due to their accumulated linguistic and cultural experiences and knowledge. Additionally, students may rely on bilingual dictionaries (e.g., https://papago.naver.com/; https://translate.google.com/) to translate their intended meanings. Therefore, it can be helpful for teachers to make concerted efforts to understand writers' intentions first by having an individual conference. Teachers can further encourage students to use online English dictionaries and thesaurus (e.g., https://www.britannica.com/; https://www.thefreedictionary.com/; https://www.wordreference.com/) judiciously to examine nuances of the expressions that they find in bilingual dictionaries. Therefore, students could benefit from exploring how their word choices and ways to construct meaning can become further clarified.

CONCLUDING REMARKS

This chapter discussed Korean-speaking English learners' characteristics in their speech and written production in English due to the first language influence and *Konglish*. Although we discussed only a few features in this chapter, other characteristics may likely appear in Korean-speaking English learners' speech and writing. Vygotsky (1987) pointed out that mastering complex linguistic features (e.g., phonetic, syntactic, semantic features) is necessitated in second language acquisition. This may not happen in first language acquisition because first language acquisition takes place in spontaneous speech events. In processing such complex linguistic features in another language, second language learners become conscious of the various phonetic, syntactic, and semantic features of the target language while making conscientious efforts to approximate how native speakers use the language (García & Li, 2014; Mahn & John-Steiner, 2012). Furthermore, second language learners' meaning-making processes are mediated by meanings in their first language and further facilitated by their access to both of their two languages (Vygotsky, 1987).

As we conclude this chapter, we would like to point out that the first language influence on second language acquisition is a very complex phenomenon. As shown in the students' examples, Korean-speaking English learners bring in their linguistic resources and cultural experiences when constructing meaning in their second language, English. This indicates that some of the features Korean-speaking English learners demonstrate in their English production evidence their active and creative use of their linguistic and cultural repertoires from their native language, by which they make sense of linguistic features in an additional language. Therefore, teachers' understanding of Korean-speaking English learners' potential challenges in learning English and unique features in their production can be the essential first step toward developing caring and mindful approaches to support Korean-speaking English learners in their meaning-making in English.

REFERENCES

Abelmann, N., Kwon, S. A., Lo, A., & Okazaki, S. (2015). Introduction: South Korea's education exodus: History, context, and motivations. In N. Abelmann, S. A. Kwon, A. Lo, & S. Okazaki (Eds.), *South Korea's education exodus: The life and times of early study abroad* (pp. 1–22). The University of Washington Press.

Back, J. (2011). Preposition errors in writing and speaking by Korean EFL learners: A corpus-based approach. 영어와 문학, *99*, 227–247.

Baratta, A. (2013). Semantic and lexical issues in writings by Korean children. *ESL Journal.* http://www.esljournal.org/tools/qp.dwp?task=show_post&post_id=5706.

Brimo, D., Apel, K., & Fountain, T. (2017). Examining the contributions of syntactic awareness and syntactic knowledge to reading comprehension. *Journal of Research in Reading, 40*(1), 57–74.

Cho, M.-H., & Jeong, S. (2013). Perception and production of English vowels by Korean learners: A case study.음성음운형태론연구, *19*(1), 155–177.

Derwing, T. M., & Munro, M. J. (2005). Second language accent and pronunciation teaching: A research-based approach *TESOL Quarterly, 39*, 379–397. http://dx.doi.org/10.2307/3588486.

Ethnologue. (2013). www.ethnologue.com/.

Flege, J. E., Munro, M. J., & MacKay, I. R. A. (1995). Effects of age of second language learning on the production of English consonants. *Speech Communication, 16*, 1–26.

García, O., & Li, W. (2014). *Translanguaging: Language, bilingualism, and education.* Palgrave.

Ha, S., Johnson, C. J., & Kuehn, D. P. (2009). Characteristics of Korean phonology: Review, tutorial, and case studies of Korean children speaking English. *Journal of Communication Disorders, 42*(3), 163–179.

Hadikin, G. (2014). *Korean English: A corpus-driven study of a new English.* John Benjamins Publishing Company.

Hong, H., Kim, S., & Chung, M. (2014). A corpus-based analysis of English segments produced by Korean learners. *Journal of Phonetics, 46*, 52–67. https://doi.org/10.1016/j.wocn.2014.06.002.

Jahng, K. E. (2011). English education for young children in South Korea: Not just a collective neurosis of English fever! *Perspectives in Education, 29*(2), 61–69.

Jang, M. (2014). Perception of English consonants in different prosodic positions by Korean learners of English. *Phonetics and Speech Sciences, 6*(1), 11–19. http://dx.doi.org/10.13064/KSSS.2014.6.1.011.

Kang, A. (2021). Marking definiteness in an articleless language: The role of the domain restrictor KU in Korean. *Language & Linguistics, 22*(2), 302–337. https://doi.org/10.1075/lali.00084.kan.

Kiaer, J. (2014). *The history of English loanwords in Korean.* Lincom.

Kiaer, J., & Ahn, H. (2021). Emerging patterns of Korean English. In E. L. Low, & A. Pakir (Eds.), *English in East and South Asia: Policy, features, and language in use* (pp. 133–148). Routledge.

Kil, I. (2003). The interlanguage development of five Korean English learners. *The Linguistic Association of Korea Journal, 11*(4), 247–264.

Ko, H., Ionin, T., & Wexler, K. (2009). L2 acquisition of English articles by Korean speakers. In C. Lee, G. Simpson, & Y. Kim (Eds.), *The handbook of East Asian psycholinguistics* (pp. 286–304). Cambridge University Press. https://doi.org/10 .1017/CBO9780511596865.023.

Korean Educational Statistics Service. (2021). 연도별 학생 만명당 유학생 수 [*Yearly number of early study abroad students*]. https://kess.kedi.re.kr/mobile /stats/school?menuCd=0101&cd=5498&survSeq=2021&itemCode=01&menuId =m_010105&uppCd1=010105&uppCd2=010105&flag=A.

Kuhn, M., Rasinski, T., & Young, C. (2019). Best practices in fluency instruction. In L. M. Morrow & L. B. Gambrell (Eds.), *Best practices in literacy instruction* (6th ed., pp. 217–288). The Guilford Press.

Lasagabaster, D., & Sierra, J. M. (2005). Error correction: Students' versus teachers' perceptions. *Language Awareness, 14*(2&3), 112–127.

Lee, J. (2020). On the source words for loanwords of the 2015 Revised National Curriculum of English. *Korean Journal of English Language and Linguistics, 20*, 851–880.

Lee, S. (2011). Perception and production of English fricative sounds by advanced Korean EFL learners. *Studies in Phonetics, Phonology, and Morphology, 17*(2), 259–281.

Leslie, L., & Caldwell, J. S. (2011). *Qualitative reading inventory* (5th ed.). Pearson.

Lyster, R., Saito, K., & Sato, M. (2013). Oral corrective feedback in second language classrooms. *Language Teaching, 46*(1), 1–40. https://doi.org/10.1017/ S0261444812000365.

Mahn, H., & John-Steiner, V. (2012). Vygotsky and sociocultural approaches to teaching and learning. In I. Weiner, W. M. Reynolds, & G. E. Miller (Eds.), *Handbook of psychology* (2nd ed., pp. 117–136). Wiley. https://doi.org/10.1002 /9781118133880.hop207006.

Munro, M. J., Flege, J. E., & MacKay, I. R. A. (1996). The effects of age of second language learning on the production of English vowels. *Applied Psycholinguistics, 17*, 313–334.

Nelson, C. L., & Kang, S.-Y. (2015). Pronunciation and world Englishes. In M. Reed & J. M. Levis (Eds.), *The handbook of English pronunciation* (pp. 320–329). Wiley Blackwell.

Park, J.-K. (2009). 'English fever' in South Korea: Its history and symptoms. *English Today, 25*(1), 50–57.

Park, J. S.-Y. (2011). The promise of English: Linguistic capital and the neoliberal worker in the South Korean job market. *International Journal of Bilingualism and Bilingual Education, 14*(4), 443–455.

Park, S. B. (2006). *The acquisition of written English articles by Korean learners* [Unpublished doctoral dissertation, Southern Illinois University at Carborndale].

Rüdiger, S. (2019). *Morpho-syntactic patterns in spoken Korean English*. John Benjamins Publishing Company.

Ryoo, M.-L. (2013). A corpus-based study of the use of phrasal verbs in Korean EFL students' writing. *Journal of Asia TEFL, 10*(2), 63–89.

Seong, M.-H., & Lee, K.-Y. (2008). Syntactic features of Korea English: Word order, ellipsis, articles, prepositions, passive, miscellaneous. *Journal of Pan-Pacific Association of Applied Linguistics, 12*(1), 81–95.

Song, J. J. (2005). *The Korean language: Structure, use and context.* Routledge.

Tsukada, K., Birdsong, D., Bialystock, E., Mack, M., Sung, H., & Flege, J. (2005). A developmental study of English vowel production and perception Oby native Korean adults and children. *Journal of Phonetics, 33*, 263–290.

U. S. Immigration and Custom Enforcement. (2020). *Student and exchange visitor program (SEVP) 2020 SEVIS by the numbers report.* https://www.ice.gov/doclib/sevis/pdf/sevisBTN2020.pdf.

Vovin, A. (2010). *Koreo-Japonica: A re-evaluation of a common genetic origin.* University of Hawai'i Press.

Vygotsky, L. S. (1987). *The collected works of L. S. Vygotsky: Problems of general psychology* (R. W. Rieber & A. S. Carton, Eds.). Plenum.

Wang, H.-S., & Pyun, D. O. (2020). Hallyu and Korean language learning: Gender and ethnicity factors. *The Korean Language in America, 24*(2), 30–59. https://doi.org/10.5325/korelangamer.24.2.0030.

Wang, L. (2003). Switching to first language among writers with differing second-language proficiency. *Journal of Second Language Writing, 12*, 347–375.

Woodall, B. (2002). Language-switching: Using the first language while writing in a second language. *Journal of Second Language Writing, 11*, 7–28.

Yeni-Komshian, G. H., Flege, J. E., & Liu, S. (2000). Pronunciation proficiency in the first and second languages of Korean–English bilinguals. *Bilingualism: Language and Cognition, 3*, 131–149.

Yoon, H.-K. (2012). Grammar errors in Korean EFL learners' TOEIC speaking test. *English Teaching, 67*(4), 287–309.

Zdorenko, T., & Paradis, J. (2008). The acquisition of articles in child second language English: Fluctuation, transfer or both? *Second Language Research, 24*(2), 227–250. https://doi.org/10.1177/0267658307086302.

Zielinski, B. (2015). The segmental/suprasegmental debate. In M. Reed & J. M. Levis (Eds.), *The handbook of English pronunciation* (pp. 397–412). Wiley Blackwell.

Chapter 4

Supporting Russian-Speaking English Language Learners

Lyudmyla Ivanyuk

Russian is one of the top ten non-English spoken languages in U.S. public schools (Office of English Language Acquisition, 2019). More than 38,000 English language learners (0.8 percent) in public schools reported speaking Russian at home in the fall of 2018 (National Center for Education Statistics, 2021). To effectively support these learners, teachers need to understand how students' knowledge of Russian influences and intersects with their learning of English. The purpose of this chapter is to discuss the most common grammatical concepts in the Russian language and the typical challenges created for Russian-speaking English language learners (RELLs). Such understanding will assist pre- and in-service teachers who do not speak Russian in developing a general knowledge of the challenges RELLs may face in learning English.

According to Fillmore and Snow (2002), teachers need to know more about language and how language works. They argue that the study of language should expand beyond the once traditional attention to grammar and include sociolinguistics topics, such as patterns of language use in different social settings and communities. Attention to such knowledge is of particular importance for teachers who work with students learning English as an additional language. Given that language is inextricably intertwined with culture (Heath, 1983; Street, 1984), teachers need to honor, validate, and sustain language practices that multilingual students bring to school. When students are encouraged to draw on their linguistic repertoires, they experience deeper learning and enhanced language development. Research suggests that teachers who promote bilingual instructional strategies (Cummins, 2005), translingual practices (Canagarajah, 2012), and translanguaging (Garcia & Wei, 2014) enhance students' literacy and language learning.

Often, monolingual teachers who have multilingual students in their classrooms feel hesitant to engage their students' first languages (L1) in their instruction (Pappamihiel & Lynn, 2014). Teachers might feel uncomfortable acknowledging other languages and may lack confidence in their own language competence (Bachman, 1990) if they do not speak the L1 of their students. Yet, research suggests that students' bilingual and biliteracy development is enhanced when teachers promote students' multilingual competence (Pacheo et al., 2019; Rowe, 2018). This call for teachers to know more about the language and how it works brings attention to the need for knowledge about the Russian language for teachers who work with these students.

A BRIEF HISTORY OF THE RUSSIAN LANGUAGE

Russian is a member of the East Slavic subgroup of the Slavic languages, along with Belarusian and Ukrainian (Cubberley, 2002). Around AD 880, the territories of modern-day Belarus, Ukraine, and part of Russia were unified into Kievan Rus. With the conversion to Christianity by Prince Vladimir in 988–989, the East Slavs were introduced to the Old Church Slavonic language (Grenoble, 2010). Until the seventeenth century, this language influenced the development of the Russian language which began to distinguish itself following the break-up of Kievan Rus in approximately 1100 (Vick, 2022).

Since Russia emerged as a unified country in the sixteenth century (Kadochnikov, 2016), the Russian language has been influenced by several sources (Argent et al., 2015). The written language was used in varieties of Church Slavonic for religious purposes as well as new secular genres of writing. The so-called "chancery" language was used for record-keeping by the administration of the autocratic Muscovite state (Argent et al., 2015). In addition, there was a spoken Russian vernacular. In order to orient Russia toward Europe and to facilitate printing in 1708, Peter the Great introduced the *grazhdankii shrift* (civil script or alphabet), thus separating a secular written language from a written language for the Church (Argent et al., 2015; Yefimov, 2013). Despite the positive contribution by Peter the Great, there was a need to bring more order into the written language. Building on the work of eighteenth-century writers and grammarians, the nineteenth-century poet Aleksandr Pushkin laid the groundwork for modern Russian by rejecting archaic written grammar and vocabulary in favor of those used in the vernacular of that time (Cubberley, 2002; Vick, 2022). The most recent language reform took place after the Bolshevik Revolution—the spelling reform of 1918. The Soviet government intended to simplify Russian writing to eliminate illiteracy. According to various estimates, only 40 percent of the Russian population could read and write before the Bolshevik Revolution (Guzeva, 2020). Despite the size of the country, there is little variation in how Russian is spoken. Russians tend to speak standard Russian with very minor regional variations.

Today, Russian is the eighth most spoken language in the world with 258 million native speakers (Emery, 2022). In the United States, more than 919,000 Americans speak Russian at home (Zeigler & Camarota, 2019). Russian-speaking immigrants predominantly reside in United States major metropolitan areas, such as New York, Philadelphia, Boston, Chicago, and Los Angeles (Dubinina & Polinsky, 2013). It is important for educators to learn about the nuances of cross-linguistic transfer between Russian and English to support this group of students in U.S. schools.

DIFFERENCES BETWEEN RUSSIAN AND ENGLISH GRAMMAR

Russian and English grammars have evolved differently. Although both languages take their roots in the Indo-European language family, they belong to different branches. Russian is from the Slavonic branch, while English is from the Germanic branch. Russian does not have some grammar concepts that are typical for English and vice versa. Moreover, both languages share some grammar concepts that are expressed differently. The subsequent sections explain some of these grammatical differences and provide examples that illustrate challenges RELLs may face when they must learn particular grammatical concepts in English along with some suggestions for instructional activities to support positive transfer for RELLs.

Challenges in Articles

English articles, such as *a*, *an*, and *the*, pose many challenges for RELLs. In English, the definite article (e.g., I have *the* book) and the indefinite article (e.g., I have *a* book.) are used to mark the definite and indefinite interpretation of nouns. In addition, other determiners, such as demonstratives (e.g., *this* student), possessives (e.g., *our* students), quantifiers (e.g., *each* student), and numerals (e.g., *the first* student), could be used to express definiteness in English (White et al., 2011). Russian does not have articles per se. Instead, it uses lexical means, such as demonstrative pronouns, to indicate definiteness or indefiniteness. Consider the following examples from Borik et al. (2020):

(1) a. Я люблю *этот фильм.*
        I like *this movie.*
     b. *Одна знакомая* преподает в этой школе.
        A (particular) friend teaches in this school.

In 1(a), the noun *фильм* (movie) is preceded by a demonstrative *этот* (this). This noun phrase indicates a particular and identifiable movie and functions like the definite article in English. In 1(b), the quantifier *одна* literally means "one." Thus, instead of using an indefinite article like *a* in English, the whole nominal phrase is indefinite.

In addition, syntactic means are used indirectly to express definiteness in Russian. In particular, topicality is used to interpret subjects before the verb as definite in languages with relatively free word order, such as Russian (Borik et al., 2020). Topics, or words that precede the verb, usually contain information that is familiar to the speaker and hearer thus indicating definiteness. On the other hand, focused words that follow the verb contain new information to the hearer, thus indicating indefiniteness. Consider examples from Cho and Slabakova (2014).

(2) a. На столе стояла *лампа*.
     A lamp was on the desk / there was a lamp on the desk.
     b. *Лампа* стояла на столе.
     The lamp was on a desk.

In 2(a), the prepositional phrase *на столе* (on the table) precedes the verb, while the noun *лампа* (lamp) follows the verb. Therefore, the former is definite, and the latter is indefinite. In 2(b), the noun *лампа* (lamp) is in the preverbal position, thus being interpreted as definite. The prepositional phrase *на столе* (on a table) is postverbal position, thus being interpreted as indefinite.

Therefore, unlike English, lexical and syntactic means are used to mark this grammatical category in Russian (see table 4.1). Although these options are not strong enough to encode definiteness and indefiniteness in all possible cases (Seres & Borik, 2021), the foregoing principles illustrate the conditions under which nouns can be interpreted as definite and indefinite in Russian.

Table 4.1 Examples of Definite and Indefinite Marking in Russian

Means	Definiteness	Indefiniteness
Lexical	Determiners (i.e., *this, that, these, those*) + Noun	The quantifier *один* (i.e., one) + Noun
Syntactic	Preverbal position: Noun + Verb	Postverbal position: Verb + Noun

The category of definiteness and indefiniteness may pose challenges for RELLs because RELLs tend to omit or misuse articles while acquiring English. For example, Yanovskaya and Neskreba (2020) observed students learning English in grades 5, 8, and 11 in Russia. They analyzed common errors in both oral and written English. Their analysis showed that article omission was one of the most common grammatical errors. Consider the following examples:

(3)   a. I would like to tell you _____ joke.
      b. My friend is _____ waiter.

In certain situations, both the definite and indefinite articles can be used before the noun *joke* in 3(a) and the noun *waiter* in 3(b). RELLs are not likely to see the distinction between *a* and *the* and may omit either of those articles because there is no equivalent word in Russian.

RELLs may also overuse articles once they have learned them. For example, Čampulová (2015) analyzed common mistakes students make whose primary language was Russian and who studied English to be accepted to a university in the Czech Republic. The results showed that students overused articles in special cases, such as certain geographical names and holidays. Consider the following examples:

(4)   a. He went to *the* Germany.
      b. I got a nice sweater for *the* Christmas.

RELLs may struggle to distinguish when to use the definite and indefinite articles in English. For example, Monk and Burak (2001) provide examples that illustrate the problem of this choice. Consider the following examples:

(5)   a. Do you have *the* mother?
      b. Is she *a* woman you told us about?

In 5(a), the definite article is used because an RELL refers to a particular mother. In 5(b), the indefinite article is used before the noun *woman* because an RELL may be guided by a general rule taught at the beginning level: The indefinite article is used before singular, countable nouns in English.

Application

The correct use of the English articles may be acquired slowly for RELLs. Although there are only four options for using articles (*a, an, the,* or no article), they have various complex functions in English. Students would benefit from focused lessons on how to use articles with particular types of words. At the beginning level, RELLs need to learn that (1) *a* or *an* must be used before a singular, countable noun (e.g., *a student*), (2) *the* is used when a speaker is referring to a particular thing, person, or group (e.g., *the Russians*), (3) *the* or no article is used with proper nouns (e.g., *the USA*), and (4) no article for general meaning (e.g., *students*) and abstract nouns (e.g., *happiness*). To help

RELLs master, for example, the first general rule, explicit instruction that every time they write a singular, countable noun, they need to write *a* or *an* before that noun (Folse, 2016) would be helpful.

The following activity can be used to help students distinguish between the definite and indefinite articles. Lay some identical items, such as books, in front of your students. Use books of different sizes and/or colors. In addition, place a different item, such as a cell phone. Call on different students by saying: "Give me a book." "Give me a big book." "Give me a red book." Repeat this until you run out of items. Then put the items back in the pile. Call on a student saying: "Give me the book." When a student gives you a book, you reply: "Not that book." Repeat this action until the students realize that they do not know which book you mean. After that, call on another student saying: "Give me the cell phone." They will give you the right item. Explain to the students that the definite article is used in this way to refer to things that the speaker and listener expect to find in the situation.

Challenges in Tense and Aspect

RELLs may also face challenges in acquiring tense and aspect. These two grammatical features are expressed differently in Russian and English. Given the analytic-synthetic distinction in classical work on the cross-linguistic typology of languages, Russian is known to be predominantly a synthetic language (Szmrecsanyi, 2016). Synthetic or inflectional languages add inflections to words to indicate grammatical relations in a sentence. Consider the following examples:

(6) a. коробка (a box)
  b. в коробке (in the box)
  c. под коробкой (under the box)

In Russian, the word *коробка* (box) changes case inflections to indicate the function it is performing in a sentence. Without these endings, it will not be clear if a noun is the subject (nominative), the direct object (accusative), the indirect object (dative), or if it is a possessive (genitive) form. In contrast, analytic languages, such as English, use specific auxiliary words rather than inflections to convey grammatical relations within sentences (Szmrecsanyi, 2016). For example: He *has been writing* his new book for two years. In addition to the main verb *writing*, the English sentence has two auxiliary verbs (*has* and *been*) to indicate the action that began in the past and is continuing now.

Being a synthetic language, Russian has rich verb morphology, which is mainly expressed through inflections in all three tenses (i.e., present, past, and future) and two aspects (i.e., perfective and imperfective). The future tense also has an analytic form, which includes the auxiliary verb *byt'* (to be) and the imperfective infinitive. See table 4.2 which was adapted from Gülzow and Gagarina (2008). The three tenses show a distinction between perfective (PFV) and imperfective (IPFV) aspects in active verb constructions.

Table 4.2 smotret' (IMPV) vs. posmotret' (PFV) "to look"

Tense	Number	Person (gender for past)	IPFV (incomplete actions)	PFV (completed actions)
Past	Sg.	masculine	smotre-l	posmotre-l
		feminine	smotre-l-a	posmotre-l-a
		neutral	smotre-l-o	posmotre-l-o
	Pl.		smotre-l-i	posmotre-l-i
Present	Sg.	1	smotr-u	
		2	smotr-ish	
		3	smotr-it	
	Pl.	1	smotr-im	
		2	smotr-ite	
		3	smotr-iat	
Future Synthetic (PFV)	Sg.	1		posmotr-u
		2		posmotr-ish
		3		posmot-it
	Pl.	1		posmotr-im
		2		posmotr-ite
		3		posmotr-iat
Future Analytic (IPFV)			byt'(1,2,3 in sg. or pl.) + infinitive smotre-t'	

Source: Adapted from Gagarina & Gulzow (2008).

Unlike the rich verb morphology in Russian, verbal constructions in English are predominantly analytical. Auxiliary verbs are used together with a main verb to show the verb's tense and aspect. English has an elaborate system of tenses—12 verb tense-aspect combinations (Larsen-Freeman et al., 2002). The three tenses (i.e., present, past, and future) show distinctions between four aspects (i.e., simple, progressive, perfect, and perfect progressive). The verb system also includes a few suffixes (i.e., synthetic means) that mark the categories of person, number, tense, and aspect (Gülzow & Gagarina, 2008). The distinctions between the two verb systems pose challenges for RELLs. These challenges are too numerous to list here; therefore, I will focus on a few examples.

RELLs may find it challenging to distinguish between past simple, present perfect, and past perfect in English. This distinction does not exist in Russian. Consider the examples from Monk and Burak (2011):

(7)   a. I read when he came. (Meaning: *I was reading when he came.*)
        b. He said he already finished work. (Meaning: *He said he had already finished work.*)

In both examples, the past simple tense is used to refer to actions and events expressed through progressive and perfect tenses in English.

Likewise, RELLs may struggle with distinguishing between present perfect and present progressive forms. Given that these forms do not exist in Russian, learners may make the following mistakes as presented in Monk and Burak (2011):

(8)   a. Where you go now? (Meaning: *Where are you going?*)
        b. How long you be/are here? (Meaning: *How long have you been here?*)

Both sentences are used in the present simple tense, which is the only present tense in Russian.

Formulating question tags and short answers also poses challenges for RELLs. Due to the synthetic nature of its verb system, Russian does not have auxiliary verbs, such as *do*, *have*, or *will*. RELLs tend to omit them or make mistakes while employing them. Consider the following examples:

(9)   a. Don't forget to bring a towel. No. (Meaning: *No, I won't.*)
        b. You enjoy it, doesn't it? (Meaning: You enjoy it, don't you?)

In 9(a) the short answer only includes *No*. The subject *I* and the auxiliary verb *won't* are omitted. The second example contains an incorrect form of the auxiliary verb *do*. The questions tag should have *don't* instead of *doesn't*.

Application

Given the elaborate system of tenses in English, learning what they are and how to use them correctly may take years to master. There are many readily available resources to introduce these grammatical points in the classroom. A verb tense chart is an excellent way to consolidate and present key information. For example, teachers can adapt a chart created by New York Language Center to introduce present tenses, then past tenses, and finally future tenses. See table 4.3. Students can also be provided with the following chart to help them analyze the differences in tense and aspect between English and Russian. In addition, they can use it as a reference every time they practice these tenses while reading, writing, or speaking.

Table 4.3 English Grammar Tenses

	Present	Past	Future
INDEFINITE	Form: (+) V_1 or V_1 (s/es when he, she, or it) (?) Do/Does + V_1 (-) do/does + not + V_1 Example: - I <u>write</u> blog posts every week.	Form: (+) V_2 or V_1 (ed) (?) Did + V_1 (-) did + not + V_1 Example: - I <u>wrote</u> a blog post yesterday.	Form: (+) shall/will + V_1 (?) Shall/Will + V_1 (-) shall/will + not + V_1 Example: - I <u>will write</u> another blog post next week.
CONTINUOUS	Form: (+) am/is/are + V_1 (ing) (?) Am/Is/Are + V_1 (ing) (-) am/is/are + not + V_1 (ing) Example: - I <u>am writing</u> a blog post right now. (Please don't interrupt me.)	Form: (+) was/were + V_1 (ing) (?) Was/Were + V_1 (ing) (-) was/were + not + V_1 (ing) Example: - I <u>was writing</u> a blog post at 5:00 p.m. yesterday.	Form: (+) shall/will + be + V_1 (ing) (?) Shall/Will + be + V_1 (ing) (-) shall/will + not + be + V_1 (ing) Example: - I <u>will be writing</u> a blog post at 10:00 a.m. tomorrow.

(continued)

Table 4.3 (Continued)

	Present	Past	Future
PERFECT	Form: (+) have/has + V$_3$ or V$_1$ (ed) (?) Have/Has + V$_3$ or V$_1$ (ed) (-) have/has + not + V$_3$ or V$_1$ (ed) Example: - I have already written a blog post today.	Form: (+) had + V$_3$ or V$_1$ (ed) (?) Had + V$_3$ or V$_1$ (ed) (-) had + not + V$_3$ or V$_1$ (ed) Example: - When my friend came, I had already finished writing my blog post.	Form: (+) shall/will + have + V$_3$ or V$_1$ (ed) (?) Shall/Will + have + V$_3$ or V$_1$ (ed) (-) shall/will+ not + have + V$_3$ or V$_1$ (ed) Example: - I will have written a blog post by 12:00 p.m. for sure. (It is 11:00 a.m. right now.)
PERFECT CONTINUOUS	Form: (+) have/has + been + V$_1$ (ing) (?) Have/Has + been + V$_1$ (ing) (-) have/has + not + been + V$_1$ (ing) Example: - I have already been writing a blog post for 2 hours.	Form: (+) had + been + V$_1$ (ing) (?) Had + been + V$_1$ (ing) (-) had + not + been + V$_1$ (ing) Example: - I had been writing a blog post for 2 hours when you called me yesterday. (That's why I did not answer.)	Form: (+) shall/will + have + been + V$_1$ (ing) (?) Shall/Will + have + been + V$_1$ (ing) (-) shall/will + not + have + been + V$_1$ (ing) Example: - I will have been writing blog posts for a year on the 15th of May.

(+) Affirmative
(?) Question
(–) Negative

V$_1$ Base form
V$_2$ Past simple
V$_3$ Past Participle

(irregular verbs)

Source: Adapted from New York Language Learning Center (n.d.).

Challenges in Phrasal Verbs

RELLs face challenges in using phrasal verbs in English. Phrasal verbs are idiomatic combinations of a verb and an adverbial particle, such as *take in, put on, keep up,* or a preposition, such as *wait for, look for, listen to,* or an adverb, such as *look through, take apart, bring together* (White, 2012). Although this semantically rich group of verbs is common in English, Russian does not have phrasal verbs. Instead, various grammatical means are used to convey the meaning expressed by English phrasal verbs in Russian. According to Mudraya et al. (2005), Russian equivalents of English phrasal verbs may have three distinct trends. First, some phrasal verbs with function words such as *in, on, out, up,* and *down* are usually translated into Russian as single verbs with an additional prefix. For example:

(10) a. die down—**за**мирать
       b. wipe out—**вы**тирать

Each Russian prefix (*за-* and *вы-*) indicates various actions that closely resemble the semantic functions of the English phrasal verbs. To illustrate, Mudraya et al. (2005) provide the literal translation of the Russian word **вы***тирать* (wipe out), which is *outwipe.*

Second, some English phrasal verbs can have adverbs that act as independent content words, such as *forward, ahead, apart, behind, together.* Such instances are translated into Russian as a combination of the verb and adverb. For example:

(11) a. bring together—сводить (verb) вместе (adverb)
       b. leave behind—оставлять (verb) позади (adverb)

Finally, some English phrasal verbs can be translated into Russian by means of different verbs for different meanings. For example, the English phrasal verb *wipe out* can be translated as:

(12) a. уничтожать, уничтожить, истребить (similar to English *destroy*)
       b. стирать, вытирать (similar to English *erase*)

These examples shed light on the grammatical relations between equivalent expressions across the two languages. They illustrate that there are no rigid rules in expressing the meanings of English phrasal verbs in Russian. Acquiring phrasal verbs in English may pose two challenges for RELLs. The first challenge is the omission of a preposition. For example, RELLs may say:

(13)   a. Explain me. (Meaning: *Explain **to** me.*)
       b. Wait me. (Meaning: *Wait **for** me.*)

In each example, the preposition (*to* and *for*) is missing. RELLs may tend to omit these grammatical elements because they are not used after verbs in their native language. The second challenge is the avoidance of phrasal verbs. For example, RELLs may use *continue* for *carry on*, *support* instead of *back someone up* or *faint* instead of *pass out* (Čampulová, 2015). Given the nature of the Russian language, RELLs may prefer one-word verbs to phrasal verbs.

Application

Although phrasal verbs are difficult, students need to learn them to become proficient in the English language. It may be wise to avoid overwhelming students with a long list of words they have to memorize. Instead, phrasal verbs can be organized into categories and presented a few at a time. For example, when students learn how to do things around the house, they can study the following phrasal verbs:

• hang up
• take down
• turn off
• turn on
• clean up
• take out

After introducing these phrases and discussing their meanings, students can be invited to describe what they do around the house or create a story using those verbs. Teaching phrasal verbs in this way enables students to apply and remember meanings within a familiar context.

Challenges in Prepositions

Prepositions are another common challenge RELLs may face when they learn English. In English, these are small words, such as *in*, *under*, and *for*, or groups of words, such as *along with*, *away from*, and *out of*. They are used before nouns, pronouns, or noun phrases to show direction (e.g., *to school*), time (e.g., *at noon*), place (e.g., *in the office*), and spatial relations (e.g., *walk toward the garage*) (Writing Center, 2021). The Russian language has a rich system of prepositions. In fact, almost every sentence in Russian contains prepositions (Zakharov & Mikhailova, 2017).

Given the pervasive use of prepositions in the Russian language, RELLs may misuse English prepositions. For example, speakers may say *on the North* instead of *in the North*, *to get rid from* instead of *to get rid of*, *to depend from* instead of *to depend on*. These misuses are the result of word-for-word translation from Russian into English. Moreover, Karpeieva and Sveklova (2015) state that the most common preposition mistakes are after transitive verbs (i.e., verbs that may have a direct object and an indirect object) in English. Consider the following examples:

(14) a. I play *in* chess.
      b. She wrote _ him.

In 14(a) the preposition *in* is used because this preposition is used in the Russian phrase—*играть в шахматы* (literally, *to play in chess*). In 14(b) a RELL omitted the preposition *to*. The preposition is not used in the Russian equivalent. Due to these differences in the use of prepositions after transitive verbs between English and Russian, RELLs may insert or omit prepositions where they are not used or are used in English.

Application

Given that prepositions are often unstressed in natural conversations, students, such as RELLs, need activities that allow them to hear and see the various ways in which prepositions are used (Folse, 2016). When reading and listening to English, RELLs need to attend to how prepositions are generally used. They can keep a notebook in which they write down verbs and nouns that require certain prepositions and their Russian equivalents. Students should be encouraged to compare English and Russian equivalents, review them regularly, and use them when speaking and writing.

INSTRUCTIONAL IMPLICATIONS FOR EDUCATORS

Understanding the grammatical principles that are potentially challenging for RELLs to master when learning English can help educators become more aware of potential difficulties and to plan instruction accordingly. Specifically, such awareness and knowledge will enable educators to better understand the differences between the two languages, know what language behaviors to expect based on students' language background, and address miscues effectively. Given the renewed focus on contextualized grammar, teachers' instructional decisions about the grammatical concepts outlined here can be shaped by the principles of contrastive analysis and culturally responsive instruction.

The principle of contrastive analysis can be used to promote awareness of the grammatical concepts and typical challenges among RELLs. A contrastive approach is a method of language analysis used to investigate the differences between two languages (Gast, 2013). This approach has attracted the attention of many language teachers, as it enables them to compare how certain grammatical concepts function in English with how they function in their students' first language. For example, teachers can introduce students to the following contrastive analysis steps:

- Identify a pattern that reflects students' native languages in their speech or writing samples.
- Invite students to generate more examples of how they would say or write a certain grammatical structure in their native language.
- Compare and contrast their examples with English equivalents.
- Create a paper or digital chart to visually represent those differences and invite students to reference it as needed.
- Create opportunities for students to engage in contrastive analysis as writers and speakers.(Sanford Inspire, 2017)

By adopting the steps of contrastive analysis outlined above, students can analyze typical errors, thus becoming more efficient in identifying those errors. By inviting RELLs to compare, reflect on, and manipulate the two languages, teachers promote students' metalinguistic and metacognitive development (Bialystok & Barac, 2012; Goodwin & Jiménez, 2021).

Culturally responsive instruction can be an important tool to promote grammar knowledge contextualized in RELLs' homes and communities. In homes and communities, students possess knowledge and ways of knowing called *funds of knowledge* (Moll et al., 1992). Funds of knowledge are historically and culturally accumulated knowledge and expertise that students acquire in their households. Academic knowledge, such as the aforementioned grammar concepts, are more meaningful and are learned more easily and thoroughly if they are grounded in instruction and opportunities that are situated within the lived experiences of students (Gay, 2002). Teachers who welcome students' language assets and contributions in classrooms demonstrate their understanding of language learning and teaching. Teachers can use the following examples of multimodal tools to help connect learning a language like Russian to students' lives outside the classroom and opportunities to point out grammar concepts that students have learned.

- Dialogue Journals: It is a written conversation between a teacher and a student or between students. Dialogue entries arise not in response to the prompt, but rather out of the relationships that students develop with the teacher and peers. Students write about what they care and know (Stillman et al., 2014).
- Interviews: Students can interview their friends, family and community members to generate information for their writing pieces (Rogovin, 1998). This tool enables students to apply their knowledge of grammar and language in authentic ways.
- Picture Word Inductive Model (PWIM): PWIM is an inquiry-oriented language arts strategy. Students are presented with pictures that contain familiar objects and actions to elicit words (Calhoun, 1999).
- Songs: Students choose a song in their home language, translate it into English, and help the class learn the home language version. Students are also invited to recognize any grammar points they have studied (Folse, 2016).

Being guided by the principles of contrastive analysis and culturally responsive instruction practices, teachers can act as important agents of socialization through learning a language. They can promote instruction that recognizes RELLs' linguistic and cultural strengths and that enhances their metalinguistic awareness. By respecting and building on those strengths, teachers can nurture students' social, emotional, and cognitive growth and enable them to function with greater comfort within another language and culture.

CONCLUDING THOUGHTS

RELLs, like others learning English, deserve to be accepted wholeheartedly into a community of learners and to receive instruction that builds on their linguistic resources. That goal can be better achieved when teachers are informed about the main differences between a student's first language and English. My goal throughout this chapter has been to help pre- and in-service teachers of RELLs to understand the key grammatical differences between Russian and English and to share tools to address those differences effectively. By thoughtfully considering the suggested steps and applying them creatively in their classrooms, teachers will be able to design and deliver grammar instruction that is responsive to students' needs and shaped by the principles of contrastive and contextualized grammar. Such instruction will better equip RELLs to learn a new language while promoting the level of social acceptance they often seek.

REFERENCES

Argent, G., Offord, D., & Rjéoutski, V. (2015). The functions and value of foreign languages in eighteenth-century Russia. *The Russian Review, 74*(1), 1–19.

Bachman, L. F. (1990). *Fundamental considerations in language testing.* Oxford University Press.

Bialystok, E., & Barac, R. (2012). Emerging bilingualism: Dissociating advantages for metalinguistic awareness and executive control. *Cognition, 122*(1), 67–73. DOI: 10.1016/j.cognition.2011.08.003.

Borik, O., Borràs-Comes, J., & Seres, D. (2020). Preverbal (in)definites in Russian: An experimental study. In K. Balogh, A. Latrouite, & R. D. Van Valin, Jr. (Eds.), *Nominal anchoring: Specificity, definiteness and article systems across languages* (pp. 51–80). Language Science Press.

Calhoun, E. F. (1999). *Teaching beginning reading and writing with the Picture Word Inductive Model.* Association for Supervision and Curriculum Development.

Čampulová, R. (2015). *Analysis of common mistakes of Russian students of English* [Diploma thesis, Masaryk University in Brno]. https://is.muni.cz/th/k7ogc/Analysis_of_Common_Mistakes_of_Russian_Students_of_English.pdf.

Canagarajah, S. (2012). *Translingual practice: Global Englishes and cosmopolitan relations.* Routledge.

Cho, J., & Slabakova, R. (2014). Interpreting definiteness in a second language without articles: The case of L2 Russian. *Second Language Research, 30*(2), 159–190. DOI: 10.1177/0267658313509647.

Cubberley, P. (2002). *Russian: A linguistic introduction.* Cambridge University Press.

Cummins, J. (2005). A proposal for action: Strategies for recognizing heritage language competence as a learning resource within the mainstream classroom. *Modern Language Journal, 89*, 585–592.

Dubinina, I., & Polinsky, M. (2013). Russian in the USA. In M. Moser & M. Polinsky (Eds.), *Slavic languages in migration* (pp. 123–154). University of Vienna Press.

Emery, C. (2022, March 22). *The 27 most spoken languages in the world (2021).* The Ultimate Language Resource. https://www.langoly.com/most-spoken-languages/.

Fillmore, L. W., & Snow, C. E. (2002). What teachers need to know about language. In C. T. Adger, C. E. Snow, & D. Christian (Eds.), *What teachers need to know about language* (pp. 7–54). Center for Applied Linguistics and Delta Systems.

Folse, K. S. (2016). *Keys to teaching grammar to English language learners: A practical handbook.* University of Michigan Press.

Garcia, O., & Wei, L. (2013). *Translanguaging: Language, bilingualism and education.* Palgrave Macmillan.

Gast, V. (2013). Contrastive analysis. In M. Byram & A. Hu (Eds.), *Routledge encyclopedia of language teaching and language learning* (2nd ed., pp. 153–158). Routledge.

Gay, G. (2002). Preparing for culturally responsive teaching. *Journal of Teacher Education, 53*(2), 106–116.

Goodwin, A. P., & Jiménez, R. (2021). *Instruction that works with emergent bilingual students.* International Literacy Association. https://www.literacyworldwide.org

/get-resources/instructional-practices/instruction-that-works-with-emergent-bilingual-students.

Grenoble, L. A. (2010). Contact and the development of the Slavic languages. In R. Hickey (Ed.), *Handbook of language contact* (pp. 581–597). Basil Blackwell.

Gülzow, I., & Gagarina, N. (2008). Analytical and synthetic verb constructions in Russian and English child language. In N. Gagarina & I. Gülzow (Eds.), *The acquisition of verbs and their grammar: The effect of particular languages* (pp. 229–259). Springer.

Guzeva, A. (2020, July 29). *How the Bolsheviks revolutionized the Russian language.* Russia Beyond. https://www.rbth.com/education/332502-bolsheviks-russian-language-reform.

Heath, S. B. (1984). *Ways with words: Language, life and work in communities and classrooms.* Cambridge University Press.

Kadochnikov, D. (2016) Languages, regional conflicts, and economic development: Russia. In V. Ginsburgh & S. Weber (Eds.), *The Palgrave handbook of economics and language* (pp. 538–580). Palgrave Macmillan.

Karpeieva, O. Y., & Sveklova, O. V. (2015). Лексико-грамматические аналогии при обучении английскому языку [Lexico-grammatically analogies in teaching English as a second language]. *Chuvash University Bulletin, 4*, 243–246.

Larsen-Freeman, D., Kuehn, T., & Haccius, M. (2002). Helping students make appropriate English verb tense-aspect choices. *TESOL Journal, 11*(4), 3–9.

Moll, L. C., Amanti, C., Neff, D., & Gonzalez, N. (1992). Funds of knowledge for teaching: Using a qualitative approach to connect homes to schools. *Theory into Practice, 31*(2), 132–141.

Monk, B., & Burak, A. (2001). Russian speakers. In M. Swan & B. Smith (Eds.), *Learner English* (2nd. ed., pp. 145–161). Cambridge University Press.

Mudraya, O., Piao, S. S. L., Löfberg, L., Rayson, P., & Archer, D. (2005). English–Russian–Finnish cross-language comparison of phrasal verb translation equivalents. In *Proceedings of the phraseology 2005 conference* (pp. 277–281).

National Center for Education Statistics. (2021, May). *English language learners in public schools.* https://nces.ed.gov/programs/coe/indicator/cgf.

New York Language Learning Center. (n.d.). *Chart of grammar tenses.* https://avatars.mds.yandex.net/i?id=1f1a3b0d2f2911e86155a3005eb796be_l-5169470-images-thumbs&ref=rim&n=13&w=988&h=827.

Office of English Language Acquisition. (2019, October). *The top languages spoken by English Learners (ELs) in the United States.* National Clearinghouse for English Language Acquisition. https://ncela.ed.gov/files/fast_facts/olea-top-languages-fact-sheet-20191021-508.pdf.

Pacheo, M. B., Daniel, S. M., Pray, L. C., & Jiménez, R. T. (2019). Translingual practice, strategic participation, and meaning-making. *Journal of Literacy Research, 51*(1), 75–99. DOI: 10.1177/1086296X18820642.

Pappamihiel, E., & Lynn, C. A. (2014). How can monolingual teachers take advantage of Learners' native language in class? *Childhood Education, 90*(4), 291–297. DOI: 10.1080/00094056.2014.937258.

Rogovin, P. (1998). *Classroom interviews: A world of learning.* Heinemann.

Rowe, L. W. (2018). Say it in your language: Supporting translanguaging in multilingual classes. *The Reading Teacher, 72*(1), 31–38. DOI: 10.1002/trtr.1673.

Sanford Inspire. (2017). *Contrastive analysis: Learn and affirm language*. https://modules.sanfordinspire.org/wp-content/uploads/2017/06/Contrastive_Analysis _Learn_and_Affirm_Language_Resource.pdf.

Seres, D., & Borik, O. (2021). Definiteness in the absence of uniqueness: the case of Russian. In A. Blümel, J. Gajić, U. Junghanns, & H. Pitsch (Eds.), *Advances in formal Slavic linguistics 2018* (pp. 339–363). Language Science Press.

Stillman, J., Anderson, L., & Struthers, K. (2014). Returning to reciprocity: Using dialogue journals to teach and learn. *Language Arts, 91*(3), 146–160.

Street, B. (1984). *Literacy in theory and practice*. Cambridge University Press.

Szmrecsanyi, B. (2016). An analytic-synthetic spiral in the history of English. In E. van Gelderen (Ed.), *Cyclical change continued* (pp. 93–112). John Benjamins Publishing Company.

Vick, J. (2022, May 3). *The Russian language*. Expatica. https://www.expatica.com/ru/education/language-learning/the-russian-language-119711/.

White, B. J. (2012). A conceptual approach to the instruction of phrasal verbs. *The Modern Language Journal, 96*(3), 419–438. DOI: 10.1lll/j.1540-4781. 2012.

White, L., Belikova, A., Hagstrom, P., Kupisch, T., & Özçelik, Ö. (2011). *There aren't many difficulties with definiteness: Negative existentials in the L2 English of Turkish and Russian speakers*. Proceedings of GALANA 4, Cascadilla Proceedings Project.

Writing Center. (2021). *Grammar: Prepositions*. Walden University. https://academicguides.waldenu.edu/writingcenter/grammar/prepositions.

Yanovskaya, H. A., & Neskreba, A. V. (2020). *Наиболее типичные ошибки при изучении иностранного языка и некоторые пути их преодоления* [The most typical errors made by the second language learners and some ways of their prevention]. *Иностранные языки в контексте межкультурной коммуникации. Материалы докладов XII Всероссийской научно-практической конференции с международным участием* (pp. 325–330).

Yefimov, V. (2013, September 3). Civil type and kis cyrillic. *Type Journal*. https://typejournal.ru/en/articles/Civil-Type.

Zakharov, V., & Azarova, I. (2019). Semantic structure of Russian prepositional constructions. *Lecture Notes in Computer Science, 11697*, 224–235.

Zakharov, V., & Mikhailova, M. V. (2017). A construction grammar approach to Russian prepo-sitions. *SGEM 4th International Multidisciplinary Scientific Conference on Social Sciences and Arts, 2*(3), 279–286.

Zeigler, K., & Camarota, S. A. (2019, October 29). *67.3 million in the United Statesspoke a foreign language at home in 2018*. Center for Immigration Studies. https://cis.org/Report/673-Million-United-States-Spoke-Foreign-Language-Home-2018.

Chapter 5

Cross-Linguistic Perspectives between Mandarin Chinese and English

Xia Chao

Chinese is one of the top five most spoken languages for English learners (ELs) in American K-12 public schools, representing 1.91 percent of the total U.S. ELs population (U.S. Department of Education, 2019). Among Chinese-speaking K-12 ELs, many of them speak Mandarin, the official language of China. Cantonese (also known as Yue), a Southern Chinese dialect, is one of the major languages in China. It is widely spoken in both China and South-eastern countries such as Singapore, Malaysia, Indonesia, and Vietnam. In Chinese communities in the United States, Cantonese is often the predominant form of Chinese because historically most Chinese immigrants to the United States were from Southern China. This chapter focuses on Mandarin Chinese as many recently arrived Chinese immigrants in the United States are more likely to come from China's provinces where Mandarin is the most widely used.

Of the many hard tasks facing the Chinese-speaking ELs, perhaps none is more challenging than learning the English language, which is different from their non-alphabetic first language (L1) background. Previous research has mainly focused on cross-linguistic influences on English learning of ELs with alphabetic L1 backgrounds (Gut, 2010; Leider et al., 2013). There is a body of research on cross-linguistic differences and transfer of Chinese college students to U.S. universities (Ke & Xiao, 2015; Li & Koda, 2022). Little research attention, however, has been given to cross-linguistic transfer of literacy-related skills of Chinese-speaking ELs in the U.S. K-12 context. Therefore, this chapter illustrates cross-linguistic knowledge across the Mandarin Chinese language and English language among emergent Chinese-English bilingual immigrant children in American K-12 public schools. This chapter intends to add valuable insights regarding the interrelationship between Mandarin Chinese and English literacy practices.

A BRIEF HISTORY OF THE CHINESE LANGUAGE

Chinese is one of the few contemporary languages whose history is documented back to the second-millennium BC (Norman, 1988). The earliest available written record of the Chinese language dates back to the Shang dynasty (c. seventeenth to eleventh centuries BC), slightly over 3,500 years ago (Bradley, 1991; Chen et al., 2009; Ong, 2005; Wang, 1973). A widely accepted convention (Dong, 2021; Wilkinson, 2000) illustrates four different stages of Chinese language as shown in table 5.1.

Table 5.1   Periodization of Chinese Language

Periodization	Timespan
Old Chinese	12th-century BC–3rd-century AD
Middle Chinese	4th–12th-centuries AD
Early Modern Chinese/Mandarin	13th–early 20th-centuries AD
Modern Chinese	early 20th-century AD–Present

In the period of Old Chinese, during the Han dynasty (206 BC–AD 220), Confucianism was established as the official state orthodoxy (Yao, 2000) and "the ethnic identity of the people was solidified, hence the origin of the name of the Hàn people and then the name of the Chinese language, Hànyǔ 漢語, meaning 'the language of the Hàn'" (Dong, 2021, p. 7). In the period of Middle Chinese, after the Tang dynasty, in terms of sounds, the language of Song dynasty (AD 960–1279) is considered an earlier form of Old Mandarin (Norman, 1988). Important changes in consonants and vowels were made toward Modern Chinese during the Yuan dynasty and its subsequent Ming (AD 1368–1644) and Qing (AD 1644–1911) dynasties.

In the period of Modern Chinese, in 1926, in the New National Pronunciation, or the xīn guóyīn 新國音, guóyǔ國語 (the successor of Mandarin) was positioned as the national language, the official lingua franca of the Republic of China (Dong, 2021; Li, 2004; Wilkinson, 2000). The People's Republic of China was founded in 1949 and the new government of China in 1956 announced the new national language named Pǔtōnghuà, which is based on guóyǔ 國語 and modeled on the pronunciation of Beijing Mandarin (Yao, 1998). In 1958, a Romanized form of Chinese called "Hanyu pinyin" (Chinese Phonetic Alphabet, an alphabetic system, pinyin for short) was established to use as "a way to annotate the pronunciations of Chinese characters" (Dong, 2021, p. 9). Pinyin shares the same letters as the English alphabet except for using *ü* as a replacement for the letter *v* (Institute of Linguistics, Chinese Academy of Social Sciences, 2004; Lin et al., 2010). During 1955–1964, the evolution of simplified Chinese characters was carried out by reducing the number of strokes in characters, particularly those with dense stroke composition in mainland China (Bökset, 2006). Table 5.2 presents an example of how *McDonald's*, a global fast-food company, is pronounced in pinyin and written in simplified and traditional Chinese characters.

Table 5.2   McDonald's in Pinyin, Simplified and Traditional Chinese

Pinyin	mài dāng láo
simplified Chinese	麦当劳
traditional Chinese	麥當勞

The Chinese language is not isolated from the history of China. It is embedded within and embodied throughout the civilization and history of China and the Chinese diaspora.

PRINCIPLED ELEMENTS OF CHINESE LANGUAGE

It is important for educators to learn that the Chinese language has linguistic features that are different from many other languages including English. This section discusses the principled elements of the Chinese language by comparing the English language in particular. Understanding these elements is crucial to supporting Chinese-speaking students' successes as they are in the process of learning English language and literacy.

Chinese Characters from Pictures of Objects

Compared to English which is an alphabetic-based language and does not originate from images of objects, the Chinese language is classified as logographic-phonetic, which means that Chinese characters represent both meaning or pictures of objects and speech sounds (DeFrancis, 1989; Morrison, 1815). This emphasizes the importance of visual processing when reading Chinese. Children often acquire phonological awareness in learning Chinese literacy by making use of the phonetic elements that characters contain in learning to read new words. Compared to English, there are an extensively large number of homonyms in Chinese language sharing the same syllable with different meaning or spelling, or both (Hanley et al., 1999). The number is reduced somewhat by lexical tones in Pinyin, which determine the meaning of a word and differentiate words from each other.

Pinyin is a unique phonetic system of the Mandarin Chinese. It is associated with Chinese character recognition. Compared to the English language which has 26 letters including 5 vowels and 21 consonants, the Pinyin system uses all 26 letters of the English language except for "v" not being used in

Pinyin but with an additional letter ü. Pinyin is the standard romanization of Mandarin Chinese and has 22 consonants, 12 vowels, and 4 lexical tones in which words are pronounced in Mandarin Chinese (Fung, 2009; Institute of Linguistics, Chinese Academy of Social Sciences, 2004). Different lexical tones indicate differences in pronunciation and meaning of the word (table 5.3). In this sense, Chinese is a tonal language.

Table 5.3   Different Lexical Tones, Different Corresponding Meanings in Chinese

Tones	Pinyin	Chinese Character	English Equivalent
1st tone: high-level pitch	qī	七	seven
2nd tone: high-rising	qí	骑	to ride
3rd tone: falling-rising	qǐ	起	to rise, to get up
4th tone: falling	Qì	弃	to abandon

Pinyin plays an important role in acquiring Chinese literacy abilities including listening, speaking, reading, and writing. For example, Lin et al. (2010) stress that Pinyin is a measure of phonological awareness in Chinese. Also, the study by Read et al. (1986) indicates that students who once learned Pinyin as well as characters performed literacy activities readily and accurately, compared to those who were not familiar with Pinyin. These studies indicate that learning Pinyin as well as characters may contribute to learners' awareness of and sensitivity to phonological structures of spoken language, which in turn facilitates their Chinese word reading.

When teachers work with Chinese-speaking ELs, it is important to know not only about the prominent phonological awareness—reading acquisition is based on Chinese-speaking students' phonological awareness—but also about logographic characters in Chinese. Teachers can connect literacy learning in English, an alphabetic language system, with literacy learning in Mandarin Chinese, a logographic language system. For example, in the mastery of sound-symbol correspondences, teachers can provide explicit instruction on rhyming word families (e.g., can, cap, cat) in reading and writing.

Abundant Compound Words

Compounding is commonly used in word formation in the Chinese language. Compared to the English language, which does not have many compound words, many words in Chinese are often compound words, that is, a combination of two or more characters referring to a single concept/word. For example, the word for "to notice, to pay attention to, to focus on something" in Chinese language is combined with two characters 注意("zhuyi" in Pinyin). This compound word breaks down to 注("zhu" in Pinyin) meaning "to focus, to concentrate" and 意("yi" in Pinyin) meaning "intention." Learners can predict the meanings of compound words based on the final characters with reference to the same semantic category. Therefore, mastering characters is very important in understanding Chinese words.

Sentence Structure

There are some exceptions but, similar to English, the Chinese language usually follows the pattern of subject-verb-object (SVO); however, unlike in English, verbs are not conjugated. For example, in English, "she *likes* reading." In Chinese, it is expressed as "she *like* reading." In present simple tense in English affirmative sentences with *like*, the subject defines whether or not the singular or plural form of *like*. Also, the Chinese language has some flexibility in its word order. In particular, the Chinese object is highly flexible. It is often placed after the verb, but it can be placed before the verb. For example, "那个词语我明白" in Chinese which is literally translated into English to read, "that word I understand," is the object-subject-verb order. Also, to qualify an activity, prepositional phrases are usually placed before the verb such as "林喜欢在后院踢足球" in Chinese, which is literally translated into English to read "Lin likes in the backyard playing soccer." Nevertheless, just like English, the word order pattern of SVO is often used in the Chinese language.

In contrast to the English language, another variation in Chinese language is the expression of dates and fractions (Galligan, 2001). In English, fractions can be expressed as parts of a whole and are often stated as "X parts of Y." However, this goes opposite in Chinese and is often stated as "Y 分之X" in Chinese characters and "Y fenzhi X" in Pinyin. For example, "three parts of four" means three-quarters in English. This phrase construction is opposite in Chinese, "四分之三" in Chinese characters, "sì fēn zhī sān" in Pinyin. Galligan (2001) indicates, "Chinese language is expressed from the general to the particular and from large to small" (p. 117). Her work elaborates on the impact of differences between English and Chinese on understanding mathematical texts.

No Tense in Chinese Language

Unlike the English language, there is no distinction in verb form to represent past, present, and future tenses in Chinese language. The form of Chinese verbs does not change depending on the time frame. The time expression is usually used to indicate the time expression. For example, the English verb "go" becomes "went" for past tense, whereas "去" ("qu" in Pinyin), the Chinese verb for "go," stays the same. In addition, tense in Chinese language is indicated by means of particles, whereas tense in English language is accomplished through inflected suffixes and changes in verb formation.

The particle 被 ("bei" in Pinyin) is the most common passive marker. The pattern of the passive voice is structured as subject-被-people/objects-verb.

SVO Pattern in Chinese Interrogative Sentences

In the Chinese language, question words stay in the position of the words that people ask.

Different from English, the Chinese language follows the pattern of SVO in interrogative sentences. The word order in an interrogative sentence does not differ from this pattern. The question word is often placed in the position of the word that people ask about. In Chinese, people ask questions by using an interrogative particle such as "呢" ("ne" in Pinyin) or a question word. For example, in English, "I like playing basketball, what about you?" However, in Chinese, " 我喜欢打篮球，你呢？ " ("wo xihuan da lanqiu, ni ne?" in Pinyin). The word-for-word translation for this is "I like playing basketball, you?" Also, in Chinese, people ask questions by using a question word such as "what." For example, in English, "how much is this backpack?" However, in Chinese, " 这个背包多少钱？ " ("zhe ge beibao duoshao qian?" in Pinyin), and the word-for-word translation is "this backpack is how much."

Inseparable from Chinese Culture

Like English and other languages, Chinese language includes not only linguistic elements such as sentence structure but also cultural elements embedded in the pragmatics such as habits and values. For example, unlike the typical greeting—"how are you doing?"—in American culture, a daily greeting in Chinese culture is 你吃了吗？ ("ni chi le ma" in Pinyin), which means "have you eaten yet?" This greeting is a common way to start a conversation because food is regarded as heaven and a common topic of discussion in Chinese culture. In addition, Confucianism, Taoism, and Buddhism were the most widespread philosophies and religions of ancient China and continue to remain as the most influential until today (National Geographic Society, 2022). Although many Chinese-speaking people self-identify as atheists, they are affiliated with traditional Confucian, Buddhist, and/or Taoist values.

SPECIFIC EXAMPLES: CROSS-LINGUISTIC IMPACT ON LANGUAGE USE

The Chinese Language Is Logographic-Phonetic

It is important for teachers to know that there is a strong relationship between knowing a word's meaning and its pronunciation in Chinese. Many Chinese characters are compound characters composed of two or more characters. These compound characters consist of morphemes indicating the overall meaning and phonetic elements providing clues to how these Chinese characters are pronounced (Hanley et al., 1999; Hoosain, 1991). For example, the Chinese character 钟 means "clock" in English, pronounced "Zhōng" in Pinyin, and its left part [钅] is a morpheme conveying the meaning "mental" and its right part [中] is pictophonetic indicating how the character can be pronounced. This example underscores that phonological awareness and Chinese character recognition are strong predictors of word identification in early Mandarin Chinese literacy learning. Similar to Mandarin Chinese, phonological awareness and alphabetic recognition are strong predictors of both word spelling and reading comprehension in early English literacy instruction (e.g., bat, mat, rat, fat).

Pinyin, a Phonetic System in Mandarin Chinese

As noted earlier, Chinese is a tonal language with four lexical tones: first (high-level), second (rising), third (falling-rising), and fourth (falling), respectively. Table 5.4 illustrates how four different pitches represent different meanings. For example, "ba" with high-level pitch indicates "eight" in English while "ba" with falling pitch reflects "dad" in English. From the cross-linguistic perspective, teachers may draw upon the knowledge of Pinyin among Chinese-speaking learners to conduct direct literacy instruction. For example, rhyming word families (e.g., sit, fit, lit) can help students find the patterns in word families, thus connecting these words and their sounds as well as producing the positive cross-linguistic influence of Pinyin on English pronunciation.

Table 5.4   Four Lexical Tones in Mandarin Chinese

Tones	Pinyin	Chinese Character	English Equivalent
1st tone: high-level pitch	Bā	八	eight
2nd tone: high-rising	Bá	拔	to pull out
3rd tone: falling-rising	Bǎ	把	to hold
4th tone: falling	Bà	爸	dad

Moreover, table 5.5 presents the positive cross-linguistic influence of Pinyin on English language pronunciation, which means there are similarities between Pinyin and English. This positive cross-linguistic influence may promote English language learning. For example, the pronunciation of "buy" is as same as that of "bai" in Pinyin. And as such, teachers can build on the linguistic capital students bring with them from their L1 to support the learning of their L2. For example, an anchor chart similar to table 5.5 below could be created as a reference guide for students. Also, Chao's (2013a) case study illustrates Chinese-speaking ELs with solid Chinese language literacy use Pinyin and Chinese characters to support their content area in academic vocabulary learning.

Table 5.5   Examples of Cross-linguistic Influence of Pinyin on English Language Pronunciation

English Words	Pinyin	Chinese Character
buy	bai	拜
Joe	zhou	舟
Do	du	度

Compounding, a Common Way of Chinese Word Formation

In the whole Chinese concept/word, the final character often indicates the semantic category of the word, and the other characters provide additional meaning to the whole concept/word. Table 5.6 presents an example of this

Table 5.6   Word Formation in Mandarin Chinese

Whole Chinese Word	Pinyin	English Equivalent
小学	xiao xue	elementary school
中学	Zhong xue	middle school
大学	da xue	university

combination.

For example, a combination like *xiaoxue* (小学in Chinese characters) refers to a single whole word, which means "elementary school." The three whole words all share the same character 学 (English equivalent: school) and the first character provides information regarding different levels of school. For another example, the meaning of "ball" ("qiu" in Pinyin, "球" in Chinese character) contributes directly to the meaning of the word, reflecting the influence of Chinese compounds on English compounds such as basketball ("lan qiu" in Pinyin, "篮球" in Chinese character). The example of "basketball" presents the similarity between Chinese compound awareness and English compound awareness. With this information, teachers would be able to support students by creating charts that show the differences in words with and without suffixes and prefixes in them. Teachers would also have students identify affixes in their reading materials.

Basic Word Order of Chinese Language: Subject-Verb-Object

The syllabic structure of Chinese language usually follows the pattern of SVO which is similar to the English language. This similar pattern in both languages indicates that Chinese-speaking learners may not have many difficulties with the SVO formula of English language. This similarity is exemplified in table 5.7.

Table 5.7   SVO Word Order in Chinese Language

language	Subject	Verb	Object
Chinese character	我	有	一本书。
Pinyin	Wo	you	yi ben shu
English	I	have	a book

However, there is no verb change to match the corresponding subject. For example, in English, "she *likes* reading." In Chinese, it is expressed as "she *like* reading." In present simple tense in English affirmative sentences with *like*, the subject defines whether or not the singular or plural form of *like*.

Also, compared to the English language with some distinct subject pronouns and object pronouns, the form of subject pronoun and object pronoun stays the same in Mandarin Chinese. Table 5.8 illustrates the comparison of the pronouns between the two languages as well as the negative influence of the Mandarin Chinese on the English language, which means Chinese-speaking learners may make mistakes or errors because of their native language knowledge. For example, "we" changes to "us" when "we" is used as the object. Different from the English language, Mandarin Chinese pronouns, either subject pronouns or object pronouns, remain the same.

Table 5.8   Comparison of Subject Pronouns and Object Pronouns

Chinese Pronouns	English Subject Pronouns	English Object Pronouns	Negative Influence
我们	We	us	He gave <u>we</u> a book.
我	I	me	<u>Me</u> went home.
她	she	her	He walked to <u>she</u>.
他	he	him	We left <u>he</u> a bag.

Also, the Chinese language has some flexibility in its word order. Although Chinese language follows the basic pattern of SVO, the word order pattern of Subject-Object-Verb (SOV) is often used in Chinese language as shown in the example in table 5.9. A special particle "把" (bǎ) is often used in the formula of SOV exemplified.

Table 5.9   Subject-Object-Verb Word Order in Chinese Language

Chinese characters	我把这个作业完成了。
Pinyin	wo ba zhe ge zuoye wancheng le.
Word-for-word translation	I preposition this assignment finished.
English translation	I have finished this assignment.

The Chinese language is often expressed from the general to the particular and from large to small. Tables 5.10 and 5.11 exemplify the differences in word order between Chinese and English.

Table 5.10   Expression of Dates in Chinese

Chinese characters	二零二一年十月二十七号
Word-for-word translation	Two zero two one October twenty-seven
English translation	October 27, 2021

Table 5.11   Expression of Fraction in Chinese

Chinese characters	百分之三
Word-for-word translation	Hundred parts of three
English translation	Three percent

A simple way to introduce word order between Chinese and English to Chinese-speaking students is by making a simple chart that indicates the differences in word order.

Mandarin Chinese, a Language without Tense

Unlike the English language, the form of the verbs maintains the same with the variety of different tenses in Mandarin Chinese. Adverbials of time are employed to indicate the present tense, past tense, or future tense. Table 5.12 shows the differences between the Mandarin Chinese and the English language in tense makers and the negative influence of the Mandarin Chinese on the English language.

Table 5.12   Tense Makers in the Mandarin Chinese and the English Language

Tense	Chinese Language	English Language	Negative Influence
Present	她天天做作业。	She does homework everyday.	She <u>do</u> homework everyday.
Past	我昨天看一部电影。	I watched a movie yesterday.	I <u>watch</u> a movie yesterday.
Future	他明天回家。	He will go home tomorrow.	He <u>go</u> home tomorrow.

Also, the particle 被 (*bei* in Pinyin) is the most common passive marker. For example, "这只猫昨天被收养了" in Chinese is literally translated into English to read, "this cat yesterday *bei* foster," and its English translation is "this cat was fostered yesterday." With the information on tense and passive markers, teachers would be able to support students by engaging students in natural conversation in which students can learn quickly given enough repetition such as auxiliary verbs in the context.

Question Words Stay in the Position of the Words That People Ask

Different from English, the Chinese language follows the pattern of SVO. Wh-words are often in situ in Chinese language, whereas in English language, they are placed at the beginning of the sentence. For example, "一本书多少钱" in Chinese is literally translated into English to read, "a book cost how much," which is different from the English expression of "how much does a book cost?"

Also, two particles, 吗(*ma* in Pinyin) and 呢(*ne* in Pinyin), are often used to turn statements into questions. 吗is commonly used to turn a statement sentence into a yes-no question, and 呢 is mostly used to turn a statement sentence into a query statement. The two particles are commonly placed at the end of a sentence to form questions. For example, "这是一个长方形吗" in Chinese is literally translated into English to read, "this is a rectangle ma," which is different from the English expression of "is this a rectangle?" To practice using question words, teachers would give students opportunities to ask questions such as in interview and shopping role plays.

INSTRUCTIONAL IMPLICATIONS FOR EDUCATORS

This chapter illustrates cross-linguistic perspectives between Chinese and English for educators to promote their awareness of the similarities and differences between the two language systems. These perspectives and examples offer educators specific ways not only to make the transfer to English but also to avoid problems that native Chinese-speaking students face as they learn English. As previously stated, understanding these cross-linguistic perspectives between Chinese and English can help educators support Chinese-speaking students in mastering the English script system.

Native Chinese-speaking students' acquisition of language and literacy is a complex process and their Chinese influences the use of English. Different from native English-speaking students, Chinese-speaking students learn the English language, spoken and written, simultaneously. Scholars indicate that English language learning of immigrant children such as native

Chinese-speaking children is affected by their primary language literacy proficiencies. Cummins (1981) proposes that there is a cognitive proficiency common to all academic languages and literacies. He emphasizes that this common proficiency allows interlingual transfer of language and literacy skills. Following Cummins, Chinese-speaking immigrant students, particularly those who are literate in Chinese, often transfer linguistic knowledge of the Chinese language to their English language use. Chao's (2013a) case study also finds that Chinese-speaking immigrant students with solid Chinese language literacy and academic skills often use Chinese and adopt academic skills to support their learning. Given the linguistic nature of languages, some general implications for English language learning can be considered in the classroom.

First, teachers may encourage Chinese-speaking students to see their primary language as a resource for learning and find connections between their L1 and English. To illustrate, many morphemes contribute to the meaning of many Chinese compounds, and this compound awareness seems to facilitate Chinese-speaking ELs' English compound awareness development. Teachers may increase exposure to English compounds, which offers opportunities to develop compound word awareness leading to vocabulary growth. Teachers may introduce the list of *501 Compound Words for Kids* (All About Learning Press, 2017) to ELs. In the introduction of this list, teachers may employ a multisensory learning approach to compound words. Take "blueprint" as an example, teachers may show right hand for the first word "blue," left hand for the second word "print," and clap to represent "blueprint," the combination of the words together.

Also, it is important to synthesize using the Chinese language as a resource for Chinese-speaking students' English language acquisition. Educators may interview Chinese-speaking students about the specific approaches and methods they use when learning Chinese language literacy and content area knowledge. Specifically, in terms of cross-linguistic differences between Chinese and English, educators may have Chinese-speaking students tell the differences in the way that tense is represented in Chinese and English. Educators may also encourage Chinese-speaking students to write their own language learning experiences and integrate these experiences into classroom instruction. Specifically, Mohan and Lo's (1985) student questionnaire allows Chinese-speaking students to voice how their L1 writing experiences affect their English as a second language writing, giving feedback on educators' instructional change to better support Chinese-speaking students. This student questionnaire can be modified for educators' own use and given to students at the beginning of the academic year to get to know their background and cross-linguistic influences on their acquisition of other language skills such as listening, speaking, and reading.

Second, it is important to become culturally and linguistically responsive educators. When educators have some cross-linguistic knowledge between

English and Chinese, they may better understand the causes of the interference problems. By drawing from 102 Chinese students' writing samples, Lay (1975) presents the important areas of interference. Along with the principled elements and specific cross-linguistic examples of Chinese language discussed above, Lay's work outlines contrastive analysis of language interference between Chinese and English. Educators' general knowledge of different patterns of Chinese and other languages may give a good reason for educators to understand ELs' errors in English language use. Also, culture as an integrative part of educators' general knowledge contributes to their understanding and teaching ELs. Drawing from my ethnographic study in a southeastern U.S. city (Chao, 2013b), the example as follows indicates the nuanced cultural differences in the use of English of a recently arrived immigrant student from a non-Christian society. The following excerpt stems from a conversation with her on the image of a church building.

Xia: What's this?
Student: House.
Xia: A house?
Student: Yes. A house.
Xia: It's a house of God, a church. It's a church.

The image of church was new to this student because she said that she had not seen a church in her native country. The word "church" was distant from her English language knowledge not only as a vocabulary but also in its culture behind it. ELs' cultural differences may influence how they communicate and use the English language. Hence, consideration of how immigrant students' cultural background impacts their comprehension and use of language needs to be given. Educators may engage ELs with authentic materials including newspaper articles, videos, music, movies, and podcasts. Schwartz's (2020) article presents a variety of online resources including websites and teacher-created videos for supporting ELs in the classroom and beyond. Educators may select resources closely related to their curriculum and make content more accessible for students. There is an example about the website of the National Geographic, which provides videos about various topics such as rainforest. Educators may show the video connected to the topic of rainforest. While students watch the video, educators can turn on closed captions so that students can read the text simultaneously.

Third, educators may study and collect key errors that native Chinese-speaking students make. The types of grammatical, lexical, morphological, semantic, word order, and choice errors may help educators locate persistent errors. Educators' knowledge of cross-linguistic similarities and differences can help educators explicitly draw attention to the errors and provide explicit instruction and detailed feedback on Chinese-speaking students' errors. A comparative analysis between English and Chinese can help educators and Chinese-speaking students draw multiple linguistic knowledge and resources to master English language knowledge and skills.

Moreover, given the nature of the symbol-sound patterns in Chinese language, educators may provide "the support and development of contextually appropriate pedagogic strategies" (Jones, 2018, p. 175). Educators can use multimodal journaling to stimulate ELs' writing. For example, educators encourage ELs to express themselves through words, photos, drawings, and other images. Multimodal journaling is "a visual mode of symbolic representation and closely related to literacy as dispositions and identities" (Chao & Ma, 2019, p. 413). Educators may provide detailed feedback on ELs' multimodal journals and draw ELs' attention to the use of language in cross-linguistic and cross-cultural contexts.

As previously noted in this chapter, the cross-linguistic comparison between English and Chinese is very meaningful. Cook (1992) states that "the L2 knowledge that is being created in them [learners] is connected in all sorts of ways with their L1 knowledge" (p. 584). This suggests the importance of understanding the cross-linguistic differences, since this understanding can facilitate instruction and help ELs with English language acquisition.

To conclude, there is an important concern because of the differing linguistic features embedded in each of the Chinese and English language systems. I hope the cross-linguistic examples and perspectives between the two language systems presented in this chapter will increase educators' knowledge and awareness of the differences between Chinese language and English language. I also hope this knowledge and awareness will enable educators to develop linguistically and culturally relevant instruction.

REFERENCES

Aaronson, D., & Ferres, S. (1987). The impact of language differences on language processing: An example from Chinese-English bilingualism. In P. Homel, M. Palij, & D. Aaronson (Eds.), *Childhood bilingualism: Aspects of linguistic, cognitive, and social development* (pp. 75–120). Psychology Press.

All About Learning Press. (2017). *501 compound words for kids.* https://blog.allabou tlearningpress.com/compound-words/.

Bökset, R. (2006). *Long story of short forms: The evolution of simplified Chinese characters, Stockholm East Asian monographs* (Vol. 11). Department of Oriental Languages, Stockholm University.

Bradley, D. (1991). Chinese as a pluricentric language. In M. Clyne (Ed.), *Pluricentric languages: Differing norms in different Nations* (pp. 305–324). Walter de Guyter.

Chao, X. (2013a). Class habitus: Middle-class Chinese immigrant parents' investment in their newcomer adolescents' L2 acquisition and social integration. *Anthropology and Education Quarterly, 44*(1), 58–74.

Chao, X. (2013b). *Faith-based languaculture: Church as a place of language education and community-family connecting* [Doctoral dissertation, The University of Alabama]. https://ir.ua.edu/handle/123456789/1687.

Chao, X., & Ma, X. (2019). Transnational habitus: Educational, bilingual, and biliteracy practices of Chinese sojourner families in the U.S. *Journal of Early Childhood Literacy, 19*(3), 399–423.

Chen, K., Rehren, T., Mei, J., & Zhao, C. (2009). Special alloys from remote frontiers of the Shang Kingdom: Scientific study of the Hanzhong bronzes from southwest Shaanxi, China. *Journal of Archaeological Science, 36*(10), 2108–2118.

Cook, V. J. (1992). Evidence for multicompetence. *Language Learning, 42,* 557–591.

Cummins, J. (1981). The role of primary language development in promoting educational success for language minority students. In California State Department of Education (Ed.), *Schooling and language minority students: A theoretical rationale* (pp. 3–49). Los California State University.

DeFrancis, J. (1984). *The Chinese language: Fact and fantasy.* University of Hawaii Press.

Dong, H. (2021). *A history of the Chinese language* (2nd ed.). Routledge.

Fung (2009). Characteristics of Chinese in relation to language disorders. In S. Law, B. Weekes, & A. M.-Y. Wong (Eds.), *Language disorders in speakers of Chinese* (pp. 1–19). Multilingual Learners.

Galligan, L. (2001). Possible effects of English—Chinese language differences on processing of mathematical text: A review. *Mathematics Education Research Journal, 13*(2), 112–132.

Gut, U. (2010). Cross-linguistic influence in L3 phonological acquisition. *International Journal of Multilingualism, 7*(1), 19–38.

Hanley, J. R., Tzeng, O., & Huang, H. S. (1999). Learning to read Chinese. In M. Harris & G. Hatano (Eds.), *Learning to read and write: A cross-linguistic perspective* (pp. 173–195). Cambridge University Press.

Hoosain, R. (1991). *Pyscholinguistic implications for linguistic relativity: A case study of Chinese.* Erlbaum.

Institute of Linguistics, Chinese Academy of Social Sciences. (2004). *Xinhua dictionary* (10th ed.). Commercial Press.

Ji, Y., Hendriks, H., & Hickmann, M. (2011). How children express caused motion events in Chinese and English: Universal and language-specific influences. *Lingua, 121,* 1796–1819.

Jones, S. A. (2018). Telling cases of bilingual children's reading and writing for English-medium school: Implications for pedagogy. *Australian Journal of Language and Literacy, 41*(3), 166–176.

Ke, S., & Xiao, F. (2015). Cross-linguistic transfer of morphological awareness between Chinese and English. *Language Awareness, 24*(4), 355–380.

Lay, N. D. S. (1975). Chinese language interference in written English. *Journal of Basic Writing, 1*(1), 50–61.

Leider, C. M., Proctor, C. P., Silverman, R. D., & Harring, J. R. (2013). Examining the role of vocabulary depth, cross-linguistic transfer, and types of reading measures on the reading comprehension of Latino bilinguals in elementary school. *Reading and Writing: An Interdisciplinary Journal, 26*(9), 1459–1485.

Li, C. W. C. (2004). Conflicting notions of language purity: The interplay of archaising, ethnographic, reformist, elitist and xenophobic purism in the perception of Standard Chinese. *Language & Communication, 24*(2), 97–133.

Li, X., & Koda, K. (2022). Linguistic constraints on the cross-linguistic variations in L2 word recognition. *Reading and Writing, 35*, 1401–1424.

Lin, D., McBride-Chang, C., Shu, H., Zhang, Y., Li, H., Zhang, J., Aram, D., & Levin, I. (2010). Small wins big: Analytic pinyin skills promote Chinese word reading. *Psychological Science, 21*(8), 1117–1122.

Mohan, B. A., & Lo, W. A. (1985). Academic writing and Chinese students: Transfer and development factors. *TESOL Quarterly, 19*(3), 515–534.

Morrison, R. (1815). *A dictionary of the Chinese language.* East India Company Press.

National Geographic Society. (2022). *Chinese religions and philosophies.* https://education.nationalgeographic.org/resource/chinese-religions-and-philosophies.

Norman, J. (1988). *Chinese.* Cambridge University Press.

Ong, S. C. (2005). *China condensed: 5000 years of history and culture.* Times Edition-Marshall Cavendish.

Read, C., Zhang, Y.-F., Nie, H.-Y., & Ding, B.-Q. (1986). The ability to manipulate speech sounds depends on knowing alphabetic writing. *Cognition, 24*(1–2), 31–44.

Schwartz, L. (2020). *Helpful online resources for teaching ELLs.* https://www.edutopia.org/article/helpful-online-resources-teaching-ells.

Taylor, I., & Taylor, M. M. (1983). *The psychology of reading.* Academic Press.

Tognini-Bonelli, E. (2001). *Corpus linguistics at work.* John Benjamins.

Tzeng, O. J. L., Zhong, H. L., Hung, D. L., & Lee, W. L. (1995). Learning to be a conspirator: A tale of becoming a good Chinese reader. In B. de Gelder & J. Morais (Eds.), *Speech and reading* (pp. 227–245). Taylor & Francis.

U.S. Department of Education. (2019). *The top languages spoken by English learners (ELs) in the United States.* https://ncela.ed.gov/files/fast_facts/olea-top languages -fact-sheet-20191021-508.pdf.

Wang, W. S.-Y. (1973). The Chinese language. *Scientific American, 228*, 50–60.

Wilkinson, E. (2000). *Chinese history: A manual (revised and enlarged).* Harvard University Press.

Xiao, R., & McEnery, T. (2006). Collocation, semantic prosody, and near synonymy: A cross-linguistic perspective. *Applied Linguistics, 27*, 103–129.

Yao, H. (1998). Guifan putonghua yu dazhong putonghua (Standard Mandarin and popular Mandarin). *Yuwen Jianshe Tongxun, 57*, 1–12.

Yao, X. (2000). *An introduction to confucianism.* Cambridge University Press.

Chapter 6

An Overview of Vietnamese for Teachers of English Language Learners

Hanh thi Nguyen, Huy Phung, and Hoan Nguyen

According to the National Center for Educational Statistics (2021), Vietnamese was the home language of 76,500 students across public schools in the United States in the fall of 2018, the fifth most commonly reported home language among English Language Learners (ELLs). Vietnamese immigrants in the United States arrived in three main waves. The first consisted of refugees who were military personnel and urban professionals arriving toward the end of the war in 1975. The second were "boat people," rural or coastal dwellers, who endured much hardship at sea before arriving in the United States in the late 1970s to late 1980s. The third were immigrants under the peaceful Orderly Departure Program (1980–1997) created to relocate Vietnamese associated with the former South Vietnamese government to the United States (Batalova & Alperin, 2018). A small number of Vietnamese in the United States are international students and scholars, some with children attending U.S. schools. Given the high number of Vietnamese ELLs in the U.S. educational system, it is mandatory for educators to be familiar with the Vietnamese language and culture to ensure equal access.

A BRIEF HISTORY OF VIETNAMESE

Vietnamese is spoken by more than 98 million people in Vietnam and 4.5 million overseas. The Vietnamese language belongs to the Mon-Khmer branch of the Austroasiatic family; thus genetically, Vietnamese is closer to Thai and Khmer than to Chinese. The three main dialects of Vietnamese—Northern, Central, and Southern—correspond to three main cultural regions.

Vietnamese civilization started about 4,000 years ago, but the language was largely oral until around the tenth century with the creation of a localized traditional Chinese writing system among the elites to record Vietnamese words (Nguyễn, 2001). Written Vietnamese has only been widespread since the adoption of a Latin phonetic alphabet near the end of the nineteenth century (Bianco, 2012; Nguyễn, 2001). With a long oral history, the Vietnamese has an extensive treasure of folklore including songs, poems, proverbs, and sayings.

Due to about 1,000 years of Chinese occupation (111 BCE–939 CE), during which Confucianism, Taoism, Buddhism, and Chinese rituals and beliefs heavily influenced Vietnam, Vietnamese today has many borrowed words from Chinese (up to 70 percent in formal contexts, see Alves, 2009a). These Sino-Vietnamese words tend to be used in formal registers while native Vietnamese equivalents are used in daily conversations. Due to nearly 100 years of French invasion and colonization (1858–1945), during which French education, culture, and infrastructural systems entered Vietnam, there are also many borrowed words from French in Vietnamese. Although the United States was involved in the war in South Vietnam for over ten years, it is the current influence of American technology, commerce, and pop culture that has resulted in many new and rapid borrowings from English (Alves, 2009b).

PRINCIPLED ELEMENTS OF VIETNAMESE

Described below are key elements of Vietnamese in orthography, phonology, morphology, lexicon, grammar, pragmatics, and verbal arts, with comparisons to English. To refer to sounds, we will use the International Phonetic Alphabet (see IPA Chart with Sounds, InternationalPhoneticAlphabet.org, 2022).

Orthography

While the English alphabet has 26 letters, contemporary Vietnamese uses a modified Latin alphabet with 29 letters: *a, ă, â, b, c, d, đ, e, ê, g, h, i, k, l, m, n, o, ô, ơ, p, q, r, s, t, u, ư, v, x, y*. Created by Portuguese missionaries in the seventeenth century and adopted by French colonizers and Vietnamese scholars in the nineteenth to twentieth century, it became the national script when Vietnam gained independence in 1945. As a recently created phonetic alphabet, it retains the correspondence between letters and sounds more clearly than in English. Of note, the letter *d* is pronounced /z/ (Northern dialect) or /j/ (Southern dialect), the letter *s* is pronounced /s/ (Northern dialect) or /ʃ/ (Southern dialect), and the letter *x* is pronounced /s/ in both dialects. Penmanship is widely practiced in Vietnamese schools, and ELLs who learned penmanship in Vietnam may transfer Vietnamese cursive style into their English handwriting. It is therefore important for teachers of Vietnamese ELLs to be aware of Vietnamese cursive letters (see a sample at Wikimedia Commons, 2022).

As listed above, there are no letters *f, j, w,* and *z* in Vietnamese. On the other hand, some letters are modified to indicate Vietnamese sounds, and some letters are combined into digraphs to indicate single sounds (table 6.1).

Table 6.1   Vietnamese Orthographic Features That Are Different From English

Modified Letters Indicating Vietnamese Sounds	Combined Letters Indicating Single Sounds
• *ă* for short /ă/, e.g., *ăn* [eat] • *â* for short /ɤ̆/, e.g., *sân* [yard] • *ê* for /e/, e.g., *tên* /name/ • *ô* for /o/, e.g., *ôm* [hug] • *ơ* for /ɤ/, e.g., *cơm* [cooked rice] • *ư* for /ɯ/, e.g., *từ* [word] • *đ* for /d/, e.g., *đi* [go]	• *ch* for /t͡ɕ/, e.g., *chân* [leg/foot] • *gh* for /ɣ/ before *e, ê* and *i,* e.g., *ghe* [small boat], *ghế* [chair], *ghi* [write down] • *gi* for /z/, e.g., *giấy* [paper] • *kh* for /x/, e.g., *không* [no, not] • *nh* for /ɲ/, e.g., *nhà* [house] • *ng* for /ŋ/, e.g., *người* [person, people] • *ph* for /f/, e.g., *phim* [film] • *qu* for /kʷ/, e.g., *quên* [forget] • *th* for /th/, e.g., *thi* [exam] • *tr* for /ʈ/ (close to English [tr]), e.g., *trang* [page]

Given the above information, educators can anticipate challenges for Vietnamese ELLs, such as new letters, different cursive styles, and the lack of letter-sound correspondence in many English words.

Phonology

Due to some phonological differences between Vietnamese and English, Vietnamese ELLs may have challenges in pronouncing English words. Knowing these differences can help teachers pinpoint pronunciation difficulties Vietnamese ELLs encounter (see also Kirby, 2011; Tang, 2007). First, Vietnamese ELLs may have difficulties pronouncing some consonants that exist in English but not Vietnamese, including /θ/ in words such as <u>*thing*</u>, /ð/ in words such as <u>*this*</u>, /ʒ/ in words such as *plea<u>s</u>ure,* and /dʒ/ in words such as *ju<u>dg</u>e.* Conversely, Vietnamese ELLs might transfer into English consonants that exist in Vietnamese but not English, including /t͡ɕ/ (e.g., *chân* [leg/foot]) and /ɣ/ (e.g., *gà* [chicken]). Since English and Vietnamese use the same letters for these two sounds, educators can help Vietnamese ELLs hear the difference by focusing on how the sounds are made rather than how the words are written.

The short-long contrast in English vowels (e.g., *hit* vs. *heat*; *foot* vs. *food*) may be difficult for Vietnamese ELLs because short vowels /ɪ/ (as in *hit*) and /ʊ/ (as in *foot*) do not exist in Vietnamese. Although Vietnamese also makes a short-long contrast between some vowels, these vowels do not exist in English. Thus, educators should still practice the recognition and production of vowel length contrast in English for Vietnamese ELLs. Additionally, Vietnamese /e/ and /o/ are not produced with the added glide /w/ and /j/, respectively, as in English. This may lead some Vietnamese ELLs to drop the glide in English words such as *bay* [bej] and *boat* [bowt], pronouncing them as [be] and [bot].

Vietnamese has six lexical tones to mark differences in word meaning: high-level (*ngang*), smooth falling (*huyền*), rising (*sắc*), glottalized sharp falling (*nặng*), deep falling (*hỏi*), and glottalized falling-rising (*ngã*). All six are present in Northern dialect, but the latter two are merged into one in Central and Southern dialects. Each word has a tone, and when a word ends with a voiceless stop, it can only have a rising tone or glottalized sharp falling tone. Tones in Vietnamese are sometimes inserted into English words by learners, and words ending with a voiceless stop tend to receive a rising tone (e.g., *tap, bat, buck*).

Vietnamese syllables have the canonical structure Consonant-Vowel-Consonant plus a tone (+T). Unlike English, Vietnamese has no consonant clusters, and only voiceless stops and nasals are allowed in the final position (e.g., *bắp, bát, bác, băm, bán, bánh, bằng*). As a result, Vietnamese ELLs tend to devoice English final consonants (e.g., *bad* may sound like *bat*). Also unlike English, Vietnamese initial voiceless stops are not aspirated, so some Vietnamese ELLs may not aspirate initial consonants in words such as *pan, tan, can* in English. Finally, when a round vowel, /ɔ/, /o/, or /u/, precedes a velar consonant, /k/ or /ŋ/, the velar consonant is pronounced as a coarticulation of a bilabial and a velar (the sound is produced in the throat while the lips are closed). For example, *khóc* [cry] is pronounced [kʰɔ́k͡p + rising tone] (Đoàn, 1977).

In contrast to English, which is a stress-timed language, Vietnamese is a syllable-timed language (i.e., every syllable receives about equal time in pronunciation). Vietnamese intonation tends to be carried by sentence-final words rather than spreading out throughout the sentence as in English. When these patterns are transferred into English, learners may sound choppy to English speakers' ears. Further, English word stress may be challenging for Vietnamese ELLs to recognize and produce, such as the distinction between *present* /ˈprez.ənt/ and /prɪˈzent/.

Table 6.2 summarizes common pronunciation patterns by Vietnamese ELLs. For samples of Vietnamese accents in English with brief error analysis, see Speech Accent Archives: Vietnamese speakers (Weinberger, 2022).

Table 6.2   Common Pronunciation Errors by Vietnamese ELLs

Types of Error	Examples
1. *Final consonant omission/simplification*	
(a) dropping some final consonants	(a) I li<u>ke</u> [laɪ] chicken becau<u>se</u> [bɪˈkɒ] it's [it] yummy.
(b) simplifying final consonant clusters	(b) He a<u>sks</u> [æk] many question<u>s</u> [kwɛtʃən].
2. *Sound substitution*	
(a) substituting [θ] with [tʰ] and [ð] with [z] or [d]	(a) I <u>think</u> [tʰɪŋ] <u>this</u> [dɪs] is a big house.
(b) substituting final [d] with [t], [g] with [k] (devoicing), [l] with [n] and [s] with [t]	(b) The foo<u>d</u> [fuːt] in the bag [bæk] wi<u>ll</u> [wɪn] be deliciou<u>s</u> [dɪˈlɪʃət].
(c) substituting final [k] after [u, ʊ, ɔ] with coarticulation [kp͡]	(c) Loo<u>k</u> [lʊkp͡]! It's a green boo<u>k</u> [bʊkp͡].
(d) substituting /g/ with /ɣ/	
	(d) Very good [ɣut]!
3. *Merging short and long vowels:*	
(a) [ɪ] sounds like [i]	(a) I see a sh<u>i</u>p [ʃip] in the picture.
(b) [u] is shortened due to devoicing of final consonant	(b) She is in a bad m<u>oo</u>d [mut] now.
4. *Misplacement of word stress:*	
(a) all syllables in a word receive equal stress	(a) I am happy [ˈhæˈpiː] when I practice [ˈpræk ˈtɪs] music [ˈmjuːˈzɪk].
(b) syllable stress is misplaced	(b) I want to buy a present /prɪˈzent/.
5. *Lack of intonation contour or sentence stress:*	
(a) Each syllable is pronounced with the same duration and stress	(a) I go to school on the bus [ˈaɪ ˈgəʊ ˈtu ˈskuːn ˈɒn ˈzə ˈbʌt].
6. *Tone insertion:*	
(a) Words ending with a stop tend to receive a rising tone	(a) That sounds very bad [bat + rising tone].

Even though these pronunciation patterns may sound unnatural in English, not all of them interfere with meaning. Thus, educators want to target those that are more likely to cause communication breakdowns.

Morphology

Morphological differences between English and Vietnamese necessitate explicit instructions on English word formation for Vietnamese ELLs. Unlike English, which uses suffixes to indicate parts of speech, as an analytic language, Vietnamese does not use affixation. For example, there is no singular/

plural marker on nouns in Vietnamese (e.g., *sách* can refer to either "book" or "books"). Similarly, verbs are not marked grammatically for tense and aspect as in English (e.g., *Hôm qua em học bài* [gloss: yesterday—I—study—lesson; translation: Yesterday I studied] (cp. *Hôm nay em học bài* [gloss: Today—I—study])). Possession is only expressed by a particle and not with a possessive marker (e.g., *sách của em* [gloss: book—of—me; translation: my book]). For these reasons, it may take Vietnamese ELLs longer to master English grammatical markers, and they may underuse the possessive marker.

While English uses suffixes to change a word's parts of speech, Vietnamese uses markers that precede the word. Formal nouns can be formed from verbs by adding a noun marker (e.g., *sự đổ vỡ* [the collapse] (cp. *đổ vỡ* [to collapse])). Adverbs can be formed from adjectives by adding an adverb marker (e.g., *một cách nhanh nhẹn* [quickly] (cp. *nhanh nhẹn* [quick])). Educators can point out to learners that both English and Vietnamese have part-of-speech shift but differ in how the shift is done.

Lexicon

Aspects of the Vietnamese lexicon that are pertinent for teachers of Vietnamese ELLs are borrowings, pronouns, and numeracy. The Vietnamese language consists of native words, Sino-Vietnamese words, and borrowings from other languages, mostly French and English, often with phonological adaptation. Teachers can draw on borrowed words to help Vietnamese ELLs make appropriate connections with the target language through the use of instructional strategies such as explicitly teaching cognates and creating a cognate word wall. For example, a host of French words entered the Vietnamese lexicon as the colonizers introduced plants, food, technology, and Western lifestyle to Vietnam. Examples are *cà phê* [coffee, from French *café*], *cà rốt* [carrot, from French *carotte*], *kem* [ice-cream, from French *crème de glace*], *ô tô* [car, from French *auto*], *xe buýt* [bus, from French *autobus*], *mốt* [fashion, from French *mode*], *xà phòng* [soap, from French *savon*], *sơ mi* [*shirt*, from French *chemise*]. These words are so well integrated into everyday vocabulary that many Vietnamese are not aware that they are borrowed from French. Currently, an influx of English borrowings is rapidly entering the Vietnamese lexicon, such as *game, internet, hacker, on sale, shop, idol, hot boy/girl, rock, fan,* and *live show.* Many foreign words have shifted their meaning when borrowed into Vietnamese (e.g., *shipper* [deliverer of ordered goods], *amateur* [non-serious], or *baby* [cute]).

The Vietnamese personal pronoun and terms of address systems are much more complex than in English with the use of many kinship terms and separate terms for formal and informal contexts. Choice of pronouns and terms of address depends on the age difference between the speaker and listener, their social relationship, the listener's gender, the speaker's attitude, and the social context. Neutral pronouns for *I, you,* and *we* do exist but are often used in formal contexts when speakers and listeners do not have preexisting relationships. Since social relationships are established, maintained, and renewed every time a pronoun or term of address is used in Vietnamese, Vietnamese ELLs may seek ways to express their relationship to the listener, such as the transfer of kinship terms or the use of gestures and other expressions. Of note, teachers in Vietnam are addressed with specific pronouns to show respect, *cô* (for female teachers, literal meaning: Miss) and *thầy* (for male teachers, literal meaning: Teacher). Some Vietnamese ELLs may use the literal translation of these terms to show respect.

Vietnamese numbers have a decimal basis. Thus, *eleven* is *mười một* [gloss: ten—one], *twenty* is *hai mươi* [gloss: two—ten], and *one million two hundred fifty-six* is *một triệu hai trăm năm mươi sáu* [gloss: one—million—two—hundred—five—ten—six]. Following the French style, decimals are marked with commas and not periods (e.g., 1.2 is written as 1,2 in Vietnamese), and periods are used to separate zeroes in large numbers (e.g., 1,000,000 is written as 1.000.000 in Vietnamese).

Grammar

At the phrasal level, Vietnamese ELLs may transfer some habits with word order as well as noun and verb phrase structures into English. Regarding word order, Vietnamese is a head-initial language, that is, modifiers follow, rather than precede, the head word in a phrase (e.g., *cuốn sách này* [gloss: classifier—book—this; translation: this book], *nhà to* [gloss: house—big; translation: big house], *đẹp lắm* [gloss: beautiful—much; translation: so beautiful]).

Vietnamese noun phrases can contain determiners (e.g., articles, demonstratives, quantifiers) as in English, but Vietnamese article and classifier usage does not parallel English (Nguyễn, 2013). Although there are some lexical items that function as articles (e.g., indefinite and singular *một*, plural *những, các*), they are not mandatory in all contexts and are often used only for emphasis or clarification. Classifiers are mandatory in specific reference or expressions of quantity (e.g., *Em thích con cá này* [gloss: I—like—animal—fish—this]) but are disallowed when referring to a noun in general (e.g., *Anh ấy thích ăn cá* [gloss: He—like—eat—fish]) (Brunelle, 2015). Finally, Vietnamese does not differentiate between count and non-count nouns. Educators can help Vietnamese ELLs by guiding their discovery of patterns of English article usage and nouns' countability.

Regarding Vietnamese verbs and adjectives, the overlap in their grammatical behaviors may lead to confusion in English by some Vietnamese ELLs. The verb/adjective distinction in English does not apply in Vietnamese (Cao, 1993).

Cognitive/Stative verbs such as *like, love, want, know* function as adjectives (e.g., *Tôi rất thích quyển sách này* [gloss: I—very—like—book—this]). At the same time, some adjectives behave as verbs (e.g., *Em đang vui* [gloss: I—progressive aspect—happy; translation: I'm having fun]). Unlike in English, in Vietnamese, the copula *be* is required with noun complements but must be omitted with adjective or preposition complements (e.g., *Tôi là học sinh* [gloss: I—be—student; translation: I am a student] vs. *Tôi vui lắm* [gloss: I—happy—very; translation: I'm very happy]) or *Nhà trên đồi cao* [gloss: house—on—hill—high; translation: The house is on a high hill] (Nguyễn, 2001).

Vietnamese uses many serial verbs, that is, verb sequences that act as a single unit without any grammatical marking. The relationship between the verbs in a serial combination may be causative or sequential (e.g., *đi chơi* [gloss: go—play], *chú ý nghe* [gloss: pay attention—listen], *vào ăn cơm* [gloss: enter—eat—rice]) (Lâm, 2012). ELLs who transfer serial verb constructions into English may omit grammatical markings between verbs in English phrases.

Because there is no direct mapping between Vietnamese and English tenses and aspects, Vietnamese learners usually find this area challenging. In Vietnamese, tense is often understood in context or indicated by adverbs of time except in formal speech or for emphasis. Aspect, as well as mood, is expressed by a range of particles (Brunelle, 2015; Cao, 1998; Đinh, 2012; Thompson, 1965). Tense marking is absent in sentences such as *Hôm qua mẹ ở nhà. Ngày mai mẹ đi làm.* [gloss: yesterday—mother—stay—home. Tomorrow—mother—go—work]. However, for emphasis, tense markers can be inserted (e.g., *Cháu hứa sẽ cố gắng hơn ạ* [I—promise—future marker—try—more—politeness marker; translation: I promise I will try harder]) (Cao, 1998). Aspect and mood are marked by particles such as *đã* [perfect aspect marker], *đang* [progressive aspect marker], *sẽ* [future projection marker], *còn* [still], *chưa* [not yet], *vừa* [just], *từng* [experience marker], *xong* [completion marker], or *rồi* [already] (Đinh, 2012). Educators may need to provide examples, explanations, and practice of English tenses and aspects in context for Vietnamese ELLs.

At the sentential level, Vietnamese learners may transfer sentence structures into English without being aware that this results in ungrammatical sentences. Teachers can address these issues by pointing out the differences between two languages using charts or comparison tables. Below are cross-linguistic comparisons of some areas that can be difficult for Vietnamese ELLs: topic-comment structures, subject and object omission, passive voice, question formation, and complex sentences.

Vietnamese canonical sentences follow the subject-verb-object word order (e.g., *Tôi đọc sách* [gloss: I—read—book; translation: I read a book]). However, sentence structures in Vietnamese are highly flexible, and in spoken language, topic-comment structure is very common (Cao, 1991) (e.g., in the sentence *Áo này mẹ mua* [gloss: shirt—this—mother—buy; translation: As for this shirt, my mom bought it], the focus is on the shirt; in *Mẹ mua áo này* [gloss: mother—buy—shirt—this; translation: My mom bought this shirt]), the focus is on who bought the shirt. A specific type of topic-comment structure is existential sentences (e.g., *Trong nhà có ba người* [gloss: In—house—have—three—people; translation: In the house there are three people]).

Unlike in English, subjects and objects in Vietnamese are frequently omitted in conversations (Phạm, 2002). For example, the utterance *Đang đi thì gặp bạn* [gloss: progressive marker—go—then—meet—friend; translation: I was on the road when I saw my friend] has an omitted subject, and the utterance *Không thích* [gloss: no—like; translation: I don't like it] has both an omitted subject and an omitted object. The omission of subjects together with the topic-comment structure can result in sentences that parallel infinitive structure or passive voice in English (e.g., *Chỗ này ngồi rất tốt* [gloss: place—this—(omitted subject) sit—very—good; translation: This is a very good place to sit], *Bàn đã lau sạch* [gloss: table—perfect aspect marker—(omitted subject) wipe—clean; translation: The table has been wiped clean]).

Regarding passive voice, challenges for Vietnamese ELLs tend to come from differences in syntactic construction and voice selection. Passive sentences in Vietnamese do not involve fronting the object or grammatical marking on the verb (Nguyễn & Bùi, 2004). However, unlike English, Vietnamese mark passive voice sentences as a neutral, positive, or negative (e.g., *Bài này do em viết* [gloss: lesson—this—neutral passive marker—I—write; translation: This essay was written by me]), in contrast with *Em được cô giáo khen* [gloss: I—positive passive marker—female teacher—praise; translation: I was praised by the teacher], or *Em bị cô giáo phê bình* [gloss: I—negative passive marker—female teacher—criticize; translation: I was criticized by the teacher]. These positive and negative markers are also used in active sentences (e.g., *Em được điểm tốt* [gloss: I—positive marker—grade—good; translation: I got a good grade], or *Em bị ốm* [gloss: I—negative marker—sick; translation: I got sick]).

Since Vietnamese question formation does not involve fronting the question word and inverting auxiliary verbs, Vietnamese ELLs may face challenges when learning to form English questions. Vietnamese questions are formed by adding question words in the answer slot rather than through inversion as in English (e.g., *Ai đi học?* [gloss: who—go—study; translation: Who goes to school?] vs. *Anh gặp ai?* [gloss: You—meet—who; translation: Who did you meet?]).

Vietnamese embedded clauses in complex sentences are not marked with complementizers (e.g., *that*) as in English (Brunelle, 2015; Nguyễn, 2001). For example, there is no complementizer to indicate that the subject is a clause in *Em làm được là giỏi* [gloss: you—do—possible—be—good; translation: That you can do it is good]. In a similar pattern, the relative pronouns in relative clauses are optional in Vietnamese (e.g., *Người (mà) cho em mượn sách là cô giáo.* [gloss: person—(who)—give—I—borrow—book—be—teacher; translation: The person who lent me the book is my teacher], and *Quyển sách có bìa rất đẹp* [gloss: classifier—book—have—cover- very—beautiful; translation: The book has a cover that is very beautiful]). Table 6.3 summarizes and exemplifies common grammatical patterns by Vietnamese ELLs.

Table 6.3   Common Grammatical Errors by Vietnamese ELLs

Type of Error	Examples
1. *Noun phrase issues:*	
(a) Mixing count and non-count nouns	(a) Great! I want more video. I have a good news for you.
(b) Missing or misusing English articles *a, an, the*	(b) I want to be scientist.
(c) Omission of plural markers	(c) I like apple.
2. *Verb phrase issues:*	
(a) Omission of inflections: Missing past tense maker *-ed* or irregular verbs	(a) We go camping last weekend.
(b) Lacking subject-verb agreement for 3rd person singular nouns or pronouns	(b) Tony don't like my drawing.
(c) Missing the copula *be* with adjective as the predicate.	(c) She hungry.
(d) Use of adverbs *very* with stative verbs	(d) I very like this book.
(e) Omission of infinitive markers in verb sequences	(e) I want go home.
(f) Tense and aspect errors	(f) I wish you can come to the movies last night.
(g) Inappropriate use of passive voice	(g) He was died last year.
3. *Adjective phrase issues:*	
(a) Using both *more* and the inflectional suffix *er'* for comparison	(a) My friend is more taller than me. It is worser than my idea.
4. *Sentence structure issues:*	
(a) Transfer of topic-comment structure into English existential sentences	(a) Around the lake have many houses.
5. *Question formation issues:*	
(a) Lack of auxiliary verbs, lack of fronting of auxiliary verbs	(a) You want it? What the topic is?
6. *Complex sentence issues:*	
(a) Omission of complementizers	(a) Do you understand we speak English?
(b) Adding connectives not required in English	(b) Although she is rich, <u>but</u> she is very mean. If you study hard, <u>then</u> you pass the exam.

Pragmatics

Being familiar with Vietnamese verbal/non-verbal communication practices and pragmatic routines could help teachers avoid misunderstandings with Vietnamese students. Vietnamese people use honorifics such as *ạ* at the end of a sentence (Northern dialect) and *dạ* at the beginning of a sentence (Southern dialect) to mark politeness toward people of higher status or seniority. Some ELLs might equate English *please* with these honorifics and insert it in English sentences to mark politeness. In conversations, Vietnamese listeners produce frequent back-channelers, *vâng* (Northern dialect) or *dạ* (Central and Southern dialects), to show respect to the speaker. These words also mean "yes" in Vietnamese, so Vietnamese ELLs may produce *yes* frequently as back-channeling, which does not always indicate understanding or agreement.

Vietnamese has a rich inventory of stance markers, discourse markers, emphasis markers, and other particles to indicate the speaker's perspective toward what is being said (which in English may be expressed through word choice, modals, and subjunctive mood in addition to particles). For example, *ơi* is used with vocatives to express affection (e.g., *Hoa ơi!* [Hoa dear!], *nhé* (Northern)/ *nghe* (Southern) are used at the end of an utterance to express or seek agreement, e.g., *Nhớ nhé/nghe* [Remember to do it, OK?], and *chứ* is used in responses to mark the asked question as questioning the obvious, e.g., *Anh có đi chơi không?—Có chứ! Đợi nãy giờ rồi* [Are you going out with us?—Yes of course! I've been waiting this whole time]) (see Roever & Nguyen, 2013).

Vietnamese speakers tend to prefer an indirect communication style when dealing with delicate topics and often maintain reservedness toward new acquaintances. Hints rather than direct speech acts are often used. For example, a speaker may describe a hardship in detail to elicit an offer from the listener rather than producing an actual request. Although this pattern is also present in English, it is more prevalent in Vietnamese. In addition, shyness is common in first encounters or in large groups, and Vietnamese students may take longer to warm up to classmates and teachers than their American counterparts. They also may not actively volunteer to express their ideas or opinions except when asked. In contrast, in close relationships or in small groups, Vietnamese people can be quite involved in others' affairs, such as asking about personal details and volunteering advice.

There are many non-verbal communication routines that are different between Vietnamese and English. For instance, the good luck gesture of crossing the fingers is a vulgar expression in Central and Southern Vietnam. On the other hand, the middle finger gesture, while offensive in English, is not a taboo in Vietnamese. The English gesture of beckoning someone with the motion of an up-turned index finger is seen as condescending to Vietnamese, as it is only used to call a dog (and dogs are traditionally considered lowly animals). When handing an object to a senior person, Vietnamese use both hands to show respect, sometimes also accompanied by lowering of the head. Vietnamese in general do not gaze directly at the interlocutor during conversations, and a downward gaze is usually to show respect.

Due to their upbringing and cultural influence, Vietnamese ELLs may use some pragmatic routines that are different from native English speakers. As conversation openers, Vietnamese ELLs may ask, "What are you doing?" "Where are you going?" or "Have you eaten lunch yet?" These are simply used to get the conversation going and are not challenges or preliminaries to invitations, as they might be in English. Vietnamese ELLs may also ask personal questions that are acceptable in Vietnamese but may not be appropriate in English (e.g., "How many people in your family?" "How old are you?" and "Are you married?")

Some Vietnamese pragmatic routines may be unfamiliar to American English speakers. Typical responses to compliments are not thanking but refusal and self-deprecating comments to show modesty (e.g., "A: What a nice shirt! B: Oh, no, this is just an ugly one!"). Also to indicate humbleness, responses to invitations and offers are typically refused multiple times, and acceptance may be produced only after insistence with several repetitions of the invitation or offer. In communication with Vietnamese who are not familiar with English invitation responses and offer responses, it is thus important to not take the initial refusal at face value. Vietnamese tend to say "thank you" and "sorry" only to outsiders, not among close friends and family members (they use expressions of gratitude such as "it must have taken you a long time to make this for me" or "I've caused you much hardship"). As a result, Vietnamese students may not say "thank you" and "sorry" in English when expected. Finally, requests in Vietnamese are formulated by the expression "Please give me X" even when speaking politely. A direct translation of this formulation might sound rude to English speakers.

Verbal Art

In addition to pragmatic routines, knowing about forms of verbal art such as wordplay in Vietnamese could help teachers see the potential for creativity and play by ELLs. Some common forms of wordplay in Vietnamese are puns, nói lái, and play with foreign words. Since the last two are different from English, we will describe them here. Nói lái [speaking backward] is a prolific form of wordplay in Vietnamese in which consonants, vowels, or tones may be swapped between words to create a new message (Macken & Nguyễn, 2006). Although the mechanism may be similar to Spoonerism in English (e.g., "you have hissed my mystery lesson"—"you have missed my history lesson"), nói lái usage is more widespread in Vietnamese than Spoonerism is in English. Nói lái is common in humor, riddles, and subversion (e.g., *Tại mày xui* [Because you are unlucky]—*Tụi mày sai* [You are all wrong], *hiện đại* [modernity]—*hại điện* [using much electricity]).

Another form of wordplay common in Vietnamese is turning foreign words into Vietnamese words of similar sounds, sometimes by adding tones. Some examples are *non nớt* [young and immature; from English *non-nerd*], *ăn ít* [eat a little; the second word, *ít*, sounds like English "eat"], *I thought you could*, pronounced as *I thọt* [I have a lame leg] *you cụt* [you have an amputated leg].

INSTRUCTIONAL SUGGESTIONS FOR EDUCATORS

Although Vietnamese ELLs often transfer features of their mother tongue into the target language, not all errors can be traced back to their first language. Their English might follow its own developmental trajectory. Therefore, teachers may need to consider several factors that may underlie ELLs' errors. In helping Vietnamese ELLs, educators can consider:

- *Celebrating.* Rather than treating Vietnamese ELLs as deficient English speakers, drawing on the rich linguistic resources a Vietnamese ELL brings to classrooms can be valuable for both learners and teachers. Teachers can encourage Vietnamese ELLs to share their own language in collaborative activities such as "How do we say, ____ in your language" (Vietnamese ELLs write translations and draw illustrations of objects or concepts on posters around the classroom) to foster students' self-esteem and cultivate a sense of belonging.
- *Awareness Raising.* ELLs learn best if they are able to attend to the gaps between their language and the target language (Schmidt, 1990). Raising awareness about English language patterns and how they are different from Vietnamese can help ELLs notice and avoid errors. For example, teachers can encourage learners to be detectives to identify errors and cross out incorrect placement of adverbs before cognitive/stative verbs. Teachers can guide learners to discover English sentence structures by underlining subjects, verbs, and objects in complex English sentences or to spot the contrast between Vietnamese and English regarding when passive voice is used. Teachers can use visual aids, videos, corpus concordances, demonstrations, teacher-made tongue twisters, minimal pairs, drills, and exercises to help ELLs notice specific features of the target language.
- *Corrective Feedback.* Teachers can draw learners' attention to linguistic forms in meaning-based contexts through focused corrective feedback. The feedback sequence can be input providing + prompting, recasts, and

explicit correction. For example, when a learner says "I want go home," teachers can reformulate the sentence, with emphasis on the correction, "Oh you want *to* go home." They can also briefly explain that "*to*" is needed between *want* and *go*.

- *Selective Focus.* A given ELL may have many errors in many areas all at once. Rather than trying to address all the errors, which can be overwhelming, it is more effective to select and focus on specific language forms to work on consistently until they are resolved. For instance, instead of correcting all final consonant omissions or simplification, teachers can focus on only some high-frequency words in ELLs' language (e.g., *because, house*). Correction on these words should be sustained consistently to draw learners' attention to final consonants in general until improvement is made.
- *Make it Fun.* Language practice can be fun with visualization, games, and interactive exercises. Stress and intonation can be introduced and practiced by using sound and pitch visualization (e.g., with Praat (Boersma & Weenink, 2022) or Sonic Visualiser (Cannam et al., 2022)). To practice syllable-timed rhythm, stress, and intonation, teachers can use tapping/clapping in Jazz chants style (Bridge-Linguatec Inc., 2008). To tell the difference between two sounds, ELLs can work in pairs on minimal pair exercises.

ACKNOWLEDGMENTS

We thank Guy Kellogg for his helpful feedback on an earlier version of this paper. All errors remain ours.

REFERENCES

Alves, M. J. (2009a). Sino-Vietnamese grammatical vocabulary and sociolinguistic conditions for borrowing. *Journal of the Southeast Asian Linguistics Society, 1*, 1–9.

Alves, M. J. (2009b). Loanwords in Vietnamese. In M. Haspelmath & U. Tadmor (Eds.), *Loanwords in the world's languages: A comparative handbook* (pp. 617–637). Walter de Gruyter.

Batalova, J. B., & Alperin, E. (2018, September 13). *Vietnamese immigrants in the United States.* Migrationpolicy.Org.

Bianco, J. L. (2012). Romanization of Vietnamese. In C. Chapelle (Ed.), *The encyclopedia of applied linguistics* (pp. 1–5). John Wiley & Sons, Inc.

Boersma, P., & Weenink, D. (2022). *Praat: Doing phonetics by computer* (6.2.14) [Computer software]. http://www.fon.hum.uva.nl/praat/.

Bridge-Linguatec Inc. (2008). *Teaching sentence stress with Jazz chants.* https://www
.youtube.com/watch?v=mAYwoLZso7s.

Brunelle, M. (2015). Vietnamese (Tiếng Việt). In M. Jenny & P. Sidwell (Eds.), *The
handbook of Austroasiatic languages* (pp. 909–953). Brill.

Cannam, C., Landone, C., & Sandler, M. (2022). Sonic visualiser (4.5) [Computer
Software]. https://sonicvisualiser.org/.

Cao, Xuân Hạo. (1991). *Tiếng Việt: Sơ Thảo Ngữ Pháp Chức Năng. [Vietnamese:
Preliminaries on a functional grammar]* (Vol. 1). Nhà Xuất Bản Khoa Học Xã Hội.

Cao, Xuân Hạo. (1993). Some preliminaries to the syntactic analysis of the Vietnamese sentence. *Mon-Khmer Studies, 20,* 137–151.

Cao, Xuân Hạo. (1998). Về ý nghĩa thì và thể trong tiếng Việt [On the meaning of
tense and aspect in Vietnamese]. *Ngôn Ngữ [Language], 5,* 1–31.

Đinh, Văn Đức. (2012). THỜI và THỂ trong tiếng Việt: Nhìn từ hai phía NGỮ PHÁP
và TÌNH THÁI. *Tạp chí Từ điển học & Bách khoa thư [Journal of Lexicography
and Encyclopedia], 5*(19). Vietlex.com.

Đoàn, Thiện Thuật. (1977). *Ngữ âm tiếng Việt [Vietnamese phonology].* Nhà Xuất
Bản Đại Học và Trung Học Chuyên Nghiệp.

InternationalPhoneticAlphabet.org. (2022). *IPA chart with sounds.* International
Phonetic Alphabet. https://www.internationalphoneticalphabet.org/ipa-sounds/ipa
-chart-with-sounds/.

Kirby, J. P. (2011). Vietnamese (Hanoi Vietnamese). *Journal of the International
Phonetic Association, 41*(3), 381–392.

Lâm, Quang Đông. (2012). Some relevant terms in the study of Vietnamese serial
verb constructions. *VNU Journal of Social Sciences and Humanities, 28*(5), 40–46.

Macken, M. A., & Nguyen, H. T. (2006). "Nói lái" and the structure of the syllable.
Linguistics of the Tibeto-Burmese Area, 29(2), 1–61.

National Center for Educational Statistics. (2021, May). *English language learners in
public schools.* https://nces.ed.gov/programs/coe/indicator/cgf.

Nguyễn, Hồng Cổn & Bùi, Thị Diên. (2004). Dạng bị động và câu bị động trong tiếng
Việt [Passive voice and passive sentence in Vietnamese]. *Ngôn Ngữ [Language],
7–8,* 1–12; 8–18.

Nguyễn, Hùng Tưởng (2013). The Vietnamese noun phrase. In D. Hole & E. Löbel
(Eds.), *Linguistics of Vietnamese: An international survey* (pp. 57–86). De Gruyter.

Nguyễn, Hữu Quỳnh. (2001). *Ngữ pháp tiếng Việt [Vietnamese grammar].* Nhà Xuất
Bản Từ Điển Bách Khoa.

Phạm, Văn Tình (2002). *Phép tỉnh lược và ngữ trực thuộc tỉnh lược trong tiếng Việt.*
Nhà xuất bản Khoa học xã hội.

Roever, C., & Nguyen, H. T. (Eds.). (2013). *Pragmatics of Vietnamese as native and
target language.* National Foreign Language Resource Center.

Schmidt, R. W. (1990). The role of consciousness in second language learning.
Applied Linguistics, 11(2), 129–158.

Tang, G. (2007). Cross-linguistic analysis of Vietnamese and English with impli-
cations for Vietnamese language acquisition and maintenance in the United
States. *Journal of Southeast Asian American Education and Advancement, 2*(1),
Article 3.

Thompson, L. C. (1965). *A Vietnamese grammar*. University of Washington Press.

Weinberger, S. H. (2022, June 6). *The speech accent archive*. https://accent.gmu.edu/browse_language.php?function=find&language=vietnamese.

Wikimedia Commons. (2022). *Handwritten Vietnamese alphabet*. Wikipedia. https://en.wikipedia.org/wiki/Vietnamese_alphabet#/media/File:Vietnamese_Decision_31_Cursive_Chart.svg.

Chapter 7

First Language Impact

Bengali

Yvonne Pratt-Johnson and Medha Bhattacharyya

The present chapter provides an overview of similar and contrasting features with respect to Bengali and English. Scholars in applied linguistics have long debated whether there is such a thing as "transfer" in new language learning and, if so, what the underlying mechanism might be (see Epstein et al., 1996; Odlin, 1989; Schwartz & Sprouse, 1996). Today, consensus still seems far off. Nevertheless, there is both anecdotal and research-based evidence that speakers of a given first language (L1) often show common traits in their usage and/or path of acquisition with respect to a second language (L2). In other words, these individuals appear to share common acquisition challenges/advantages (relative to speakers of other L1s) that can be mapped against (and thus suspected to have been "impacted by") features of their first language. Hence, just as knowledge of heritage cultures benefits teachers by helping them connect content to students' experiences and home lives (Banks & McGee-Banks, 2016; Catto, 2018; Delpit, 2012; Ladson-Billings, 2014), knowledge of similar and contrasting features of a given L1/L2 pair can help educators predict usage/learning patterns and provide targeted instruction.

This chapter is intended primarily for teachers of L1 Bengali students in an English-speaking context. For this reason, the chapter begins with a brief account of Bengali students in the United States, followed by a brief history of the Bengali language. This, in turn, is followed by a discussion of similarities and differences between Bengali and English, in which the authors identify and discuss potential challenges for Bengali students. The chapter concludes with a section on pedagogical implications, in which the authors suggest strategies teachers can use to help overcome these challenges. Thereafter, the authors provide a section on Bengali literature that teachers might incorporate into their lesson plans and, in their conclusion, reflect on some

113

of the advantages and challenges associated with bringing knowledge of students' first languages to bear in the classroom.

BENGALI STUDENTS IN THE UNITED STATES

Bengali, also known as Bangla, is the first language for approximately 228 million people worldwide, making it (at least) the world's seventh most spoken native tongue (Hasan, 2020). Currently, around 100 million Bengalis (in English, "Bengali" refers to both the language and its speakers) reside in Bangladesh and around 85 million in India, mostly in the states of West Bengal, Assam, and Tripura (Bengali Language, 2021). Of the remainder, the largest contingents are found in the United Kingdom and the United States (Budiman, 2021).

In the United States, the immigration of Bengali speakers has increased considerably in the current millennium. In 2000, the U.S. Bengali population stood at about 57,000; by 2019, however, it had risen to around 208,000—an increase of nearly 265 percent (Pew Research Center, 2021). Currently, large populations of Bengali speakers can be found in such U.S. cities as Los Angeles, Boston, Buffalo, Chicago, Detroit, Atlantic City, and Washington, D.C. New York City (NYC), however, is home to the largest U.S. Bangladeshi community: approximately two-thirds of the nation's Bangladeshis and about 90 percent of those in New York State (Asian American Federation Census Information Center, 2019).

The NYC public school system, which is the largest in the country, serves approximately 1.3 million K-12 students (New York City Department of Education [NYC DOE], 2019). Of these, more than 6,500 are Bengalis (Luna, 2015), making theirs the fourth most common language system-wide (NYC DOE, 2019). Nonetheless, Bengali-speaking teachers and administrators are few, and basic knowledge of the Bengali language is rare (Luna, 2015). In fact, only three schools in the city offer bilingual English–Bengali programs (Luna, 2015). Thus, most L1 Bengali students—in NYC and, indeed, across the country—develop their skills in the language of instruction through English as a new language services.

A BRIEF HISTORY OF THE BENGALI LANGUAGE

A member of the Indo-Aryan group of the Indo-Iranian branch of the Indo-European language family, Bengali originates from the eastern Middle Indic languages of Prakrit, Pāli, and Sanskrit. Scholars debate when and how Bengali emerged as a distinct language. One main camp claims that Bengali had its beginnings in the tenth century CE from a spoken form of Magahi Prakrit, while the other holds that it already possessed distinct spoken and written forms in the seventh century CE, the era of the Gauda Kingdom (Bengali Language, 2017).

By the twelfth century, in any case, literature in Bengali had become well established. Modern scholars divide Bengali literature into the following periods: Ancient (650–1200), Medieval (1200–1800), Modern (1800–1980s), and Postmodern (1980s–Present). The first surviving work from the ancient period is *Caryapāda*, a collection of mystical verse songs in the Vajrayana tradition, composed by Buddhist monks between the eighth and twelfth centuries. Notable in the Medieval period is the work of Kashiram Das, a sixteenth-century poet who composed a Bengali version of the *Mahābhārata* (*Kashidasi Mahabharat*, 1604 CE). Among many luminaries of the Modern period, poet and playwright Michael Madhusudan Dutt (1824–1873) experimented with both meter and theme in his masterpiece *Meghnad Badh Kavya* (Poem about Slaying Meghnad, 1861) and Bankim Chandra Chattopadhyay (1838–1894), a novelist and poet, composed the *Vande Mataram* (Hail Motherland), which became the national song of India. Also noteworthy is Rabindranath Tagore (1861–1941), the first Nobel Laureate of Asia, who distinguished himself by writing in all literary genres in Bengali (Bhattacharyya, 2020). Later, in the twentieth century, Kazi Nazrul Islam (1899–1976) composed nearly 4,000 Bengali songs, but he remains most famous for his 1922 revolutionary poem *Bidrahi* (The Rebel) (Sen, 1992). Prominent contemporary Bengali Postmodernists include Syed Manzoorul Islam and Swapnamoy Chakraborty.

Although modern Bengali retains a largely Sanskrit vocabulary base, it has acquired words and structures from language families outside the Indo-Aryan group, such as the Dravidian, the Austroasiatic, and the Tibeto-Burman families (Bengali Language, 2017). In terms of writing, the Bengali alphabet, like almost all scripts known to have been used in South Asia, originates in the ancient Brahmi script. The classic literary form was established by the twelfth century, but the alphabet underwent further changes, particularly in the sixteenth and nineteenth centuries (Bengali Language, 2021).

KEY CHARACTERISTICS OF BENGALI AS COMPARED TO ENGLISH

The discussion of similar and contrasting features of Bengali and English is organized into eight categories: word order, pronoun use, negation, empty subjects, verb inflection, copula use (object complement), pluralization, and auxiliary verbs. In what follows, literal translations of sample Bengali expressions—along with quoted examples of English discourse from Bengali speakers that are likewise ungrammatical in English—are marked with an asterisk (*).

Word Order

The order of a typical English sentence is Subject + Verb + Object (SVO) (e.g., *Susana jumped rope*). Bengali, however, is an SOV language. This difference presents challenges for Bengali students, especially beginners, who often appear to impose SOV structure onto English. In simple utterances, this may have little impact, as when Bengali speakers say things like **He high jump* for target-like *He jumps high*. When other elements are involved, however, the problem may be compounded. For example, adverbs in English are placed either before or after the verb. In Bengali, however, adverbs always come before the verb and, if there is an object preceding the verb, the adverb is placed between the subject and the object. Teachers may encounter non-target-like utterances (aka "errors") of the following form from Bengali-speaking English language learners (ELLs): **They the mall went yesterday; *I very much cake like; *I fast run.*

Pronoun Use

In English, although some individuals prefer to be referred to by the non-gender-marked pronouns "they/them," traditional singular third-person personal pronouns have gender-based forms: she/he, her/him, her/his, herself/himself. Bengali, on the other hand, is a genderless or gender-neutral language, and Bengali pronouns do not differentiate gender. Table 7.1 shows the third-person singular personal pronouns in English and their Bengali equivalents.

Table 7.1   Third-Person Singular Personal Pronouns in English and Bengali

English	Bengali
she/he	sē
her/him	tāke
her/his	tārā

The lack of gender differentiation in pronouns in their L1 may represent a special challenge for Bengali speakers. At any rate, these learners are often observed to make incorrect or inconsistent use of the gender-based pronouns in English. Typically, these are errors of *he* for *she, she* for *he,* and so on, as in the following examples (where not otherwise indicated, examples were noted by the authors in the course of their teaching):

> *John is my brother, and <u>she</u> [referring to John] my house live.
> * This my new classmate. <u>She</u> name Pierre.
> *I think Uni [a girl], <u>he</u> is my best friend. (Islam, 2004)

Negation

In English, negation is most commonly achieved using the particle *not*, either separately or contracted with an auxiliary (aka "helping") or modal verb. Rules for placement of the negative particle depend on the grammar and meaning of the sentence. Thus, the basic English sentence cited in the section on Word Order has several negative equivalents, such as *Susana does not jump rope* (or, in past tense, *did not*) and *Susana is not jumping rope*. In constructions that use the auxiliary *have*, the negative particle is placed between the auxiliary and the main verb: that is, subject + auxiliary + <u>*not*</u> + main verb. When a modal verb (can/could, will/would, may/might, shall/should, and must) is used on its own, however, the particle *follows* the verb: *I will not!*

Negation in English can be said to be somewhat complex. Negation in Bengali, however, at least in terms of particle use, is much simpler: the element <u>*nā*</u> is always placed at the *end* of the sentence, as in the following examples:

āmi boli *nā.*
(I do <u>*not*</u> speak.)

tārā aktā gāḍī chālābe *nā.*
(They should <u>*not*</u> be driving a car.)

Islam (2004) reports a beginning-level L1 Bengali student describing his school as "very good not, very bad not," which can be interpreted as a calque (i.e., an unaltered "loan translation") of how the utterance would be ordered in Bengali. The following examples were also culled by Islam (2004) from L1 Bengali students' beginning-level English writing samples:

*I rice eat <u>*not*</u>.
(I do <u>*not*</u> eat rice.)
(āmi bhāt khāi <u>*na*</u>.)

*I well <u>*not*</u>.
(I am <u>*not*</u> well.)
(āmi bhālo <u>*nāi*</u>.)

*his money no.
(He has no money.)
(tār tākā nāi).

The fact that their first language and English both use a particle for negation may be theorized as presenting L1 Bengali students with a sort of "tantalizing similarity," and this may stand in some relation to the fact that many seem to ignore the difference in the placement of the particle and produce utterances that are, in this regard, more "correct" in relation to Bengali than to English. As noted above, however, there is no agreement regarding what "causes" so-called language transfer, or even that learners can technically be said to "transfer" structures across languages. Nevertheless, classroom experience shows that L1 Bengali students, particularly those at the beginner or lower intermediate levels, often generate spoken or written utterances with the English negative particle "wrongly" placed at the end—just as it would be in their L1: *My school is very good* not; *We happy* not; *I have job* not.

Empty Subjects

English possesses a relatively uncommon feature known as "pleonastic" subjects. Commonly referred to as "empty" or "dummy" subjects, they function as a type of placeholder in utterances in which the subject cannot be stated using a noun or personal pronoun. The two pronouns or particles used in these constructions are *there* and *it*. Both are used in conjunction with forms of the verb *be*, as in the following examples:

> *There* is a need for new blood in this organization.
> *It* is clear that her work has improved.
> *It* is raining.

Bengali, however, does not employ empty subjects to express impersonal action or states. In the authors' experience, the typical response of beginning and intermediate L1 Bengali students to the need to produce subject-less utterances in English is either (1) to treat what would be the grammatical object of the target-like sentence as the subject or (2) to place some other object in the subject position—as in the following examples:

> *Snow falling.
> (It is snowing.)
> *3rd grader—high beginner ELL*

> *In New York City many people.
> (There are many people in New York City.)
> *5th grader—intermediate ELL*

Verb Inflection in Present Tense

From an earlier, more complex system of verb endings, modern English retains only the -s that marks third-person singular in the simple present tense: *She* walks *every day; He* works; *It* makes *sense.* Although slight in form and narrow in distribution, this "-s" feature is important, since failure to apply the rule correctly can prevent the receiver from understanding the message. Table 7.2 shows samples of verb inflection in the present tense for all five personal subject pronouns in English and their Bengali equivalents.

Table 7.2   Verb Inflection in Present Tense in English and Bengali

English	Bengali
I travel a lot	āmi khub ghure baeṛāi
You travel a lot	āpni khub ghure baeṛān
He/She travels a lot	tini khub ghure baeṛān
They travel a lot	baeṛān ora khub ghure
We travel a lot	āmrā khub ghure beṛāi

As teachers of ELLs can attest, learners from many L1 groups take time to acquire this feature, and some never do. Underlying this challenge may be the fact that, even if a given learner's L1 has a more complex system (and hence, intuitively, one might expect such a learner to find the English system "easier"), there is seldom a one-to-one correspondence between rule systems. In Bengali, for example, as table 7.2 shows, there is a distinct verb form for the *first* person in the present tense, but not for the third. Again, there is no proof that this difference is the "source" of a developmental delay or acquisitional challenge. Nonetheless, in the authors' experience, many Bengali students take longer to acquire English third-person singular verb marking than they do to acquire some of the other features discussed in this chapter, and omission of the marker often persists for learners otherwise functioning at the upper intermediate or advanced levels.

Copula Use (Object Complement)

English constructions involving the so-called object complement (i.e., those in which an adjective functions as the grammatical object) require the use of a form of the copula (i.e., the verb *be*): *I am tall; she is nervous; we are nervous.* This, however, is not the case in Bengali, as table 7.3 demonstrates based on examples encompassing the three present tense *be* forms in English.

Table 7.3   Copula Use (Object Complement) in English and Bengali

English	Bengali
I am happy	āmi khuśi
	Literally: *I happy
She/He is happy	tini khuśi
	Literally: *She/He happy
We are happy	āmrā khuśi
	Literally: *We happy
They are happy	onārā khuśi
	Literally: *They happy

In the authors' experience, beginning and lower intermediate L1 Bengali students tend to omit the *be* verb in constructions of this kind in English. In other words, they appear to follow the Bengali, not the English rule, as in the following examples:

*I sad.
(I am sad.)

*It cold.
(It is cold.)
*Book long.
(The book is long.)

Pluralization

In English, both the determiner (e.g., *this*) and the noun (e.g., *car*) indicate pluralization: *this car/these cars; a table/many tables*. In Bengali, however, the plural marker can appear before or after the noun, but not both in the same phrase. In the authors' observation, L1 Bengali students commonly omit one or the other of the required English plural markers in both speech and writing, as in the following classroom examples:

*Those cookie mine
(Those cookies are mine.)

*this books
(these books)

*I have 4 teacher
(I have four teachers.)

Auxiliary Verbs

English makes extensive and complex use of auxiliary and modal verbs to express tense, mood, and voice: *I am/was writing; I have/would have written; It is being written*. Bengali has no equivalent to this system. The following are examples of L1 Bengali students' attempts to generate utterances for which the target-like English form would require an auxiliary:

*They facing many problems.
(They *are* facing many problems.)

*I mango eaten.
(I *have* eaten a mango.)

*She talking me.
(She <u>was</u> talking to me.)

The students who generated the above examples were intermediate to advanced level ELLs participating in tenth and eleventh-grade English language arts classes in NYC. Even at this level, they appear to have followed the rule system of Bengali (which lacks auxiliaries) instead of that of English. Their reason for doing so may never be known.

Nevertheless, the resulting "error" may be considered a predictable or likely phenomenon. At the outset of this chapter, the authors suggested that knowledge of such *predictable usage/learning patterns* can be useful to teachers of L1 Bengali students in English-speaking contexts. In the following section, the authors demonstrate how this comparative and predictive knowledge can be applied by providing sample strategies (classroom practices) that are tailored to address the error patterns identified as typical of Bengali students.

PEDAGOGICAL IMPLICATIONS

This section provides examples of strategies that may be effective in promoting acquisition of the features of English identified above as challenging for Bengali students. Suggestions are provided in each of the categories treated above: *word order, pronoun use, negation, empty subjects, verb inflection, copula use, pluralization,* and *auxiliary verbs.* As with the information provided in the preceding section, the techniques and strategies suggested here are intended merely as a starting point for teachers of Bengali students. For further guidance, readers may wish to consult the works cited (where citations are lacking, the exercises are described based on the authors' classroom experience).

Strategy for Word Order

One strategy that teachers of L1 Bengali students can use to help foster the acquisition of English SVO word order is *unscrambling sentences.* This activity can be used: (1) with all proficiency levels, (2) individually or as a group activity, and (3) as a timed game (Larsen-Freeman & Anderson, 2011; Picksychick, 2012). In this activity, students receive words in jumbled order and are asked to re-sequence them to form grammatical sentences. This exercise can be differentiated for more advanced students by using more words (and more advanced vocabulary) to form longer, more complex sentences. This activity not only helps students to understand and acquire English sentence structure, but it also offers practice for reading. Similar activities that teachers can use to help their Bengali students acquire English word order include putting sentences together by matching, copying, or manipulating given parts of a sentence.

Strategy for Pronoun Use

As noted, Bengali pronouns do not distinguish gender. To help L1 Bengali students master the use of English masculine and feminine pronouns, one activity that teachers can use is a substitution drill with visual aids. Such an activity can begin with writing a few basic sentences on the board, such as:

1. *Tom* is a good student.
2. *Linda* is my sister.
3. *Tom and Linda* eat lunch in school.

Then, ask students to replace the underlined subjects with the appropriate subject pronouns:

1. *He* is a good student.
2. *She* is my sister.
3. *They* eat lunch in school.

Especially when teaching beginning-level students, it may be helpful to use pictures that correspond to these pronouns and to have students post the appropriate picture next to the sentence. For intermediate students, pictures of gendered or group subjects engaged in activities can be used as cues to produce sentences in which students also practice their verb use: *He* is running; *She* is studying; *They* are swimming.

Strategy for Negation

Recall that Bengali sentences are negated by adding *nā* at the end. In English, the relationship between form and function for this parameter is more complex (i.e., different rules apply depending upon the features/purpose of the utterance; see Vaidyanathan, 1991). To help L1 Bengali students acquire the English rules, teachers can, as suggested in the case of *word order,* present students with sentences to transform: *I can talk—I cannot talk; I work hard—I do not work hard; I am a teacher—I am not a teacher.* Transformation can also be from negative to positive, and sentence complexity can be adjusted to suit the English level of students in the class (see Rogge, n.d.).

Strategy for Empty Subjects

As the so-called "existential *there*" has no equivalent in Bengali, teachers may find that Bengali students need extra practice to acquire this construction. Here, again, visual aids can be useful. Teachers can post or distribute pictures and, individually or in groups, students can try to work out how to describe them; though help is often required, this typically leads to formulations such as: *There is a boy in the room; There is a magazine on the floor; There are apples on the table.* Role play can also be used, with students creating their own mini-skits on themes like expressing complaints—for example at a restaurant or on a picnic: *"Waiter, there is a fly in my soup!" "There are ants in my potato salad!"* (Case, 2015).

Strategy for Verb Inflection

Teachers of Bengali students should bear in mind that their students' first language also has no equivalent to the English third-person singular present tense -*s* marker. A great way to engage students in active use of this feature is the interview strategy (Jin et al., 2014). Teachers should assign students to work in pairs and should instruct each participant to interview the other, asking about the partner's daily routine. Then, students should introduce their partners to the class—that is, transform the partner's "I . . ." statements into "He/she/they . . ." statements. This activity generates contexts in which the -*s* marker will be required; it also provides students with opportunities to practice not only the English subject pronouns but the object (her/him/them) and possessive (her/his/theirs) pronouns as well.

Strategy for Copula Use

As observed, English requires a form of *be* in sentences with an adjective in the object position: *I am tall.* This structure is absent in Bengali, and Bengali speakers often omit *be* when speaking or writing such expressions in English. It may be helpful to teach these students to think of this use of *be* as part of a *description*—or as a *link* between the subject and the adjective. Here, again, visual aids or manipulatives can help. Teachers should prepare a collection of pictures of people, animals, and things that manifest an unmistakable feature—or pass out magazines and start the activity by having students choose and cut out pictures in groups, discussing the reasons for their choices as they proceed. Then, as groups or individuals, students should try to generate the "proper" description in a grammatical English sentence: *The man is happy; The dog is big; The dress is blue.*

Strategy for Pluralization

While English often calls for double plural marking (e.g., *many cars*), Bengali never uses two plural markers in a single phrase. Bengali students can therefore benefit from guided practice placing plural nouns after such words as *many, most, these,* and *those.* For this purpose, an identification/description exercise using simple objects in the classroom can be useful. In this activity, teachers instruct students to look "here" or "there" and to provide the appropriate description: *I see many books (on the shelf); those pencils (on the teacher's desk) are yellow.*

Strategy for Auxiliary Verbs

Bengali students, even those of intermediate or advanced English proficiency, often omit English auxiliary verbs—for example in the perfect or progressive tenses—which have no equivalent in their L1. For the present progressive tense, the well-known game of *charades* can provide the basis for exercises in which students practice the use of forms of the auxiliary *be.* For example, students can act out a common activity, such as vacuuming, brushing teeth, or swimming. They can then take turns guessing/identifying: *He is vacuuming; He is swimming.* For variety, teachers can introduce "wrong" guesses, prompting "corrections" like: *No, I am shaving!* For full coverage of the range of pronouns and verb forms, teachers can also call for a switch from individuals to groups: *Look, they are dancing!* And, to expand the exercise to cover the past progressive, individuals/groups can be instructed to switch tasks: *They were dancing, but now they are singing!* (The perfect tenses, by contrast, are less intuitive/visual, and practice using written materials may be more effective—e.g., worksheets with missing *have* forms: *I ___ eaten; She ___ slept; The students ___ studied.*)

USING BENGALI LITERATURE IN THE CLASSROOM

Using Bengali literature in the classroom can assist teachers to build a classroom community that is supportive, empathetic, and accepting of Bengali students. More specifically, learning about popular and/or historically important texts helps to create an atmosphere of cultural celebration, and this both heightens classmates' appreciation of and respect for Bengali students (Hseu & Hetzel, 2000) and bolsters Bengali students' individual and cultural self-concept (Colby & Lyon, 2004; Hefflin & Barksdale-Ladd, 2001; Steiner et al., 2008). Moreover, lessons that incorporate Bengali literature not only build bonds among Bengali students and their teachers and classmates, but they also provide opportunities to make connections and associations with Bengali students' daily lives, which is an important element in student engagement (Banks & McGee-Banks, 2016; Ladson-Billings, 2014). Such lessons, furthermore, provide a valuable learning experience for all participants, and they can be used as a starting point for broader explorations of diversity among world cultures.

Teachers of Bengali students in middle or high school who would like to add Bengali literature to their classroom libraries or to incorporate selected works or genres into their teaching might start by referring to the summary account of important Bengali authors and works provided earlier in this chapter. They may also find that the poetry of Rabindranath Tagore (2005) is well-suited to teaching a variety of literature-and-culture-based lessons, as are the stories in *Tales of India: Folktales from Bengal, Punjab, and Tamil Nadu* (2018).

For elementary school teachers, meanwhile, the authors recommend the works on the following list. This selected bibliography is presented alphabetically by title to help teachers locate works by topics that might be of particular interest to their students; it is also divided into two sections: works in English and works that incorporate both Bengali and English versions of the text.

Recommended Books in English

- *Binny's Diwali* by Thirty Umrigar (2020)
- *Home Is in Between* by Mitali Perkins (2021)
- *In My Mosque* by M. O. Yuksel (2021)
- *It's Ramadan, Curious George* by Hena Khan (2016)
- *Lailah's Lunchbox: A Ramadan Story* by Reem Faruqi (2015)
- *Ramadan around the World* by Ndaa Hassan (2018)
- *The Proudest Blue: A Story of Hijab and Family* by Ibtihaj Muhammad (2019)

Recommended Bilingual Works

- *Am I Small?* by Phillipp Winterberg and Nadja Wichmann (2013)
- *Farm Animals* by Brian Wildsmith (2008)
- *My Most Beautiful Dream* (with audio) by Ulrich Renz (2020)
- *Sleep Tight, Little Wolf* (with audio) by Ulrich Renz (2016)
- *Where Is the Baby?* by Sujatha Lalgudi (2016)

CONCLUSION

Knowledge of students' heritage cultures, which many teacher training programs now recognize, can have a positive impact on pedagogical practices in the classroom. The present authors, however, also believe that training should emphasize the benefits of learning about the *language* backgrounds of ELLs, including how their first languages can impact the miscues they make as they acquire English. True, one can teach ELLs armed only with knowledge of the methods and strategies that research has demonstrated to be effective with learners in general. Nonetheless, many experienced teachers believe that knowledge of "habits," "error patterns," and paths of development common to individuals from a given L1 group can be helpful in teaching new students with the same language background.

Based on this widely held premise, the authors of the present chapter have sought to provide information about English and Bengali that can help teachers of Bengali students understand and support these students' language learning journeys by making them more sensitive to the factors at play in this large and growing sector of the U.S. K-12 population. One of the reasons that such information may be valuable to teachers is that it can enable them to replace generic lesson plans with ones that offer targeted, specific, and timely practice (Baecher et al., 2012). In keeping with this viewpoint, the authors have presented some of the elements that lesson plans targeted to classes that include L1 Bengali students might encompass.

Arguments in favor of what one might call "linguistically informed pedagogy," however, are not limited to its impact on the nuts and bolts of classroom practice. Rather, from a more holistic standpoint, when teachers take the time to acquire knowledge of their students' first languages and to develop an appreciation for their challenges and struggles, the students are likely to feel not only understood but *valued*, and they may respond with better effort and focus both in and out of the classroom. Teachers who are equipped with such knowledge, moreover, can creatively seek opportunities to use examples from students' languages in ways that can help learners to better understand the challenges they face and to engage more actively and reflectively in learning English.

In this regard, teachers need to be unafraid to make mistakes, just as they encourage their students to be. In fact, when teachers accept—as do adherents of the now-popular translanguage movement (Beiler, 2021)—that they, too, are *learners* who communicate using elements of a variety of linguistic and non-linguistic idioms, some of which they have not mastered, this acceptance can have an equalizing effect on classroom dynamics (i.e., the "sage on the stage" takes on the role of learning partner) and, at least potentially, a positive impact on learner self-efficacy and motivation

(Dörnyei et al., 2016). In other words, the present authors have the following message for teachers: *Go ahead, try to pronounce that Bengali word or phrase you learned—if you get it wrong, the interest that you demonstrate and the courageous effort that you model will still have a positive impact on your students' learning!*

Today, tens of millions of L1 Bengali students reside in English-speaking nations, and millions more live in countries where facility in English may represent their best chance to participate meaningfully in competitive education and employment (Budiman, 2021). However, in the United States, at least, it is not yet the case that many teachers possess knowledge of Bengali, even within the limited frame of key points of similarity and difference vis-à-vis English. As this chapter has argued, however, such knowledge is important, as it enables teachers to anticipate and more effectively respond to the types of *non-target-like utterances* that L1 Bengali students are likely to produce as well as conferring a better understanding of their overall pattern of development in English.

Throughout this chapter, the authors have tried to avoid, minimize, or explain technical jargon. It is important to note, however, that the phrase "non-target-like utterance" is not just a technical term: rather, it can be used deliberately to avoid value-laden terms like "errors" or "mistakes." In a seminal article titled "The Study of Error," American composition and literacy scholar David Bartholomae (1980) made two points that remain critical in this regard, and that can be said to have anticipated certain tenets of the "translanguage" movement: "Errors," Bartholomae argues, "are [to be] seen as (1) necessary stages of individual development and (2) data that provide insight into the idiosyncratic strategies of a particular language user at a particular point in his [or her] acquisition of a target language" (p. 256). To take Bartholomae's first point, the non-target-like utterances that learners generate are not aberrations but rather an inevitable feature of the acquisition process. Indeed, if ELLs did not make "errors," they would not be "learners," and they would not be making the necessary *effort* to learn English! This seems obvious enough, but it should be treated as an important reminder not to "cringe" or knowingly allow any form of shaming to occur when errors are encountered in the classroom; rather, one should treat all student-generated speech and writing as positive learning attempts, and all "mistakes" as constructive teaching points.

If, moreover, one is to accept Bartholomae's (1980) dictum and treat errors as "data that provide insight" (p. 256), then one ought to do so authentically and systematically—not just at the level of individual learners but, where available information is sufficient to support conclusions, with respect to *groups* of learners as well. In other words, it is essential for teachers of ELLs and the institutions that train them to embrace "errors" both as a necessary byproduct (in fact, the very medium!) of authentic learning efforts and as grist for the language-teaching mill: that is, as "data" that can be used to analyze and respond to patterns in the learning efforts of individuals, subgroups (such as Bengali speakers), and ELLs in general. Such analysis, this chapter argues, can facilitate targeted and hence more effective language and literacy instruction. The effort of acquiring such knowledge on the part of teachers, the chapter further argued, can have a positive impact on student motivation and learning, as can the habit of practicing stigma-free language pedagogy. Therefore, teachers should be not only encouraged but *supported* in learning all that they can about students' first languages, and teacher training and professional development programs should make "linguistically informed pedagogy" a part of their curriculum for all teachers of ELLs.

REFERENCES

Asian American Federation Census Information Center. (2019). *Profile of New York City's Bangladeshi Americans*. Retrieved December 29, 2021, from https://www .aafederation.org/wp-content/uploads/2020/12/2019bn.pdf.

Baecher, L., Artigliere, M., Patterson, D. K., & Spatzer, A. (2012). Differentiated instruction for English language learners as "variations on a theme": Teachers can differentiate instruction to support English language learners. *Middle School Journal, 43*(3), 14–21. Retrieved December 15, 2021, from http://www.jstor.org/stable/23074855.

Banks, J. A., & McGee-Banks, C. A. (2016). *Multicultural education: Issues and perspectives* (9th ed.). Wiley/Jossey Bass.

Bartholomae, D. (1980). The study of error. *College Composition and Communication, 31*(3), 253–269.

Beiler, I. (2021). Marked and unmarked translanguaging in accelerated, mainstream, and sheltered English classrooms. *Multilingual, 40*(1), 107–138. https://doi.org/10 .1515/multi-2020-0022.

Bengali. (n.d.). *Omniglot: The online encyclopedia of writing systems and languages*. Retrieved September 22, 2021, from https://omniglot.com/writing/bengali.htm.

Bengali Language. (2017, July 28). *Encyclopedia Britannica*. https://www.britannica .com/topic/Bengali-language.

Bengali Language. (2021, March 17). *New world encyclopedia*. Retrieved September 3, 2021, from https://www.newworldencyclopedia.org/p/index.php?title=Bengali _language&oldid=1050679.

Bhattacharyya, M. (2020). *Rabindranath Tagore's Śāntiniketan essays: Religion, spirituality, and philosophy*. Routledge.

Budiman, A. (2021). *Bangladeshis in the U.S.: Fact sheet*. Pew Research Center. Retrieved October 4, 2021, from https://www.pewresearch.org/social-trends/fact -sheet/asian-americans-bangladeshis-in-the-u-s/.

Case, A. (2015). How to teach *There is* and *There are. Using English.com.* Retrieved October 12, 2021, from https://www.usingenglish.com/teachers/articles/how-to-teach-there-there-are.html.

Catto, S. (2018). More than one voice: Utilizing students' home languages and cultural experiences in reading recovery. In E. Ortlieb & E. H. Cheek, Jr. (Eds.), *Literacy research, practice and evaluation: Addressing diversity in literacy instruction* (pp. 17–36). Emerald Publishing Limited.

Chamorro, G., & Paz, B. (2017). Improving language learning strategies and performance of pre-service language teachers through a CALLA-TBLT model. *Issues in Teachers' Professional Development, 19*(2), 101–120.

Colby, S. A., & Lyon, A. (2004). Heightening awareness about the importance of using multicultural literature. *Multicultural Education, 11*, 24–28.

Delpit, L. D. (2012). *"Multiplication is for white people": Raising expectations for other people's children.* New Press.

Dörnyei, Z., Henry, A., & Muir, C. (2016). *Motivational currents in language learning: Frameworks for focused interventions.* Routledge.

Epstein, S., Flynn, S., & Martohardjono, G (1996). Second language acquisition: Theoretical and experimental issues in contemporary research. *Brain and Behavioral Sciences, 19*, 677–758.

Faruqi, R. (2015). *Lailah's lunchbox: A Ramadan story.* Tilbury House.

Hasan, M. (2020, February 17). Bangla ranked at 7th among 100 most spoken languages worldwide. *Dhaka Tribune.* Retrieved August 22, 2021, from https://www.dhakatribune.com/world/2020/02/17/bengali-ranked-at-7th-among-100-most-spoken-languages-worldwide.

Hassan, N. (2018). *Ramadan around the world.* Beyond Books.

Hefflin, B. R., & Barksdale-Ladd, M. A. (2001). African American children's literature that helps students find themselves: Selection guidelines for grades k–3. *The Reading Teacher, 54*(8), 810–819.

Hseu, M., & Hetzel, J. (2000). *Bridging the cultural divide through multicultural children's literature.* Retrieved August 22, 2021, from http://buddies.org/articles/Literature.html.

Islam, S. M. A. (2004). *L1 influence on the spoken English proficiency of Bengali speakers.* Dalarna University.

Jin, B., Odabasi, G., & Kim, J. (2014). Teaching simple present tense in third-person singular. *CATESOL News.* Retrieved December 15, 2021, from http://www.catesolnews.org/2014/12/teaching-simple-present-in-third-singular/.

Khan, H. (2016). *It's Ramadan, curious George.* HarperCollins.

Ladson-Billings, G. (2014). Culturally relevant pedagogy 2.0: Aka the remix. *Harvard Educational Review, 84*, 74–84. https://doi.org/10.17763/haer.84.1.p2rj131485484751.

Lalgudi, S. (2016). *Where is the baby?* CreateSpace Independent Publishing Platform.

Larsen-Freeman, D., & Anderson, M. (2011). *Techniques and principles in language teaching.* Oxford University Press.

Luna, J. (2015, October 2). Bengali students need teachers who speak their language [Radio broadcast]. *WNYC.*

Muhammad, I. (2019). *The proudest blue: A story of hijab and family.* Little, Brown and Company.

New York City Department of Education, Division of Multilingual Learners. (2019). *2018–2019 English language learner demographic report.* Retrieved December 29, 2021, from https://infohub.nyced.org/docs/default-source/default-document -library/ell-demographic-report.pdf.

Odlin, T. (1989). *Language transfer: Cross-linguistic influence in language learning.* Cambridge University Press.

Perkins, M. (2021). *Home is in between.* Farrar Straus.

Pew Research Center. (2021). *Bangladeshis in the U.S. fact sheet.* Retrieved December 29, 2021, from https://www.pewresearch.org/social-trends/fact-sheet/asian -americans-bangladeshis-in-the-u-s/.

Picksychick [pseud.]. (2012). *All mixed up: Sentence scramble.* Retrieved December 15, 2021, from https://en.islcollective.com/resources/printables/worksheets_doc _docx/all_mixed_up__sentence-scramble/28124.

Renz, U. (2016). *Sleep tight, little wolf* (with audio). Sefa.

Renz, U. (2020). *My most beautiful dream* (with audio). Sefa.

Rogge, R. (n.d.). *Activities for teaching negative sentences.* Retrieved October 12, 2021, from https://www.theclassroom.com/activities-teaching-negative-sentences -8600764.html.

Schwartz, B., & Sprouse, R. (1996). L2 cognitive states and the full transfer/full access model. *Second Language Research, 12,* 40–72.

Sen, S. (1992). *History of Bengali literature.* Sahitya Akademi.

Steiner, S. F., Nash, C. P., & Chase, M. (2008). Multicultural literature that brings people together. *The Reading Teacher, 62*(1), 88–92.

Tagore, R. (2005). *Selected poems.* Penguin Books.

Tales of India: Folktales from Bengal, Punjab, and Tamil Nadu. (2018). Chronicle Books.

Umrigar, T. (2020). *Binny's Diwali.* Scholastic Press.

Vaidyanathan, R. (1991). Development of forms and functions of negation in the early stages of language acquisition: A study in Tamil. *Journal of Child Language, 18*(1), 51–66. https://doi.org/10.1017/S0305000900013295.

Wildsmith, B. (2008). *Farm animals.* Star Bright Books.

Winterberg, P., & Wichmann, N. (2013). *Am I small?* CreateSpace Independent Publishing Platform.

Yuksel, M. O. (2021). *In my mosque.* Harper.

Zare, P. (2012). Language learning strategies among EFL/ESL learners: A review of literature. *International Journal of Humanities and Social Science, 2*(5), 162–169.

Chapter 8

Arabic Language's Impact on English Language Learners' Literacy Development

Implications for Educators

Alaa Mohammed M. Shakoori and
Eliane Rubinstein-Avila

LITERACY DEVELOPMENT: IMPLICATIONS FOR EDUCATORS

The increase of Arabic-speaking English language learners (ELLs) in K-12 American public schools varies across geographical regions. Although this group accounts for less than three percent of the entire ELL (K-12) student population in the United States (Corey, 2020), a Pew Research Report revealed that Arabic is now the second-most common spoken language in the homes of ELLs in 16 states (Bialik et al., 2018). In fact, *Education Week* has recently claimed that Arabic-speaking ELLs have increased by 75 percent over the past eight years (Corey, 2020).

With about 300 million Arabic speakers across 25 countries, it behooves educators to understand the history of Arabic, its basic elements, and the main differences between Arabic and English. This chapter begins with a brief overview of Arabic and Arab immigration to the United States. Next, the chapter addresses the basic elements of Arabic and its differences from English. Finally, the chapter ends by discussing the challenges that Arabic-speaking ELLs (K-12) tend to find as they develop English literacy and proposes several effective instructional strategies to encourage English literacy development for this student population.

A BRIEF HISTORY OF ARABIC LANGUAGE

Arabic is the fifth most-spoken language in the world (Ibanez, 2020). It is spoken across Northern Africa, the Arabian Peninsula, and the Middle East and is spoken by immigrants and refugees around the world in Australia, Brazil, the United States, and Europe. Also of importance is the fact that "Arabic is not just a language of communication" (Ahmed, 2010, p. 199). Indeed, it is the liturgical language of Islam, which consists of more than 1.5 billion followers around the world. Arabic is believed to have evolved from Aramaic over a millennium ago in the Arabian Peninsula among nomadic Bedouin tribes (Versteegh, 2014). In fact, the word "Arab" means nomad. It is part of a language group known as the Central Semitic languages, which includes Hebrew, Aramaic, and Phoenician.

The Arabic language is emerging alongside English and Portuguese as one of the fastest growing languages in the world (Tirosh, 2021), and gaining social, economic, and political power. Consequently, the teaching of Arabic across American colleges has vastly grown in the United States, especially after the U.S. government designated Arabic as a "strategic" language (Abdelghany, 2016). Currently, there are 35 public schools nationwide that offer dual language programs in many languages—including Arabic (Corey, 2020).

Arab immigration to the United States is not a recent phenomenon. The first Arab immigration to the United States was in the1880s, mostly Christians from Syria, Lebanon, and Palestine. The rapid growth of this population is a phenomenon that ought to be of great interest to educators. The most recent U.S. Census report released in 2020 indicates that the Arab population is about two million, with the largest Arab American communities residing in California and Michigan (Statista Research Department, 2022). By the same token, the number of Arabic ELLs in public schools has become the second-largest after Spanish ELLs, with a total of 131,554 students across the United States (National Center for Education Statistics, 2022). Given the increase of Arabic ELLs in K-12 American public schools, it is important for educators to be familiar with key elements of the Arabic language that may have an impact on the students' English language learning and literacy.

PRINCIPLE ELEMENTS OF ARABIC LANGUAGE

In this section, we highlight the main characteristics of the Arabic language that have proven to interfere with ELLs' ability to read and write in English. Classical Arabic is a version found in literary texts from the seventh to ninth centuries and in the Quran, the Holy Book of Islam. However, there are two current major varieties of Arabic: Standard Arabic (SA) and Spoken Arabic (SPA). SA differs from SPA in terms of grammar, vocabulary, and pronunciation (Abu Rabia et al., 2003). SA, also known as Modern Standard Arabic or Modern Classic Arabic, is used in textbooks, official documents, and overall formalities. SPA refers to the many spoken varieties of Arabic across different Arab countries and regions. It continues to evolve over time and reflects changing sociopolitical, sociocultural, and geopolitical contexts. Both SA and SPA have characteristics that may interfere with those of English, yet the differences are more obvious in the case of SA. Moreover, Arab children develop literacy skills in SA. For these reasons, we will be focusing on eight major characteristics of SA and the ways they may interfere with English literacy. These characteristics include: direction and sounds, letter-sound correspondence, vowels, word order, adjectives, verbs, articles, and prepositions.

Direction and Sounds

Arabic has 28 letters whereas English has 26 letters. Even though both languages are alphabetic, their orthography (e.g., spelling) and phonology (e.g., sounds) are very different. Compared to English, which runs from left to right, Arabic is read and written from right to left. This difference in directionality leads some ELLs to make mistakes when they read and write in English; for example, it is not unusual for Arabic ELLs to confuse "mirror-shaped" letters such as **b** vs. **d** and **q** vs. **p** (Smith, 2001, p. 199). Likewise, mistakes in reading or writing words such as *twon* instead of **town** could be attributed to "right to left eye movements" (Ibid, p. 200).

Even though English and Arabic share most of their consonant sounds (Allaith & Joshi, 2011), some sounds in English do not have an equivalent in Arabic. For instance, the following sounds in English do not exist in Arabic:

/g/ [as in **g**lass]
/p/ [as in **p**aper]
/v/ [as in **v**ase]
/ʧ/ [as in **ch**ild]
/ŋ/ [as in ki**ng**]

Due to the absence of those sounds in Arabic, Arabic ELLs are likely to struggle with pronouncing and spelling them appropriately. Ahmad (2011), for example, found that the sounds /p/ and /v/ were significantly mispronounced by ELLs and were replaced with /b/ [as in **b**ook] and /f/ [as in **f**air], respectively. Likewise, Allaith and Joshi (2011) found that English sounds that do not exist in Arabic were misspelled. ELLs mistakenly replaced /p/ and /v/ with /b/ and /f/.

Educators who work with Arabic ELLs should consider these variations in direction (e.g., right to left) and sounds (e.g., /p/ and /v/ as /b/ and /f/). Such elements mainly affect the students' reading, spelling, and pronunciation competencies. Equipped with this knowledge, educators can better understand the origin and nature of some Arabic ELLs' struggles and help students to be more conscious of differences between Arabic and English.

Letter-Sound Correspondence

Arabic is a transparent language—each letter in Arabic is represented by one sound only (Alshaboul et al., 2014). This means that words in Arabic are typically written in the same way they are pronounced. In contrast, the phonological system (sound system) in English is more complex. A letter can be represented by more than one sound in English (Palmer et al., 2007). For example, the letter [c] can be represented by different sounds such as /s/ as in ice, /k/ as in car, and /ʃ/ as in ocean. Moreover, two letters can be combined to produce multiple sounds in English (Farghaly & Shaalan, 2009). For instance, the letter [c] can be combined with the letter [h] to produce three different sounds: /k/ [as in school], /sh/ [as in machine], and /tʃ/ [as in chair]. By the same token, silent letters are common in English words but do not exist in Arabic.

Educators need to understand these issues of correspondence between letters and their sounds because it has a significant impact on Arabic ELLs' literacy skills in English (Al Sobhi et al., 2017; Fender, 2003). Fender (2003) has argued that Arabic ELLs associate one particular sound with one letter when they read in English as they usually do when they read in Arabic. Therefore, the lack of consistency between letters and sounds contributes to the struggles Arabic ELLs experience when reading and writing in English.

Vowels

Compared to the multiple sounds of vowels in English, Arabic vowels only have three fundamental sounds: **/a/, /o/,** and **/e/**. These three vowels are used to represent all vowel sounds in English (Smith, 2001). For this reason, Arabic ELLs have difficulty differentiating between the sounds of vowels in words such as "**boot, boat,** and **bought**" (Thompson-Panos & Thomas-Ruzic, 1983, p. 612). The vowels in those words are distinctive in English but are signified by only one sound in Arabic: **/o/**.

To illustrate, each vowel sound in Arabic has a long and a short phonation. Long vowels are represented by letters (e.g., ١, و,ي) while their short phonations/vowels are represented by diacritic marks (e.g., ٰ , , ٰ), respectively. For example, the sound of **/a/** in (car) represents the **long vowel /aa/** in Arabic whereas the sound of /a/ in (family) represents the Arabic **short vowel /a/**. Similarly, the pronunciation of **/oo/** (room) is an example of the **long vowel / oo/** in Arabic whereas **/oo/** in (good) is an example of the Arabic **short vowel /o/**. Finally, the sound of **/ea/** in (sheet) represents the **long vowel /ee/** in Arabic while **/e/** in (led) represents the **short vowel /e/** (see table 8.1).

Table 8.1 Long and Short Vowels in Arabic: Representation and Pronunciation in English

Long Vowels in Arabic	Representation in English	Pronunciation of Long Vowels	Short Vowels in Arabic (diacritic marks)	Representation in English	Pronunciation of Short Vowels
ا	/aa/	C<u>a</u>r	´	/a/	f<u>a</u>mily
و	/oo/	r<u>oo</u>m	؍	/o/	g<u>oo</u>d
ي	/ee/	sh<u>ee</u>t	ٜ	/e/	l<u>e</u>d

As shown in the table 8.1, the diacritic marks (e.g., ´ , ,) represent short vowels in Arabic. These diacritic marks can be omitted from the word/text. On the other hand, long vowels are essential and must be written in the word. This feature of Arabic, in which short vowels (diacritic marks) are omitted from the text, may impede Arabic ELLs' ability not only to read in English but also to process English words. That is, efforts to apply their Arabic word process strategies to English may lead to challenges in reading comprehension (Hayes-Harb, 2006). Because they tend to depend more on consonants when reading English words, Arabic ELLs have more difficulty reading or identifying words with missing consonants than those with missing vowels (Jiang, 2018). For instance, it would be more challenging for Arabic ELLs to identify the word *carpet* when consonants are missing [ca..pe..] compared to missing vowels [c..rp..t].

Word Order: (V + S + O)

Arabic and English have different word order. Unlike English, which follows a subject **(S)**, verb **(V)**, and object **(O)** structure **(S + V + O)**, the verb in Arabic must come first **(V + S + O)** (Al Khresheh, 2010) (see table 8.2).

Table 8.2 Word Order in Arabic versus English

Arabic	English
أكل الولد التفاحات	The boy **ate** the apples
Akal al-walad attufaahaat	(S) (V) (O)
(V) (S) (O)	

Due to this nature of Arabic, some students tend to apply Arabic word order when they write in English. They write English sentences in the order of **(V + S + O)** and, consequently, make mistakes such as: (*ate the boy the apples**). Educators need to explicitly emphasize that the subject should precede the verb in English sentences in order to help students avoid this type of mistake.

Adjectives

There are three key points that highlight the differences between Arabic and English concerning the use of adjectives. As shown in table 8.3, Arabic and English have distinctive structures in terms of adjectives. In Arabic, adjectives follow the nouns they modify (Zawahreh, 2013), can take a plural form (Diab, 1997), and must agree with the modified noun in definiteness (Shamsan & Attayib, 2015).

Table 8.3   The Use of Adjectives in Arabic versus English

Arabic	English	Examples
1. Adjectives succeed the noun they modify.	Adjectives precede the noun they modify.	
2. Plural nouns are modified by plural adjectives.	Adjectives should be singular regardless of the numerical status of the noun.	In Arabic: *girls nices. In English: nice girls.
3. Adjectives must agree with the noun they modify in definiteness. The definite article should precede the noun and the adjective.	The definite article precedes the adjective only.	In Arabic: * the girls the nices volunteered to teach children. In English: the nice girls volunteered to teach children.

Most of the errors Arabic ELLs make when using adjectives stem from direct translation from Arabic into English (Diab, 1997). For instance, the students would write (* **the girls the nices**) because this would be the correct sequence in Arabic, but not the correct sequence in English (**the nice girls**). With this in mind, it would be particularly helpful for educators to discourage literal translation and assist students to grasp the rules of using adjectives in English.

Verbs

Unlike English, a sentence in Arabic can be grammatically correct without the presence of a verb (Al Horais, 2006). In addition, auxiliary verbs (e.g., **do/does/did**) and verb "to be" (e.g., **am/is/are**) do not exist in Arabic. For this reason, some Arabic ELLs overlook these verbs when they write in English (Al Zoubi & Abu Eid, 2014; Farghaly & Shaalan, 2009; Smith, 2001). Some students transfer these features to English when they leave out the verbs that have no equivalent in Arabic as discussed above.

Furthermore, the lack of auxiliaries in Arabic has an impact on how Arabic ELLs use negation in English. Negation in English is expressed through a particle that consists of two words: the auxiliary verb (e.g., **did**) and the negation word (e.g., **not**) (Tawalbeh, 2013). In Arabic, however, no auxiliaries are used. Negation is expressed through stand-alone words such as (**maa**), (**laa**), (**lam**), (**lan**), all of which are equivalent to the word (**not**) in English (see table 8.4).

Table 8.4   Examples of Negation in Arabic versus English

Arabic	English
لم يذهب علي إلى المباراة	Ali **did not go** to the game
Lam yath-hab Ali ela almubarat	(S) (Au) (Neg) (V)
(Neg) (V) (S)	

A further distinction between the two languages is the way in which they form passive voice. For instance, short vowels (the diacritic marks) in Arabic play a syntactic role in a sentence even though they might not be written explicitly. Hence, the passive voice in Arabic can be formed by changing the short vowels of the verb rather than changing its form. The short vowel attached to the first consonant of the verb is shifted to /o/, and the short vowel attached to the consonant second to last is shifted to /e/. Meanwhile, forming the passive voice in English is a "morphosyntactic" process that entails changing the form of the verb into "its past participle" (Shamsan & Attayib, 2015, p. 146) (see table 8.5).

Table 8.5   Example of Passive Voice in Arabic versus Passive Voice in English

Active Voice in Arabic	Passive Voice in Arabic	Meaning in English
أخذَ أحمد القلم	أُخِذَ القلم	The pen was **taken**
Akhatha Ahmad al-qalam	**Okhetha** al-qalam	
(V) (S) (O)	(V) (O)	

Given the differences between Arabic and English in forming the passive voice, it is likely that ELLs might apply Arabic rules when forming the passive voice in English. The result would be making mistakes such as (***token the pen**) rather than the correct form (**the pen was taken**). Educators need to explain the concepts of *past participle* and *verb to be* and how they are used to form the passive voice in English. Educators should also bring the students' attention to the difference in word order between Arabic and English.

Articles

Arabic and English signify definiteness and indefiniteness in distinct ways, thus the use of articles is very likely to be confusing for Arabic ELLs (Thyab, 2016). The article (**al**) in Arabic is added before the noun or the adjective in order to express definiteness. It is similar to the definite article (**the**) in English; however, variance in use should be taken into consideration. For instance, the definite article in English cannot precede abstract nouns if these nouns were not modified, which is not the case in Arabic (Diab, 1997; Tawalbeh, 2013). As a result, many students make mistakes such as:

> * Fadi never visited *the Petra* (Tawalbeh, 2013, p. 100).
> The correct answer is: Fadi never visited *Petra*.
> * Faisal not go *the school* yesterday (Tawalbeh, 2013, p. 100).
> The correct answer is: Faisal did not go *to school* yesterday.

In terms of indefiniteness, English has two indefinite articles (**a** and **an**). Indefinite articles have no counterparts in Arabic, therefore students tend to leave them out when they write in English (Albalawi, 2016) as shown in the following example:

> *Dubai *is beautiful* city (Albalawi, 2016, p. 192).
> The correct answer is: Dubai *is a beautiful* city.

Prepositions

Some prepositions have similar meanings in both languages but are used differently. For this reason, many Arabic ELLs use prepositions incorrectly when they write or speak in English. Diab (1997) demonstrated that the prepositions (e.g., **in, on, at**) are specifically confusing for two reasons. First, the difference between these prepositions is imperceptible; therefore, inexperienced ELLs are not able to fully grasp the difference in meaning and use between these particular prepositions. Second, Arabic ELLs translate from Arabic into English when they struggle to choose the proper preposition. The following sentences are examples:

He is waiting **in** the room.
She is **at** work.
We are **on** campus.

When translated into Arabic, (**in**) is used with all of the abovementioned sentences. As a result, students make mistakes such as:

* I mean **in** this example [the correct answer is: I mean **by** this example] (Diab, 1997, p. 76).
* He is ready **to** the exam [the correct answer is: He is ready **for** the exam] (Diab, 1997, p. 77).

SPECIFIC EXAMPLES

In the following section, we provide a table that includes specific examples of Arabic ELLs' common patterns of language use. The given examples represent how Arabic ELLs' performance and mistakes would be influenced by those patterns. The table also serves as a summary of the major differences between Arabic and English as discussed in the previous section.

Table 8.6   Examples of Arabic ELLs' Errors

Elements: Arabic versus English	Examples of Arabic ELLs' Errors	Correct Answer in English
Direction and sounds: Arabic is read and written from right to left.	- The comma in Arabic is drawn upward toward the right (،). - The question mark in Arabic is shaped facing the right (؟).	- The comma is drawn downward toward the left (,). - The question mark is shaped facing the left (?).
Direction and sounds: English sounds that do not exist in Arabic such as /p/.	*Blaying	Playing
Letter-sound correspondence: Unlike Arabic, a letter can be represented by different sounds in English.	*Kar	Car
Letter-sound correspondence: Silent letters do not exist in Arabic.	*Haves	Halves

(continued)

Table 8.6   (Continued)

Elements: Arabic versus English	Examples of Arabic ELLs' Errors	Correct Answer in English
Letter-sound correspondence: Combining two or more letters to produce different sounds is a feature that does not exist in Arabic.	- Mispronouncing the sound / tʃ / [as in **ch**air] and replacing it with the sound /ʃ/ [as in **sh**are]. - Mispronouncing the sound /ʒ/ in words such as (plea**s**ure) and (mea**s**ure) and replacing it with /ʃ/ [as in **sh**are]; /s/ [as in **s**chool], or /z/ [as in **z**oo].	- Correct pronunciation: **ch**air [not *****sh**are]. - Correct pronunciation: plea**s**ure [not *****plea**sh**re, *****plea**s**re, or *****plea**z**re].
Vowels: Only three Arabic vowels are used to represent all vowels in English.	*****Brake	Break
Word Order: Arabic and English have different word order.	*****Ate the boy** the apples.	**The boy ate** the apples.
Adjectives: Adjectives in Arabic follow the noun they modify.	*****It is a **house big**.	It is a **big house**.
Adjectives: Arabic adjectives must agree with the nouns they modify in terms of plurality and definiteness.	*****My sister goes to **others shops**. *****I bought **the roses the beautifuls**.	My sister goes to **other shops**. I bought **the beautiful roses**.
Verbs: Auxiliary verbs and (verb to be) do not exist in Arabic. Also, a sentence without a verb is acceptable in Arabic syntax.	*****The book on the table. *****You** like dark chocolate?	The book **is** on the table. **Do you** like dark chocolate?
Verbs: Arabic differs from English in forming passive voice.	*****Wroten** the lesson.	The lesson **was written**.
Verbs: Arabic differs from English in forming negation.	*****Ali **not** a shy boy. *****No go** Sara to the party yesterday.	Ali **is not** a shy boy. Sara **did not go** to the party yesterday.
Articles: Indefinite articles do not exist in Arabic.	*****It is sunny day!	It is **a** sunny day!
Articles: Definite articles in Arabic can precede some proper nouns or unmodified nouns.	*****She lives in **the Cairo**.	She lives in **Cairo**.
Prepositions: Literal translation from Arabic into English.	*****I have three meetings **in** Monday.	I have three meetings **on** Monday.

As shown in table 8.6, many Arabic ELLs' mistakes can be traced to the characteristics of their first language. Such mistakes mainly affect their English writing, grammar, speaking, and pronunciation competencies. Educators can better promote these competencies by identifying and understanding the sources of the students' mistakes.

INSTRUCTIONAL IMPLICATIONS FOR EDUCATORS

This section provides instructional implications for educators in order to help Arabic ELLs overcome the potential challenges associated with language transfers. Educators' conceptualizations of bilingual education play a role in shaping their teaching practices (MacSwan, 2018). Therefore, educators' teaching practices should be informed by an understanding of how bilingual learners learn and which methods could be employed to assist them. First of all, educators need to enter their classrooms with a mind-set that speaking Arabic (or any other language) will not hamper the students' ability to learn English, and that using the students' first language in the classroom, when and if possible, should not be stigmatized or penalized. Using both of the students' languages is academically referred to as *translanguaging* (García & Kleifgen, 2020) and supporting this practice could facilitate students' engagement in classroom activities. For instance, educators could ask their students to introduce themselves to their classmates using Arabic and English words. They could also have Arabic ELLs work together in group activities and give them permission to use Arabic *and* English, allowing the two languages to scaffold each other. In addition, it is an opportunity for the students to collaborate and support each other instead of complete reliance on their educators' assistance.

In other words, bilingualism and bilingual learning should be regarded as a source of strength and enrichment rather than a burden. This entails increasing educators' awareness of transfers between Arabic and English and using this knowledge to foresee possible opportunities and/or challenges and assist the students as needed. Knowledge and competencies that individuals develop while acquiring their first language can be transmitted to their second language (L2) (Cummins, 1981), and in correspondence, ELLs can be assisted to promote *positive transfers* and minimize *negative transfers* between the two languages (Palmer et al., 2007). To give an example, ELLs' phonological awareness in Arabic could be used to promote their reading competency in English (Alshaboul et al., 2014) and minimize pronunciation mistakes. That said, many Arabic-speaking ELLs may not have learned to read or write in SA even though they may speak Arabic at home. For this reason, it is important to consider whether Arabic-speaking ELLs received formal education in Arabic. Those who did are more likely to be impacted either positively and/or negatively.

The use of proper strategies will help educators support Arabic ELLs in using their first language knowledge and competencies to further enhance their literacy skills in English. For example, providing these students with bilingual instructions and texts they can relate to culturally contributes to promoting their English proficiency (Palmer et al., 2007). At the same time, they also need to read a variety of English texts at different levels and document their own progress (Fender, 2003). Students should be encouraged to monitor their own mistakes and identify whether these mistakes are due to Arabic–English transfers or insufficient knowledge of English (Al Zoubi & Abu Eid, 2014). For this purpose, students can keep a journal or create a portfolio in order to document the characteristic of English compared to those of Arabic (e.g., direction, word order) and identify the ways their performance in English is impacted by differences between the two languages.

Given the differences between Arabic and English, providing explicit instructions when teaching English is of high importance. These instructions should be clear and direct. That is, the words and structure used to give instructions (written or oral) should be simple and focused on a particular point. To illustrate, Arabic ELLs find the irregularities and inconsistencies of English rules (e.g., lack of correspondence between letters and sounds) to be very confusing. However, many of these inconsistencies are "highly systematic" (Farghaly & Shaalan, 2009, p. 8). Hence, educators need to bring the patterned nature of these inconsistencies to students' attention and provide them with explicit, detailed instructions that demonstrate those rules. For example, they should explain the cases in which (**c**) is pronounced as /s/ as in (i**c**e) or /k/ as in (**c**ar), or /ʃ/ as in (o**c**ean). Encouraging Arabic ELLs to handwrite their assignments instead of typing them could also be a good practice (Albalawi, 2016), as it might help them remember how words are spelled despite the lack of correspondence between sounds and letters.

Likewise, educators need to increase these students' phonological awareness in order to distinguish the sounds of consonant pairs (e.g., **b** versus **p**) from each other. Some fun activities educators can incorporate in their classrooms include "rhyming, segmenting, blending, manipulation activities, games, songs, and read-alouds" (Allaith & Joshi, 2011, p. 1106), with particular focus on the sounds that are challenging for Arabic ELLs. Allaith and Joshi (2011) found that such activities helped to improve students' spelling, especially with the sounds and the letters that do not exist in Arabic. Other features of English that do not exist in Arabic (e.g., silent letters) should receive more attention and practice (Al Sobhi et al., 2017).

Similarly, teaching vowels explicitly to Arabic ELLs is highly recommended in order to help them fathom the significance of vowels in English

(Hayes-Harb, 2006). Due to the differences between Arabic and English concerning vowels, students need to grasp the correct use of vowels in order to improve their pronunciation, reading, and word identification competencies. Educators could provide students with "lists of words with similar consonant structures and ask them to define each word in the list" (Hayes-Harb, 2006, p. 337). They could also make use of technology and make learning vowels more enjoyable by using word recognition games (Fender, 2003).

Syntactic elements (e.g., word order, adjectives, verbs, articles, prepositions) require increasing students' understanding of appropriate use of English, therefore as much as possible should be taught in context. Educators can provide the students with a text and ask them to identify certain syntactic structures of a given sentence or paragraph. For example, they could ask the students to underscore a negative sentence and describe how negation is formed in English, then describe how negation is formed in Arabic and identify any possible transfers. Providing the students with ample opportunities for self-assessment in order to analyze their own errors (Albalawi, 2016) would be helpful as well.

Also, ELLs ought to be encouraged to avoid literal translation from Arabic into English as much as possible in order to gain a better understanding of English structure and use (Al Zoubi & Abu Eid, 2014; Diab, 1997; Zawahreh, 2013). For this purpose, the use of English–English dictionaries (paper or electronic) is recommended, depending on the students' ages and levels of English proficiency. Finally, educators need to encourage their students to read extensively in English, as extensive reading plays a key role in enhancing literacy skills overall and increasing one's understanding of proper use of English.

CONCLUSION

Since the Arabic-speaking population is increasing across the country, it would behoove educators to be aware of the important role of Arabic as a heritage language and have basic knowledge about Arabic. We began this chapter with a brief overview of the history of Arabic and Arab immigration to the United States. We cast light on some of its main characteristics in relation to direction and sounds, letter-sound correspondence, vowels, word order, adjectives, verbs, articles, and prepositions. We also explained how elements of Arabic differ from those of English and provided examples of how such differences could impact Arabic ELLs' literacy and overall competency in English.

Having educators acquire basic knowledge about Arabic is so important because many of the mistakes made by ELLs do not necessarily reflect a lack of understanding or motivation to learn English. Rather, it is an issue of language transfer. However, students in public schools, especially at elementary levels, are too young to recognize the concept of language transfer. As a result, they might not be able to identify the sources of their mistakes, which in turn can be very confusing and frustrating. Equipping educators with basic knowledge concerning their students' first language will enable them to identify possible interferences between Arabic and English and aid their students accordingly. This increases the students' chances of having a better and more equitable learning experience.

We value our educators and appreciate their endeavors to help Arabic ELLs overcome the challenges associated with language transfers. We strive to support their efforts and therefore concluded this chapter with instructional implications for educators in order to focus on common errors and ultimately to successfully scaffold the development of English literacy among (K-12) Arabic-speaking ELLs. Major takeaways include providing students with explicit instructions, using games and activities to make learning more interesting, avoiding literal translation from Arabic into English, and finally encouraging extensive reading.

REFERENCES

Abdelghany, L. (2016, April 28). *Why study Arabic?* Lingua Franca: Annual Newsletter of the Department of World Languages & Cultures at Salem State University. https://ssulinguafranca.org/2016/04/28/why-study-arabic/.

Abu Rabia, S., Share, D., & Mansour, M. S. (2003). Word recognition and basic cognitive processes among reading-disabled and normal readers in Arabic. *Reading and Writing, 16*, 423–442.

Ahmad, J. (2011). Pronunciation problems among Saudi learners: A case study at the preparatory year program. *Language in India, 11*(7), 22–36.

Ahmed, K. (2010). The Arabic language: Challenges in the modern world. *International Journal for Cross-Disciplinary Subjects in Education, 1*(3), 196–200.

Al Horais, N. (2006). Arabic verbless sentences: Is there a null VP? *Pragmalingüística, 14*, 101–116.

Al Khresheh, M. H. (2010). Interlingual interference in the English language word order structure of Jordanian EFL learners. *European Journal of Social Sciences, 16*(1), 105–116.

Al Sobhi, B. M. S., Rashid, S. M., Abdullah, A. N., & Darmi, R. (2017). Arab ESL secondary school students' spelling errors. *International Journal of Education and Literacy Studies, 5*(3), 16–23. http://dx.doi.org/10.7575/aiac.ijels.v.5n.3p.16.

Al Zoubi, D. M., & Abu Eid, M. A. (2014). The influence of the first language (Arabic) on learning English as a second language in Jordanian schools, and its relation to educational policy: Structural errors. *Sino-US English Teaching, 11*(5), 355–372.

Albalawi, F. S. (2016). Investigating the effect of grammatical differences between English (L2) and Arabic (L1) on Saudi female students' writing of English. *European Scientific Journal*, *12*(14), 185–197. http://dx.doi.org/10.19044/esj.2016.v12n14p185.

Allaith, Z. A., & Joshi, R. M. (2011). Spelling performance of English consonants among students whose first language is Arabic. *Reading and Writing*, *24*, 1089–1110.

Alshaboul, Y., Asassfeh, S., Alshboul, S., & Alodwan, T. (2014). The contribution of L1 phonemic awareness into L2 reading: The case of Arab EFL readers. *International Education Studies*, *7*(3), 99–110. http://dx.doi.org/10.5539/ies.v7n3p99.

Bialik, K., Scheller, A., & Walker, K. (2018, October 25). *6 facts about English language learners in U.S. public schools*. Pew Research Center. https://www.pewresearch.org/fact-tank/2018/10/25/6-facts-about-english-language-learners-in-u-s-public-schools/.

Corey, M. (2020a, January 7). U.S. schools see surge in number of Arabic and Chinese speaking English learners. *Education Week*. https://www.edweek.org/teaching-learning/u-s-schools-see-surge-in-number-of-arabic-and-chinese-speaking-english-learners/2020/01.

Corey, M. (2020b, January 21). Schools in 35 states offer dual-language programs. *Education Week*. https://www.edweek.org/teaching-learning/schools-in-35-states-offer-dual-language-programs/2020/01.

Cummins, J. (1981). The role of primary language development in promoting educational success for language minority students. In California State Department of Education (Ed.), *Schooling and language minority students: A theoretical framework* (pp. 3–49). Los Angeles Evaluation, Dissemination, and Assessment Center, California State University.

Diab, N. (1997). The transfer of Arabic in the English writings of Lebanese students. *The ESPecialist*, *18*(1), 71–83.

Farghaly, A., & Shaalan, K. (2009). Arabic natural language processing: Challenges and solutions. *ACM Transactions on Asian Language Information Processing*, *8*(4), 1–22. https://doi.org/10.1145/1644879.1644881.

Fender, M. (2003). English word recognition and word integration skills of native Arabic and Japanese-speaking learners of English as a second language. *Applied Psycholinguistics*, *24*(2), 289–315. https://doi.org/10.1017/S014271640300016X.

García, O., & Kleifgen, J. A. (2020). Translanguaging and literacies. *Reading Research Quarterly*, *55*(4), 553–571.

Hayes-Harb, R. (2006). Native speakers of Arabic and ESL texts: Evidence for the transfer of written word identification processes. *TESOL Quarterly*, *40*(2), 321–339.

Ibanez, F. (2020, September 15). *The five most spoken languages in the world*. https://www.alphatrad.co.uk/news/most-spoken-languages-world.

Jiang, X. (2018). English spelling knowledge and word reading skills of Arabic and Japanese ESL learners. *Studies in English Language Teaching*, *6*(3), 186–206.

MacSwan, J. (2018). Academic English as standard language ideology: A renewed research agenda for asset-based language education. *Language Teaching Research*, *24*(1), 28–36. https://doi.org/10.1177/1362168818777540.

National Center for Education Statistics. (2022, May). *English learners in public schools*. U.S. Department of Education, Institute of Education Sciences. https://nces.ed.gov/programs/coe/indicator/cgf.

Palmer, B. C., El-Ashry, F., Leclere, J. T., & Chang, S. (2007). Learning from Abdallah: A case study of an Arabic-speaking child in a US school. *The Reading Teacher, 61*(1), 8–17.

Shamsan, M. A. A., & Attayib, A. (2015). Inflectional morphology in Arabic and English: A contrastive study. *International Journal of English Linguistics, 5*(2), 139–150.

Smith, B. (2001). Arabic speakers. In M. Swan & B. Smith (Eds.), *Learner English: A teacher's guide to interference and other problems* (2nd ed., pp. 195–213). Cambridge University Press.

Statista Research Department. (2022, January 27). *U.S. states with the highest Arab American population in 2019*. https://www.statista.com/statistics/912643/arab-american-population-state/.

Tawalbeh, I. Z. (2013). The effect of colloquial Jordanian Arabic on learning the English definite article and negation. *English Language Teaching, 6*(8), 95–107. http://dx.doi.org/10.5539/elt.v6n8p95.

Thompson-Panos, K., & Thomas-Ruzic, M. (1983). The least you should know about Arabic: Implications for the ESL writing instructor. *TESOL Quarterly, 17*(4), 609–623.

Thyab, R. A. (2016). Mother tongue interference in the acquisition of English articles by L1 Arabic students. *Journal of Education and Practice, 7*(3), 1–4.

Tirosh, O. (2021, April 6). *The fastest growing languages in the world*. https://www.tomedes.com/translator-hub/fastest-growing-languages.

Versteegh, K. (2014). *The Arabic language*. Edinburgh University Press.

Zawahreh, F. A. S. (2013). A linguistic contrastive analysis case study: Out of context translation of Arabic adjectives into English in EFL classroom. *International Journal of Academic Research in Business and Social Sciences, 3*(2), 427–443.

Chapter 9

Japanese Language Impact on English Learning

Kinji Ito

At the present time, English language learners (ELLs) account for almost 10 percent of the total K-12 student population (i.e., 4.8 million) in the United States, and the number has been continuously growing (U.S. Department of Education, n.d.). Perhaps in this increasingly diverse academic world, the most essential issue is closing the opportunity gap between non-ELLs and ELLs.

According to the U.S. Department of Commerce (2022), the largest Asian origin populations in the United States are Chinese, Asian Indian, Filipino, Vietnamese, Korean, and Japanese, in this order. Frey (2015) explains that the decline in population from 1990 to 2010 was only for Japanese immigrants while other groups saw considerably large gains. This is similar to other statistical data on the population of immigrant Japanese speaking students in the United States provided by educational agencies (e.g., California Department of Education, 2022; National Center for Education Statistics, 2021). Though it is not a lot by any means, there are a considerable number of Japanese ELLs (JELLs) at the K-12 level who need teachers' instructional support in the United States. This chapter will make practical suggestions for educators to take into consideration while pinpointing the primary challenges that JELLs confront.

A BRIEF HISTORY OF THE JAPANESE LANGUAGE

Japanese is the national language of Japan spoken by more than 120 million people and is considered one of the most spoken languages in the world (Danesi, 2018). This is mainly attributed to its history of evolving language over 1,500 years and the adaptation of Chinese characters called *kanji*, which is perhaps the most important event in the development of the Japanese language. Today, there are three kinds of writing systems in Japanese: *kanji*, *hiragana*, and *katakana*. Below is an example of how Japanese writing is used to express the declarative statement, "I ate pizza yesterday."

昨日 (*kanji*, yesterday), ピザ (*katakana*, pizza) をたべた (*hiragana*, ate)。

Starting with *kanji*, it was originally adopted from China sometime between the third and fourth centuries (Crump, 2014) and was exclusively used for hundreds of years thereafter. The form of its characters was greatly simplified, and the strokes were omitted with the passage of time in order to make writing as fast and efficient as possible. This is how *hiragana* and *katakana* (the two syllabaries in Japanese) were created in the eighth century (Sato et al., 2014). There are 46 basic characters for each syllabary as shown in table 9.1, plus 62 other characters including ones with diacritical marks, and more.

Table 9.1   The Basic 46 Hiragana and Katakana Characters Chart

ン ん	ワ わ	ラ ら	ヤ や	マ ま	ハ は	ナ な	タ た	サ さ	カ か	ア あ
n	wa	ra	ya	ma	ha	na	ta	sa	ka	a
		リ り		ミ み	ヒ ひ	ニ に	チ ち	シ し	キ き	イ い
		ri		mi	hi	ni	chi	shi	ki	i
		ル る	ユ ゆ	ム む	フ ふ	ヌ ぬ	ツ つ	ス す	ク く	ウ う
		ru	yu	mu	fu	nu	tsu	su	ku	u
		レ れ		メ め	ヘ へ	ネ ね	テ て	セ せ	ケ け	エ え
		re		me	he	ne	te	se	ke	e
	ヲ を	ロ ろ	ヨ よ	モ も	ホ ほ	ノ の	ト と	ソ そ	コ こ	オ お
	wo	ro	yo	mo	ho	no	to	so	ko	o

Note. Each box contains *hiragana* (top-right), *katakana* (top-left), and its English pronunciation (bottom-center).

In general, *hiragana* and *katakana* are used to write Japanese origin words and foreign words, respectively. It has been said that the extensive use of the latter is ascribed to increasing pressure from Western powers that ended more than 200 years of the Edo period (1603–1867) to force Japan to form commerce diplomatic and commercial relationships with them. "During the years that followed, an unprecedented number of translations from English, French, German, and Russian into Japanese enriched and changed the Japanese language, not only in vocabulary but also in sentence structure" (Hasegawa, 2014, p. 63).

Along with the two syllabaries, today over 4,000 Chinese characters are commonly used in everyday life, but more than 50,000 characters are said to exist in the Japanese language (Ellington, 2009). This fact alone shows its complexity, and it should come as no surprise that Japanese is possibly the world's most difficult writing system when compared to other languages such as English which uses combinations of 26 letters to represent meanings.

PRINCIPLED ELEMENTS OF THE JAPANESE LANGUAGE

All languages have structural and systematic foundations that make them logical for the people who speak them. Therefore, it is important to learn the principled elements of the Japanese language to get a better understanding of the difficulties that students may have. This will also help teachers apprehend the main differences between the two languages: Japanese and English. The main differences along with suggestions for instruction will be discussed with the following three components: sounds, sentence structure, and rules of nouns.

Sounds

Unlike English which has either 14 or 15 distinct vowel sounds depending on different parts of the country (Ladefoged & Disner, 2012), the Japanese language has only five vowels: a, e, i, o, and u (see table 9.1). Due to this, JELLs tend to have difficulties in learning all different English vowel sounds. All sounds in Japanese, except vowels and "n," have a combination of a consonant plus a vowel, and consonants do not occur by themselves or at the end of a syllable (Huffman, 2013). Since a consonant is a sound that can be combined with a vowel to form a syllable, Japanese pronunciation has been said to be relatively simple, and it is therefore not that challenging for those who wish to learn the language.

For example, if individuals attempt to pronounce vowels found in a sentence, they will have their approximate sounds. In addition, Japanese is almost exclusively formatted with CV (i.e., Consonant Vowel), meaning that it allows no consonant clusters (i.e., a group of consonants with no vowels between them). Winkler (2007) provides specific examples such as Suzuki (CVCVCV) and Toyota (CVCVCV) to show that there are no two consonants in a row in the same syllable. This is distinctively different from English syllable structure as seen in the names of the American car manufacturers such as Chevrolet (CCVCCVCVC) and Chrysler (CCCCCCVC). Consequently, teachers need to bear in mind that JELLs are more likely to demonstrate difficulty in accurately pronouncing English words with consonant clusters.

Sentence Structure

In terms of basic sentence structure and key characteristics, Japanese is the language of the SOV (subject-object-verb) type while English is SVO (subject-verb-object). Due to this different structure, JELLs have challenges in speaking and writing in English in the order of SVO. Furthermore, since Japanese verbs come at the end of the sentence as shown in table 9.2, a whole sentence must be carefully read or heard to fully determine its form: affirmative, negative, or interrogative.

Table 9.2 The Comparison of Sentence Structure

Form	Japanese	Literal English Translation
Affirmative	Yamada san wa (S) kuruma o (O) unten shimasu (V).	Mr. Yamada drives a car.
Negative	Yamada san wa (S) kuruma o (O) unten shimasen (V).	Mr. Yamada doesn't drive a car.
Interrogative	Yamada san wa (S) kuruma o (O) unten shimasu ka (V).	Does Mr. Yamada drive a car?

Note. Wa, o, and ka that appeared in the Japanese sentence in the table are called particles which are equivalent in function to the English *prepositions*.

Let us use the same example of affirmative as shown above, while no change is required in English (i.e., *Mr. Yamada drives a car.*), the verb in Japanese needs to be appropriately conjugated to show respect according to social status and the relationship of the speakers when it is deemed necessary. In case of a situation where Mr. Yamada is senior to the speaker would be as follows: *Yamada san wa* (S) *kuruma o* (O) *unten nasaimasu* (V). This type of verb is called honorific which is part of an important cultural aspect that shows how people socially relate to each other.

Nickel (2016) mentions that the basic word orders in "Japanese and English are mirror images of each other" (p. 219). Because of this, particularly its verb placement, transferring Japanese sentence structure into English could be an impediment to successful communication and progress toward mastery of the target language.

Rules of Nouns

Japanese grammar is generally less explicit and thus is more confusing compared to English. Particularly, when it comes to grammatical number (i.e., singular and plural) and articles (i.e., a, an, and the), they do not exist in Japanese. Due to the absence of these elements in students' primary language, JELLs are in a position to acquire the elements as new information in English. JELLs' potential challenges can be anticipated when teachers learn the rules of nouns in Japanese.

According to Nakanishi (2007), Japanese lacks obligatory grammatical markings of plurality, therefore a noun can be interpreted as singular or plural. Henshall and Kawai (2012) give an example saying that there is no distinction made between the two, as a result, *neko* can mean cat or cats. Osawa (2022) also claims that "Japanese has no article systems, and hence the prediction is that many errors will be found in the use of articles in English writing or speaking by Japanese learners of English" (p. 88). Consequently, referring to the example above, *neko* can mean a cat, the cat, or the cats. That is, if students are to translate *neko* into English, they will need to thoroughly comprehend the context to find the appropriate equivalence. Otherwise, rules used for grammatical numbers identify countable and uncountable nouns, and articles that function to specify if the noun is general or specific in its reference could easily be unintentionally ignored.

TYPICAL PATTERNS OF PRIMARY LANGUAGE USE AND CHALLENGES

Not only the differences in principled elements of the two languages but also the fact that one's first language (L1) and second language (L2) are linguistically polar opposites have a great influence on JELLs. When they are acquiring an L2 (English in this chapter), it is inevitable for them to make comparisons to their L1 (Japanese in this chapter). This is called "language transfer" which is the process of applying knowledge from L1 to L2 and can be either positive or negative. For the former, when mastering a new language, it is helpful because some facets of L1 and L2 are quite similar. For the latter, however, it is arduous because many facets of L1 and L2 are significantly different.

To fully understand the challenges that JELLs may have, close attention was paid to a list created by the Foreign Service Institute (U.S. Department of State, n.d.) that shows how difficult it is for native English speakers to learn foreign languages. As shown in table 9.3, there are a total of four categories with a few examples for each.

Table 9.3   The Language Difficulty Ranking

Category I:	Languages more similar to English (e.g., French, Italian, Spanish).
Category II:	Languages that take a little longer to master than Category I languages (e.g., German, Indonesian, Swahili).
Category III:	"Hard languages"—Languages with significant linguistic and/or cultural differences from English (e.g., Greek, Hebrew, Russian).
Category IV:	"Super-hard languages"—Languages which are exceptionally difficult for native English speakers (e.g., Chinese, Japanese, Korean).

Note. This information is adapted from the Foreign Service Institute (U.S. Department of State, n.d.).

It is obvious that those whose native languages are English or fall into Category I would likely have the most difficult time learning Japanese. To put it the other way around, it is a painstaking process for many native Japanese speakers, especially those who have never been exposed to other languages, to acquire English. This is due to the fact that the linguistic systems related to Japanese culture, history, and geographical location are very different from the target language.

In the next few sections to follow, some examples of JELLs showing typical patterns of primary language use and challenges will be discussed. This is particularly for teachers who serve for JELLs at the K-12 level to understand the types of problems the learners have and be able to address them.

Challenge 1: Pronunciation

As mentioned previously, Japanese pronunciation is relatively simple because a consonant is a sound that can be combined with a vowel to form a syllable. Thus, Japanese sounds appropriate if pronounced how it is written, "samurai," "kimono," "karaoke," you name it. This makes JELLs' task even more difficult to pronounce the target language which does not share the same syllable structure and/or whose sounds do not exist in their L1. For JELLs, phonemes (i.e., a unit of sound) such as /o/ and /a/, and /l/ and /r/ are often confused in pronunciation. First, for the former, Japanese vowels /o/ and /a/ are pronounced as is. Consequently, when JELLs describe their daily routine "I always walk to work" in English, it may sound like "I always work to walk" to native English speakers (NESs). The pronunciation leads to the meaning change. It is therefore misleading unless the listener somehow understands the nuance contextually. Nevertheless, being unable to distinguish between these two pronunciations can cause problems in communication.

Then, what if a sentence that a JELL produces contains /r/ sound? "I correct my mistakes right away" is a case in point. It goes without saying that it changes the whole meaning of the sentence like "I collect my mistakes light away" and describes what is not even close to what the speaker intends to convey. This is another issue that JELLs often encounter since they cannot possibly avoid words and phrases that include those phonemes when using language to communicate. For /l/ and /r/, it is said to be ascribed to the difference in which English has two liquid sounds (i.e., the way the tongue moves in the mouth) while Japanese has only one (Tsujimura, 2013). Since Japanese does not have the same level of detail regarding pronunciation, it is important for teachers to understand that JELLs might pronounce /r/ as /l/ in words in English.

Another aspect that teachers need to know about is that the Japanese language does not have the /θ/ ("th") sound. "Japanese speakers use [s] instead of /θ/ in words like *thank*" (Sewell, 2016, p. 54). In other words, "thank you" sounds like "sank you" which unsurprisingly forces NESs to work to comprehend what they just heard. While the voiceless sound /θ/ involves the tongue to produce its sound, Japanese is a language that can be pronounced without any significant movement of the mouth or tongue. Imagine a JELL and an NES are having the following conversation.

NES: What do you like about your parents?
JELL: Everything [pronounce like "Every sing"]. I think ["sink"] that I have great faith ["face"] in both ["boss"] my parents.
NES: Huh?

The response the JELL produces may sound like, "Every sing. I sink that I have great face in boss my parents." Just one /θ/ sound is enough to trip them up, and thus if JELLs do not know how to properly pronounce "th" sound, they will end up miscuing the pronunciation in their daily conversation. When JELLs realize that they repeatedly struggle to make themselves understood using words that contain sounds such as /r/, /l/, and /θ/, they may feel discouraged and unsure how to amend the miscues. Teachers who work with JELLs need to understand that it is a laborious process to produce unfamiliar sounds for those who are not equipped with such tongue movement in their L1. Hence, it makes them think consciously about all the moves in their mouth which hampers the natural flow of the conversation.

Challenge 2: Word Order and Prepositions

As the name implies, negative language transfer affects various aspects of L2 learning for speakers of an SOV language learning as SVO language. This is exactly what happens to JELLs because Japanese does not have strict word order unlike English. Hence, the word order SOV can easily be rearranged in a variety of ways as seen in table 9.4 while maintaining the same meaning "Mr. Yamada drives a car" in English regardless of the word order.

Table 9.4   Sentence Structure with the Different Word Order

Word Order	Japanese	Literal English Translation
SOV	*Yamada san wa* (S) *kuruma o* (O) *unten shimasu* (V).	Mr. Yamada drives a car.
OVS	*Kuruma o* (O) *unten shimasu* (V), *Yamada san wa* (S).	A car drives Mr. Yamada.
VOS	*Unten shimasu* (V), *kuruma o* (O) *Yamada san wa* (S).	Driving a car, Mr. Yamada.

Note. The literal English translations in the table are approximate equivalence.

It is of course important to follow the basic word order; however, these examples above are commonly used in conversation regardless of age and gender in Japan. Though there are some exceptions, English is a relatively fixed word-order language while Japanese is a free word-order language (i.e., order is not tightly constrained). The word order OVS as seen in table 9.4, while Japanese maintains the same meaning as the original, English completely changes its meaning as in "A car (O) drives (V) Mr. Yamada (S)" when the word order is reorganized. Moreover, a preposition (e.g., at, in, on) is an essential part of the English language as is used to link nouns, pronouns, or phrases to other words. NESs might use it naturally to make sentences sound more expressive and informative as in a sentence "Mr. Yamada drives a car on Sundays," for example. But alas, Japanese students tend to drop prepositions when casually speaking. This is merely a habitual practice and thus there is no strict rule to follow for JELLs.

Because of these differences in word order and strict rules found within a sentence, teachers will observe that many JELLs may struggle with conversing in English. For JELLs, a whole sentence must be carefully read or heard to fully determine its form when using their L1. Therefore, this is one of the ingrained habits that creates an unavoidable delay when using their L2. If there are JELLs who struggle to improve their conversation skills, teachers can understand that the problem may be that the students are fixated on their native language sentence structure, and it may not be related to a processing concern.

Challenge 3: Articles and Plurality

Teachers can also understand that JELLs might have challenges in applying the rules of nouns. The definiteness-indefiniteness distinction and plurality of a noun are implicit in Japanese that take neither any articles nor changes for number. First, the basics of article usage may sound simple to those whose L1 contains the definite and indefinite articles to refer to specific nouns. However, since Japanese has no such part of speech equivalent to English articles, it is the most frequently occurring error among Japanese learners of English (Dykes, 2016). To rub salt into the wound, phrases like "worth the wait" and "worth a try" are troublesome. Without any clarifications, sometimes English randomly requires the definite or indefinite article before the noun. The seemingly arbitrary application makes JELLs even more confused. Below is a set of instances with or without the definite article that they often misuse, followed by an awkward situation between a JELL and an NES talking on the phone. The negative language transfer caused confusion and a need for clarification:

JELL: Do you have the time?
NES: What do you mean? (implying that you called me to ask that?)
JELL: I have a favor to ask of you . . . so do you have the time?

"Do you have time?" is used to ask if individuals have time in their schedule while "Do you have *the* time?" is used to ask what time it is. It does make a difference in overall meaning depending on whether the article is appropriately used or not. Lang (2010) states that the definite and indefinite articles constitute two of the most frequently used words in English and they are the most difficult linguistic elements to learn for ELLs, especially for those whose L1 lacks the article system.

Next, Japanese nouns have no plural form. "With few exceptions, the sense of plural is made evident by the context of the phrase or sentence" (De Mente & Kawai, 2016, p. 18). This differs greatly from English as shown in the examples given below. Note that Japanese is translated into English for the purpose of comparison.

English: I have two sisters, and both own three cars.
Japanese: I have two sister, and both own three car.

As seen in the English example above, most inflections on nouns depend on how many of something is being referred to. However, this is not the case in Japanese which does not require such a change because the numerals placed before the nouns indicate the number that the speaker is referring to. Therefore, "sister" as in "two sister" and "car" as in "three car" are considered plural. Applying the English rules of plurality for JELLs can leave students perplexed, which typically stems from an over application of the syntax form in their L1, and that it makes them overthink the grammatical differences between Japanese and English. This too inhibits JELLs from making progress in their speaking skills.

All the aforementioned examples given through challenges 1–3 are perfect demonstrations of how much impact Japanese has on English learning. Interestingly, they all are related to speech production. This is because of its culture and society in which people are expected to express themselves indirectly and ambiguously when communicating verbally (Davies & Ikeno, 2002).

INSTRUCTIONAL IMPLICATIONS FOR EDUCATORS

Today, there are ways to support JELLs in promoting language and literacy development. For instance, oral corrective feedback (OCF) is a powerful technique that teachers can use. According to Lightbown and Spada (2013), OCF is defined as "an indication to a learner that his or her use of the target language is incorrect" (p. 216). This chapter focusing solely on JELLs will highlight the effective use of OCF because, unlike written corrective feedback, teachers can attach meaning to what they say with actions, gestures, and the like. Additionally, to make OCF work more effectively, teachers can clarify the following points in advance for JELLs.

- The significance of making errors and/or mistakes to further progress and learn from it. This is very important because Japanese people are culturally said to be introverted or reserved and mindfully conscious of committing errors or mistakes.
- The reason as to why it is essential to be an active listener is to become fluent in their L2. In other words, during conversations, paying attention to the incoming information (i.e., OCF) provided by the teacher and consequently producing correct output modified by the learner based on the feedback received is a must. By repeating this process, learners might make fewer errors and/or mistakes and eventually internalize the information (i.e., knowledge).

Using Oral Corrective Feedback

Ellis et al. (2009) state that there are six different types of OCF used in language learning environments which were first reported by Lyster and Ranta (1997). In the past, many studies (e.g., Nassaji & Kartchava, 2017; Sheen, 2004) adopted the existing strategy of OCF and demonstrated how it can be used to create cognitive and affective scaffolding (Porayska-Pomsta & Pain, 2004). Below are the definitions of each feedback type in the order of explicitness along with examples. The definitions are adapted from Lyster and Ranta (1997). Note that L is for learner and T is for teacher.

- Explicit correction: The explicit provision of the correct form. As teachers provide the correct form, they clearly indicate that what learners had said was incorrect.

L: I am graduating on June.

T: Please say "in June."

- Metalinguistic feedback: Contains comments, information, or questions related to the lack of well-formedness of learners' utterance, without explicitly providing the correct form.

L: I am graduating on June.

T: Please use the appropriate preposition.

- Clarification request: Learners are asked to clarify their meaning without any indication of the presence of an error.

L: I am graduating on June.

T: Pardon?

- Repetition: Teachers repeat learners' utterance, including any error(s).

L: I am graduating on June.

T: You are graduating on June.

- Elicitation: Learners are prompted to reformulate their utterance. Teachers elicit completion of their own utterance by strategically pausing to allow learners to "fill in the blank."

L: I am graduating on June.

T: You are graduating . . .?

- Recast: Teachers reformulate all or part of learners' utterance, minus the error.

L: I am graduating on June.

T: You are graduating in June.

It is inevitable that each OCF type has its strengths so that they can be strategically employed depending on challenges that learners face, language course levels, and so on. Nevertheless, I would suggest that teachers use the implicit types of feedback: recast and elicitation for JELLs in grades K-12 for the following reasons.

- Implicit types of OCF are preferred so as not to embarrass the speaker. This is to keep JELLs motivated and interested in learning the target language.
- Explicit correction is incompatible with student-generated repair because they only elicit repetition for all practical purposes. Similarly, clarification request and repetition may allow JELLs to repeat the same error.
- Metalinguistic feedback indicates ways of negotiation of form without explicitly providing the correct form. Therefore, it is far more effective when used for JELLs who possess enough knowledge of English to modify the output.

Focusing on the first, it is a well-known fact that motivation is one of the keys to success in language learning as many studies (e.g., Benati & Angelovska, 2016; Cook & Singleton, 2014) have supported. Some are innately motivated, and others are difficult to stay motivated. It is therefore important not to demotivate JELLs, in this case, perhaps using explicit types of OCF in the classroom.

Helping with Errors in Pronunciation

As discussed earlier, many JELLs are often troubled with carrying on a natural conversation with NESs due to the differences in many aspects between the two languages; consequently, if sounds do not exist in their L1, JELLs must be fully conversant with it through the assistance of teachers who can help them improve their speaking skills. When it comes to errors in pronunciation, using recast is recommended since the proper enunciation is directly but implicitly given. Below is an example of the following challenge.

Pronunciation

T: What do you like about your parents?
L: Everything [pronounce like "Every sing"].
T: Oh, you like everything (recast: put stress on the unvoiced "th" sound).

One of the characteristics of recast is not to break off the conversation that is perhaps spontaneously flowing. This is critical due to the fact that many JELLs in general tend to get discouraged from speaking up again when interactions are constantly interrupted. While making a correction, I would suggest that teachers do the following:

- Use as much of a gesture as possible and make the learner imitate your action. Any physical movement tends to trigger memory and increase recall.
- Utilize visual aids such as pictures and videos (e.g., for pronunciation, showing the actual tongue movement to increase the learners' interest).
- Repeat similar words that have the same sound. This way, the learner has the opportunity to practice more.

Helping with Errors in Grammar Rules

Sentence structure (e.g., prepositions) and rules of nouns (e.g., plurality) may be a challenge for JELLs to overcome. However, with teachers using effective techniques such as so-called OCF, these challenges can be mitigated. Therefore, it is assumed that implicit types of feedback can be strategically employed to help JELLs retain the information and later retrieve the knowledge stored in their memory system. To reiterate, using recast is recommended because it does not break off the conversation which also helps them stay motivated. Let us look at examples of successful responses (i.e., recast works in the first place) for the following challenges.

Preposition

L: I played tennis Sunday.
T: Oh, you played tennis on Sunday (recast)
L: Yes, I played tennis on Sunday.

Plurality

L: I have two sister.
T: Oh, you have two sisters (recast)
L: Yes, I have two sisters.

The fact that the preposition "on" before the noun and the plural form "sisters" may be new to the learner. Nevertheless, if JELLs pay attention and thus notice the gap, they will be able to correct the error after receiving recast feedback. As a result, this new input may become knowledge if the learner uses or rehearses it. While making a correction, I would suggest that teachers do the following:

- Use as many nouns as possible for practice purposes (e.g., words that require different prepositions/countable and uncountable: how about people? How about information?). This will help the learner become able to differentiate one from the other.
- Utilize visual aids such as pictures and videos that show the actual use of grammar in context. Learners tend to remember and retain information presented visually/graphically.
- Avoid asking the learner "Do you remember we did this before" or "Do you really understand?" JELLs will more than likely say "Yes" to avoid a negative consequence. In other words, teachers need to be patient because basic grammar rules for them do not mean the same for JELLs.

One important thing teachers need to keep in mind is that, if recast was not noticed, a few attempts can be made using elicitation or a combination of both until the learner produces the correct form. Let us look at examples of unsuccessful responses (i.e., recast does not work in the first place) for the same challenges.

Preposition

L: I played tennis Sunday.
T: Oh, you played tennis on Sunday (recast)
L: Yes, I played tennis Sunday.
T: You played tennis . . .? (elicitation)
L: I played tennis Sunday.
T: Oh, you played tennis on Sunday (recast)

Plurality

L: I have two sister.
T: Oh, you have two sisters (recast)
L: Yes, I have two sister.
T: You have two . . .? (elicitation)
L: I have two sister.
T: Oh, you have two sisters (recast).

If neither works, teachers need to move on. This is to avoid a situation in which teachers unconsciously put undue stress on JELLs, as a result, they might disengage from learning. While making a correction, I would suggest that teachers do the following:

- Teachers talk about themselves that include the correct forms like "When I was your age, I used to play tennis on Sundays" and "I have two sisters who live in Texas." This is to have interactive conversations with students in a meaningful way.

What is important here is that teachers should leave no stone unturned to help bring JELLs' understanding of conventional ways of expressing their ideas in the target language, in this case, English.

CONCLUSION

It is recommended that teachers employ implicit types of OCF depending on what errors their students make, what grade they teach, and the like. For pronunciation, recast is effective because the proper enunciation is directly but implicitly given. For grammar, recast may work better for elementary and intermediate learners, while elicitation may be more suited for advanced learners. Teachers can also learn this through trial and error. Even though it may be time consuming, they should take all the suggestions into consideration, and deliberately use such pedagogical techniques more often with JELLs. This is because using the appropriate form of OCF at the right time will be beneficial for both teachers and learners alike.

As in Japanese and English, it is undoubtedly a daunting task for those whose L1 has a greater linguistic distance from L2 to acquire the target language. Not only the difference in sounds but also in sentence structure and rules of nouns which JELLs need to become proficient in order to develop the basic language skills: reading, listening, speaking, and writing. To achieve this, it is vital for teachers who support their language and literacy development to be aware of how much impact L1 has on L2 learning. If they understand the gap between L1 and L2, then a more effective learning environment can be provided. Future studies on JELLs at the K-12 level should build on this by comparing other foreign languages and including other language levels. Lastly, it is incumbent upon the teacher to ensure the students leave their settings with all the tools necessary to be successful in life.

REFERENCES

Benati, A. G., & Angelovska, T. (2016). *Second language acquisition: A theoretical introduction to real-world applications.* Bloomsbury Academic.

California Department of Education. (2022, April 18). *Facts about English learners in California.* https://www.cde.ca.gov/ds/ad/cefelfacts.asp.

Cook, V., & Singleton, D. M. (2014). *Key topics in second language acquisition.* Multilingual Matters.

Crump, T. (2014). *Japanese numbers game.* Routledge.

Danesi, M. (2018). *Language, society, and new media: Sociolinguistics today.* Routledge.

Davies, R. J., & Ikeno, O. (2002). *The Japanese mind: Understanding contemporary Japanese culture.* Tuttle Publishing.

De Mente, B. L., & Kawai, J. (2016). *Survival Japanese: How to communicate without fuss or fear instantly!* (2nd ed.). Tuttle Publishing.

Dykes, R. (2016). *A common error with Japanese learners of English: Article usage* [Poster session]. JALT International Conference, Nagoya, Aichi, Japan.

Ellington, L. (2009). *Japan.* ABC-CLIO.

Ellis, R., Loewen, S., Elder, C., Reinders, H., Erlam, R., & Philp, J. (2009). *Implicit and explicit knowledge in second language learning, testing and teaching.* Multilingual Matters.

Frey, W. H. (2015). *Diversity explosion: How new racial demographics are remaking America.* Brookings Institution Press.

Hasegawa, Y. (2014). *Japanese: A linguistic introduction.* Cambridge University Press.

Henshall, K. G., & Kawai, J. (2012). *Welcome to Japanese: A beginner's survey of the language; learn conversational Japanese, key vocabulary and phrases.* Tuttle Publishing.

Huffman, J. L. (2013). *Modern Japan: An encyclopedia of history, culture, and nationalism.* Taylor & Francis.

Ladefoged, P., & Disner, S. F. (2012). *Vowels and consonants.* John Wiley & Sons.

Lang, Y. (2010). *Grammar and the Chinese ESL learner: A longitudinal study on the acquisition of the English article system.* Cambria Press.

Lightbown, P. M., & Spada, N. (2013). *How languages are learned.* Oxford University Press.

Lyster, R., & Ranta, L. (1997). Corrective feedback and learner uptake: Negotiation of form in communicative classrooms. *Studies in Second Language Acquisition, 19*(1), 37–66.

Nakanishi, K. (2007). *Formal properties of measurement constructions.* Walter de Gruyter.

Nassaji, H., & Kartchava, E. (2017). *Corrective feedback in second language teaching and learning: Research, theory, applications, implications.* Routledge.

National Center for Education Statistics. (2021, May). *English language learners in public schools.* https://nces.ed.gov/programs/coe/indicator/cgf.

Nickel, B. (2016). *Between logic and the world; an integrated theory of generics.* Oxford University Press.

Osawa, F. (2022). The rivalry between definiteness and specificity: The grammaticalization of definiteness in DP emergence. In L. Sommerer & E. Keizer (Eds.), *English noun phrases from a functional-cognitive perspective* (pp. 79–106). John Benjamins.

Porayska-Pomsta, K., & Pain, H. (2004). Providing cognitive and affective scaffolding through teaching strategies: Applying linguistic politeness to the educational context. In J. C. Lester, R. M. Vicari, & F. Paraguacu (Eds.), *Intelligent tutoring systems* (pp. 77–86). Springer.

Sato, S., Sato, A. O., Roshi, G. A., & Fujiwara, S. (2014). *Shodo: The quiet art of Japanese Zen calligraphy, learn the wisdom of Zen through traditional brush painting.* Tuttle Publishing.

Sewell, A. (2016). *English pronunciation models in a globalized world: Accent, acceptability and Hong Kong English.* Routledge.

Sheen, Y. (2004). Corrective feedback and learner uptake in communicative classrooms across instructional settings. *Language Teaching Research, 8*(3), 263–300.

Tsujimura, N. (2013). *An introduction to Japanese linguistics.* John Wiley & Sons.

U.S. Department of Commerce. (2022, May 3). *U.S. census bureau releases key stats in honor of Asian American, native Hawaiian, and Pacific islander heritage month.* https://www.commerce.gov/news/blog/2022/05/us-census-bureau-releases -key-stats-honor-asian-american-native-hawaiian-and.

U.S. Department of Education. (n.d.). *Our nation's English learners.* https://www2 .ed.gov/datastory/el-characteristics/index.html.

U.S. Department of State. (n.d.). *Foreign language training.* https://www.state.gov/ foreign-language-training/.

Winkler, E. (2007). *Understanding language: A basic course in linguistics.* Bloomsbury Academic.

Chapter 10

Supporting and Engaging French Background Students Learning English

Fanny Macé and Sylvie Roy

Our goal is to help educators who work with French native speakers in the United States to examine the influence of the language on learning English. According to the U.S. Census Bureau's 2020 American Community Survey (ACS), about 22 percent of Americans spoke a language other than English at home. In addition, the number of French-speaking newcomers in the United States has continuously evolved, especially in recent years. Consequently, the number of English language learners (ELLs) with French linguistic backgrounds is also changing. Nationwide statistics from the U.S. Census Bureau's 2013 ACS and the Department of Education revealed that French/Haitian Creole was the fourth primary language spoken in ELLs' homes in 2013, representing 2 percent of ELLs enrolled in public schools throughout the United States (Ruiz Soto et al., 2015).

Today, French ranks third—after Spanish and Chinese—with more than 2 million speakers or 0.7 percent of the U.S. population (Hernandez et al., 2022). In the U.S. current context, French usually includes Cajun, Creole, and Haitian. While in the United States, French is not ranked as the top primary language spoken in ELLs' homes in any of the 50 states; it is worth noting that in Maine and Maryland, French is the second most spoken language with respectively 7 percent and 3 percent of ELLs. In Florida, Haitian-Creole-speaking students count for 10 percent of ELLs. Today in Louisiana, a state with a deep historical and cultural connection to the French-speaking world (Guidry, 2022), there is a revival of French, thanks to French immersion programs managed by the Council for the Development of French in Louisiana (CODOFIL) as the number of French heritage speakers are about 250,000.

To understand the evolving origin of French speakers immigrating to the United States, educators need to note that between 2010 and 2018, an additional 22.7 million people speaking French were reported worldwide:

90 percent of these "new" speakers come from Africa (68 percent from sub-Saharan Africa and 22 percent from North Africa or Maghreb (i.e., Algeria, Morocco, and Tunisia)), 7 percent from the Americas including Haiti, and 3 percent from Europe (Chutel, 2018). Consequently, most French speakers immigrating to the United States today come primarily from Western sub-Saharan Africa, North Africa (Maghreb), and Haiti. French is the main or the only language of instruction (Lorenzi & Batalova, 2022).

As demonstrated, the United States is characterized by double heterogeneity—the ELLs and their diverse French backgrounds. Nevertheless, general principles of second language acquisition might prove helpful to support teachers and students alike. First, the influence of students' primary language on second language acquisition is essential (Derakhsan & Karimi, 2015) as students can highly benefit from their primary language knowledge (Gass, 1987; LeBlanc, 1989).

Primary language interference or transfer refers to students applying knowledge from their primary language while learning a second or additional language. Several scholars work on looking at the connection between primary and second languages. For example, Karim and Nassaji (2013) explored primary language transfers in second language writing, while Fatemi et al. (2012) examined the differences in consonant clusters in the primary and second languages. They found that primary language influenced writing in the second language, and second language learners had difficulties pronouncing some unfamiliar phonological patterns. Whereas some of these influences were seen as barriers, others appeared as facilitating tools for teachers (Chaira, 2015). Indeed, even if linguistic transfers can be perceived as unfavorable (i.e., producing interference errors), most learners' linguistic transfers are positive (Jarvis & Pavlenko, 2008). It is also relevant to remember that positive transfers occur more often when two languages present similarities at the linguistic level (Ringbom & Jarvis, 2009), which is the case for English and French.

A BRIEF HISTORY OF FRENCH

The *Organisation Internationale de la Francophonie* (OIF, 2022) has recently estimated that there were 321 million Francophones (i.e., people able to communicate in French) worldwide in 2022. It is worth noting that within this number are not only French native speakers but also partial French speakers and speakers of numerous French dialects and creoles. Due to colonization, French is today the fifth most widely spoken language in the world, after English, Mandarin, Hindi, and Spanish (OIF, 2022). Like English, French is a global language spoken on all five continents. French is an official language in Canada, the French Caribbean, and five European countries (e.g., France, Belgium, Switzerland, Luxembourg, and Monaco). It is also either an official, an administrative, or a second language in 29 states and territories, mainly in Africa (OIF, 2022). Additionally, French is the second most learned language in the world after English, with more than 93 million students having French as one of their languages of instruction and more than 50 million individuals learning it as a second or additional language (OIF, 2022).

There are wide varieties of French worldwide. They are based on extraordinary innovation and are characterized by the formation of new terms and phrases. While remaining highly intelligible in most cases, their lexicons have evolved in their own ways, influenced by geographic specificities and local languages. Unfortunately, rather than always being perceived as linguistic gains, some variations can be considered improper by some and therefore suffer low prestige. Lodge (2013) argues that French culture and language have always been subconsciously positioned as the cornerstone of the French national heritage. In the French tradition, the *perfect state of a language* has often been defined by an *ideal of homogeneity and uniformity*. This ideology rests on the principles of one language per nation, the primacy of written over spoken, and the ideologies of norms and standards—thus placing *standard/ Parisian French* on top of the hierarchy.

According to this biased view, other unfamiliar French regional varieties, French-based creoles, and their intra-linguistic continuums, such as Haitian (Tessonneau, 1983), dialects, and patois, can be considered low prestige. The speakers of these varieties of French can therefore express feelings of linguistic insecurity. Thus, educators must remember that the diversity of contexts where students have learned and spoken French may affect their perception and performance in acquiring English as an additional language. This aspect is particularly true if ELLs with a French background have been constantly judged on the variety of the French they speak. Furthermore, another barrier to their learning of English can emerge as the myth of standard English still prevails in the United States in the form of language ideology and discrimination (Lippi-Green, 2011).

In the following part, we will introduce some features of the French language that will help teachers understand the challenges ELL students with French backgrounds may encounter.

MAIN CHARACTERISTICS AND PARTICULARITIES OF THE FRENCH LANGUAGE

To best support ELLs with a French background, educators should be aware of the main characteristics and particularities of the French language. By understanding the most salient features of the French language and getting a sense of the commonalities and differences between the French and the English languages, teachers will be better equipped to efficiently support their students with a French background in learning English as an additional language. In return, students will be more meaningfully engaged and motivated.

French Letters and Diacritics

When looking at French for the first time, educators may have noticed some written symbols that do not exist in English (i.e., except in some borrowed words, such as café, façade, and naïve). These symbols are called diacritics; accents and the cedilla are the most common. In French, accents can only be attached to vowels "a; e; i; o; u" while the cedilla is exclusively used with the letter "c." Accents and cedilla are essential in French as their roles consist in modifying the letter values (i.e., alteration in pronunciation or duration), enabling speakers to pronounce the letters differently. For example, the "c" is pronounced /k/ when followed by vowels "a, u, o" while "ç" is pronounced /s/ when followed by the same vowels. Concerning French-speaking students' learning English, it may prove interesting to note that there is a commonality in the pronunciation of some words using a cedilla in French and an "s" or "ss" sequence in English (i.e., *leçon* and lesson; *rançon* and ransom).

Moreover, in some instances, the circumflex accent in French can be a remnant of a former "s" (i.e., the "s" is still present in English: *les pâtes* and pasta; *le château* and the castle; *la forêt* and the forest; *l'île* and the island). Accents can also be used as a means to distinguish between identical written words (i.e., they are called homographs; *sûr* [sure] ≠ *sur* [on/upon]). Educators should remember that if students mix up homographs in French, this may result in inadequate translations in English. In providing these explanations and examples from French, we hope that we help teachers to better understand the possible difficulties ELLs with a French background could face when learning English.

The Sounds of French

English and French have significant variations in pronunciation. Pronunciation remains one of the significant difficulties that speakers of French as a primary language face in their learning of English (Nabine, 2013), mainly because the system of sounds in English is notoriously inconsistent. For French language speakers, one of the main difficulties in pronouncing English lies in the lack of correspondence between writing and sounding. In English, there are about 44 (19 vowel and 25 consonant sounds) phonemes (i.e., smallest units of speech distinguishing one word from another, as in "pin" and "pan" where the sound difference stands on the realization of the vowels "i" and "a" in the phonemes /ɪ/ and /æ/) whereas, in French, there are about 36 phonemes (16 vowel and 20 consonant sounds), and they are very different. There is also a lack of correspondence between the English and the French phonological systems.

From a French speaker's viewpoint, English pronunciation can be perceived as confusing given its numerous rules and exceptions.

Specific Difficulties in English Pronunciation for French Speakers

- *Various pronunciations of the same graphemes* (i.e., the written representation [from one letter to a cluster of letters] of one sound) are very common in English. For French speakers, it is difficult to predict how the grapheme will sound (especially when encountering new words).
- *Sounds that do not exist in French*: The following consonant sequence "th" has two realizations in English. They can realize either in a "soft th," which is /θ/, or in a "hard th," which is /ð/. Koffi (2015) did an intensive study with several languages to demonstrate how the "th" is complicated for several speakers. French was not included in that study, but, in our own experiences, the "th" has consistently been something difficult to achieve as native speakers of French.
- *Interferences between French and English*: Some errors result from French-speaking habits negatively transferring to the pronunciation of English words (e.g., forgetting to pronounce consonants in English because they are mute in French). The most common examples are the non-realization of the glottal "h" (at the beginning or in the middle of a word) and of the "s" (at the end of words in particular; genitive or third person of present tense verbs). Other examples might include the mis-realization of the letter "s" (i.e., /s/ or /z/), especially at the end of words. In general, students with French backgrounds, when first encountering the English language, would tend not to pronounce the final "s." However, as students become more familiar with the English language, they pronounce it but sometimes inadequately (i.e., /s/ when its realization is /z/, for instance). In table 10.1, we have compiled some examples illustrating specific difficulties for ELLs with French backgrounds that educators should consider.

Table 10.1   Illustration of Specific Difficulties in Pronunciation

Specific Difficulties	*Examples*
Various pronunciations of the same graphemes: The example of the grapheme "ea"	/iː/ (General rule): Beard; Fear; Leave; /e/ (Secondary value): Bread; Head; Measure **"ea"** + letter R (two realizations) (1) /ɪə/: Ear; Near; (2) /eə/: Bear; Pear **"ea" + letter R + consonant**: /ɜː/ Early; Learned
Sounds that do not exist in French: The example of the soft "th" versus hard "th"	**The soft "th"** (First realization): /θ/ Author /ɑθɚ/; Thing /θɪŋ/; Think /θɪŋk/ **The hard "th"** (Second realization): /ð/ That /ðæt/; Them /ðem/; They /ðeɪ/; This /ðɪs/; Those /ðoʊz

The Words of French: Lexicon

The main difference between French and English, and the difficulty for French speakers in learning English, remains in the existence of genders in French (feminine and masculine). In English, gender uses remain marginal except in a few cases (i.e., actor/actress, comedian/comedienne, waiter/waitress, host/hostess, fiancé/fiancée, and widow/widower). One consequence of French transfer over to English could be that French-speaking students may use the corresponding French gender when referring to objects (i.e., inanimate) which are not gender-neutral in French as illustrated in table 10.2.

Table 10.2   Illustration of the Gender of Inanimates

English	French
The book?	Le livre?
*He is on the table.	Il est sur la table.
	Note: In French, "Il" can either be translated by "it" or "he" according to the referent. Also note that **"table"** being feminine in French, it could be (wrongly) replaced by the subject pronoun "*she".

When teaching vocabulary, teachers might want to remember two main principles:

(1) **The use of different teaching and learning modalities** (e.g., contrasting, drawing, interacting (Gas et al., 1998), listening, reading, speaking, summarizing, teaching, translating, visualizing, writing)

(2) **The creation of networks** (e.g., mind-mapping, interconnection between words, intertextuality, and transdisciplinarity) thanks to notions such as word families (i.e., groups of words presenting common features, patterns, or meanings). In this category, we can find synonyms (i.e., words holding similar meanings), antonyms (i.e., words holding contrary meanings), hypernyms (i.e., words whose meanings include the meanings of more specific words; e.g., flower is a hypernym of daisy), hyponyms (i.e., contrary of hypernyms); words whose meanings are included in the meanings of other more general words (e.g., daisy is a hyponym for flower). These two strategies should be emphasized when teaching ELLs as they help to categorize, memorize, retain, and retrieve vocabulary.

As demonstrated above, the main principle of second language teaching and learning rests on creating and working on associations between students' primary language and English. One of the critical aspects is for educators to understand how crucial it is for ELLs to go beyond the word-by-word approach. Teachers should encourage students to acquire English by working on complete structures whenever possible. One strategy is pointing out that languages rarely translate words for words or use similar structures. Another strategy comprises bilingual children's books as a resource (e.g., Storybooks Canada (n.d.)) to encourage and meaningfully engage ELLs to independently work on their acquisition of English as a second or additional language while developing ELLs' autonomy in their learning.

Specifically, students whose primary language is French could encounter the following challenges:

- **Multiple terms versus one term**: When one term is used in French to refer to multiple terms in English;
- **"Be" versus "Have"**: When French uses "have" in expressions that request the use of "be" in English;
- **Different verbal constructions**: When there is no direct correspondence between French and English.

Some examples illustrating these three specific challenges have been compiled in table 10.3.

Table 10.3   Examples of Particular Challenges for ELLs with French Background

Specific Challenges	English	French
Multiple terms versus one term	**Multiple terms**: "dead"; "death" and "died" **Death** (noun) He is **dead**/he **died** (adjective/verb in the past)	**Only one term** for several contexts: *Mort* La ***mort*** (noun) Il est ***mort*** (adjective/past participle)

WORKING ON STRUCTURE COMMONALITIES AND DIFFERENCES

Word Order and Agreement: The Examples of Adjectives and Adverbs

Two particular distinctions occur when making French and English sentences. The most salient is the question of word orders and agreements, and the other is the choice and use of the correct prepositions when constructing sentences. Teachers need to be aware of some linguistic features specific to French so they can understand some of the particular challenges ELLs with a French background may encounter. We will briefly illustrate how two examples of specific categories of words, such as (1) adjectives and (2) adverbs, work differently in French and English (table 10.4):

Table 10.4   Illustration of Word Order and Agreement: The Examples of Adjectives and Adverbs

Specific Challenges	English	French
Adjectives: Agreement and Positioning	He wants to buy **blue *shoes***. He wants to buy a **blue *shirt***. She likes seeing the **blue *sky***. They are writing with **blue *pens***. Note: No matter the noun used, in English, the adjective **blue** remains <u>invariable</u> (i.e., it does not agree, it does not alter its form).	Il veut acheter des ***chaussure*<u>s</u>** **bleue**<u>s</u>. Il veut acheter une ***chemise* bleue**. Elle aime voir le ***ciel* bleu**. Ils écrivent avec des ***stylos* bleu**<u>s</u>. Note: In French, the adjective ***bleu*** is <u>variable</u> (i.e., it agrees or alters its form according to the gender (feminine or masculine) and number (singular or plural) of the noun).
Adverbs: Positioning	Sofia **always** <u>reads</u> before bed. Ali **often** <u>sees</u> ***his neighbor***. I <u>like</u> ***your brother*** very much. Note: In English, adverbs usually are used <u>before</u> verbs, and <u>verbs</u> and <u>object complements</u> are <u>not separated</u> by adverbs.	Sofia <u>lit</u> **toujours** avant d'aller au lit. Ali <u>voit</u> **souvent *son voisin***. J'<u>aime</u> **beaucoup *ton frère***. Note: In French, adverbs usually are used <u>after</u> verbs, and <u>verbs</u> and <u>object complements are separated</u> by adverbs.

- *Adjectives: Agreement and Positioning.* Compared to English, French is more inflected as a language, which means alterations in the forms of most of the words used. One relevant example is adjectives (i.e., words describing nouns; e.g., blue versus *bleu*; *bleue*; *bleus*; *bleues*). Whereas in French, adjectives need to agree (i.e., adjectives have to show whether they are masculine or feminine (gender) and singular or plural (number) to pair with the noun they describe); in English, they remain invariable (i.e., their form remains the same). Also, the positioning of adjectives in French and English is different. Whereas English positions adjectives before nouns, French tends to put them after nouns. Teachers working with ELLs with French backgrounds might note mistakes linked to the difference in adjective functioning between French and English. For example, a prevalent error consists of putting the English adjective after the noun.
- *Adverbs: Positioning and Functioning.* In French and English, the positioning of adverbs (i.e., types of words describing verbs in the same fashion as adjectives are associated with nouns) is different. Whereas English positions adverbs before verbs, French tends to put them after. There is a commonality in the functioning of adverbs in English and French: Adverbs are invariable (i.e., they do not alter their forms) in both languages.

As the position of adverbs is usually different in English and French, educators may notice a tendency in their ELLs with a French background to put them after rather than before verbs. Another standard error consists of students with French backgrounds separating the verb from its complement (i.e., *I like very much your brother; reflecting the French word order). A good strategy to reinforce ELLs' ability to use certain types of words in the right place in the sentence consists of inviting students to construct sentences using colored-lego bricks (i.e., one color per word category). Furthermore, educators should engage and encourage students to build more complex sentences whenever possible as a means to reinforce the learning of English.

Word Order: Asking Questions

Asking questions does not require the same structure in French and English. Contrary to French, where questions can be constructed by using statements with a simple change of intonation and the adding of a question mark, asking questions in English requires an auxiliary verb such as "be," "do," or "have" and a change in the word order. For example, French-speaking ELLs may ask, "You want water?" instead of "Do you want water?" Therefore, we can imagine a group activity based on pictures, and students work on constructing questions by using color blocks representing the different categories of words. The objective is to create questions thanks to three modalities: using the color blocks, saying them out loud, and writing them down.

The Absence versus the Presence of Determiners

Determiners are among the most challenging aspects to master even as proficient English second language speakers, as their use may differ significantly from one language to the next. To demonstrate our point, we will discuss limited occurrences of the absence of determiners in English in contrast to the presence of determiners in French.

- *In expressing generality*: French uses definite articles in the plural *les*, while English uses no determiner (or determiner ø) in the plural form.
- *Talking about quality and default*: Another example that proves hard for French speakers is the absence of a determiner when talking about qualities or defaults such as courage.

As a transfer from French, ELLs with French backgrounds might use the determiner "the" when nothing is needed in English. Table 10.5 illustrates this specific aspect.

Table 10.5   Illustration of the Absence versus the Presence of Determiners

Specific Challenges	English	French
Determiners Use: Expression of generality	**ø Dogs** are faithful animals. Note: In English, the expression of generality requires the use of no determiner (or ø) and a noun in the plural form.	**Les chiens** sont des animaux fidèles. Note: In French, the expression of generality requires the use of plural definite determiner *les* (i.e., corresponding to "the" in English) and a noun in the plural form (*chiens*).
Determiners Use: Talking about quality and default	**ø Courage** is a quality that is often lacking. Note: In English, talking about quality and default requires the use of no determiner (or ø).	**Le courage** est une qualité qui fait souvent défaut. Note: In French, talking about quality and default requires the use of singular definite determiner *le, la, or l'* (i.e., corresponding to "the" in English) and a noun in the singular form.

Educators working with ELLs with French backgrounds may have noticed these students usually overuse determiners "the" and "a/an" as direct transfers from French. One strategy consists of pointing out the contexts in which the absence of a determiner is required in English, especially when reading and writing. Additionally, teachers can create corpora of texts or use books that specifically address this topic and make sure that students often revisit these questions.

Phrasal Verbs

Another important topic for ELLs with French backgrounds is the use of phrasal verbs such as "look up" and "figure out" (i.e., "any two-part verb consisting of a lexical verb followed by an adverbial particle") (Gardner & Davies, 2007), cited in Liu, 2011, p. 663) that have no equivalent in French. It is worth noting for teachers that as these phrasal verbs have Latin counterparts (e.g., "consult" with French equivalent *"consulter"* and "solve" with French equivalent *"résoudre"*) and students who speak French could use these cognates (i.e., instead). ELLs with French backgrounds tend to abuse this option, so their teachers can perceive this as a positive linguistic transfer and might think that ELLs with French backgrounds' lexical knowledge is deeper than it is.

A suggestion to help educators support students learning and retaining phrasal verbs more efficiently is to encourage and meaningfully engage them to:

- *Refer to frequency lists or dictionaries of phrasal verbs:* Giving good habits to students may help them, in the long run, to develop autonomy in second language learning and become more efficient long-life learners. For instance, the ten most frequent phrasal verbs in spoken American English are: *go on, come back, come up, go back, come out, find out, go out, get out, come in,* and *pick up.* Refer to the appendix in Liu (2011, pp. 683–688) for phrasal verbs that are most frequent in spoken or written English.
- *Create mind-mapping systems:* Contrasting one adverbial particle with its specific uses may help students become better equipped. By keeping a growing record of new words and expressions, students will benefit as they gain additional ways of expressing themselves more precisely.

IMPLICATIONS FOR INSTRUCTION

As seen in this chapter, French-speaking ELLs usually face challenges related to some of the specificities of English pronunciation, vocabulary, and grammar structure. However, researchers have well established the importance of interlinguistic transfers or influences during the acquisition of any second or additional language (Cook, 2016). "Transfer is the influence resulting from the similarities and differences between the target language and any other language that has been previously (and perhaps imperfectly) acquired" (Odlin, 1989, p. 27, cited in Yu & Odlin, 2016). Gass and Selinker (1983) provided a consensual definition of language transfer, which refers to the use of primary or additional language knowledge in the acquisition of a second (or additional) language. Therefore, the use of already known languages is now seen as a learning strategy rather than a barrier to encourage students in their language learning journey (Reed & Callie, 2014).

The main strategies that we have addressed in this chapter can be summarized in three central ideas:

- *Using different teaching and learning modalities* (e.g., contrasting, drawing, interacting (Gas et al., 1998), listening, reading, speaking, summarizing, teaching, translating, visualizing, writing);
- *Creating networks in teaching and learning* (e.g., mind-mapping, interconnection between words and ideas, intertextuality, and transdisciplinarity);
- *Using already known languages* through interlinguistic transfers or influences (Cenoz et al., 2001), especially for the learning of vocabulary and grammar structures.

Strategies for Pronunciation

In pronunciation, French-speaking ELLs have to face sounds that do not exist in French, deal with various pronunciations of the same graphemes, and interferences between French and English. While pronunciation should not be the main focus when learning a language since accent often allows people to show their bi/multilingualism positively, it might be interesting for students to learn some differences between speaking/writing/reading in English and French. As sociolinguists, we would like to emphasize that accents should not be seen as an issue but rather as a value of having learned several languages in a lifetime.

A first approach may consist of working on contrastive pronunciation underlining the richness of the English vocalic system. Educators should make sure that they are presenting ELLs with diverse variations of the English pronunciation. Pronunciation tasks should focus on sounds that are particularly difficult for French speakers, such as the /h/ including words containing "wh-," the "th-" articulating in /θ/ and /ð/, and the three realizations of the "-s."

By contrasting French and English pronunciations, teachers are helping second language (L2) students eliminate negative transfers (i.e., direct transfers from the sounds of French to English) when the realization of these sounds should be different (e.g., particularly cognates such as hesitation, tradition, university). Therefore, a second step consists of learning the correct realization of these sounds in English. To improve the identification and the production of novel sounds in English, Iverson et al. (2012) suggested five to ten sessions of high variability training (i.e., a set of words presenting a large diversity of realizations of the same graphemes). Another strategy will be to work with minimal pairs (i.e., words that sound different because of one phoneme, here the glottal "h": hair/air/heir, ham/ am, has/as, heat/eat). A further strategy will consist in proposing songs to work on the prosody of the English language (i.e., the rhythm of the language), rather than focusing on the lexicon. As research has shown second language learners can better pronounce when singing (Baills et al., 2021; Good et al., 2015).

Generally speaking, pronunciation tasks will require students to often manipulate and repeat patterns. To better engage students, educators should develop various kinds of activities, including mind-mapping, word clouds, individual and collaborative work while reading and listening to corpora of texts presenting the studied pronunciation traits, and encourage students to record themselves while reading.

Strategies for Vocabulary, Grammar Structure, and Discourse

As developed in the chapter, French-speaking ELLs and their teachers meet several challenges (Thi Diem & Eisuke, 2014) with the teaching and learning of English. In particular, students have to deal with the fact that in English, there is no gender, word agreements do not necessarily work in the same fashion, many expressions using "be" require "have," verbal constructions do not always translate words for words, and word orders and punctuation rules can be very different.

To face their teaching challenges and support their students, educators should use all the possible occasions to highlight the commonalities and the differences between the primary language (French) and the target language (English). For example, teachers can compare and explain some of the traits of both languages, especially when dealing with the English vocabulary, grammar structures, and punctuation rules. Rather than emphasizing differences, stressing similarities between French and English prove to be more efficient. At the elementary level, topics can include French versus English pronunciation, vocabulary, grammar, and basic grammar structures, while at a more advanced level, more complex themes can emerge (e.g., discourse coherence and cohesion, rules of punctuation of complex grammar structures, sociolinguistic variations (i.e., language registers and genres), and cultural "norms" in discourse).

For instance, in the context of vocabulary, cognates are words from different languages of the same linguistic origin. The similarities could be in spelling, pronunciation, and meaning. For example, the word "doctor" in English would be almost the same as in French "*docteur.*" Teachers would then use similarities and words that French-speaking students know to help them learn English. Subtle differences between the two languages are also relevant to notice: some words might look the same, but their definitions would be slightly different. They are called false friends (Inkpen et al., 2005).

One activity on cognates may consist of students reading and exploring several texts containing examples of English and French cognates. Teachers can then ask students to find similar words in English and French. In groups, students can then write them down on sticky notes. All sticky notes can then be added to the board for future reference. Teachers can then discuss the spelling of those cognates to make sure that they are written adequately in both languages. Another essential aspect to bear in mind when teaching ELLs vocabulary is that second language students acquire vocabulary best through comprehensible input, which means that using drawing or communicating thanks to body language to communicate and make the message understood remains one of the best second language teaching and learning strategy (Krashen, 1989, 2003).

Educators should be aware that when students make mistakes, there could be a language transfer. However, there is no point in putting the students down for such matters; it simply means more practice and awareness are needed for the students. Guided by their teachers or working collaboratively with peers on their pronunciation, vocabulary, sentence structures, and discourse, ELLs can gradually shift toward self-assessing and correcting their errors in their English reading, speaking, interacting, and writing.

CONCLUSION

In sum, throughout this chapter, we explored and demonstrated how knowing French can help or even benefit the learning of English as a second or additional language in today's multilingual world. Of course, being bilingual or multilingual also means that one will be code-switching, and languages will interfere with each other. Translanguaging (Cenoz & Gorter, 2020; Garcia & Wei, 2014; Wei, 2018) exists in all classrooms where students will use their knowledge to learn something new (Creese & Blackledge, 2010). We also discussed the specificities of the French language that could help teachers better understand why French-speaking ELLs make specific errors. Moreover, this chapter also presented a reflection for future teachers as they prepare and get ready to teach English to students from diverse linguistic and cultural backgrounds and anticipate ways of including them in their teaching practices. In the end, we provided some examples supported by strategies and tips on where to start.

REFERENCES

Baills, F., Zhang, Y., Cheng, Y., Bu, Y., & Prieto, P. (2021). Listening to songs and singing benefitted initial stages of second language pronunciation but not recall of word meaning. *Language Learning, 71*(2), 369–413.

Cenoz, J., & Gorter, D. (2020). Pedagogical translanguaging: An introduction. *System, 92*, 102269. http://dx.doi.org/10.1016/j.system.2020.102269.

Cenoz, J., Hufeisen, B., & Jessner, U. (2001). *Cross-linguistic influence in third language acquisition: Psycholinguistic perspectives*. Multilingual Matters.

Chaira, S. (2015). Interference of first language in pronunciation of English segmental sounds. *English Education Journal, 6*(4), 469–483. http://www.jurnal.unsyiah.ac.id/EEJ/article/view/2856.

Chutel, L. (2018). French is now the fifth most spoken world language and growing—Thanks to Africans. *World Economic Forum*. https://www.weforum.org/agenda/2018/10/french-is-now-the-fifth-most-spoken-world-language-and-growing-thanks-to-africans.

Cook, V. (2016). Transfer and the relationships between the languages of multi-competence. In R. A. Alonso (Ed.), *Crosslinguistic influence in second language acquisition* (pp. 24–37). Multilingual Matters.

Creese, A., & Blackledge, A. (2010). Translanguaging in the bilingual classroom: A pedagogy for learning and teaching? *The Modern Language Journal, 94*(1), 103–115.

Derakhsan, A., & Karimi, E. (2015). The interference of first language and second language acquisition. *Theory and practice in language studies, 5*(10), 2112–2117. http://dx.doi.org/10.17507/tpls.0510.19.

Fatemi, M. A., Sobhani, A., & Abolhassani, H. (2012). Difficulties of Persian learners of English pronouncing some English consonant clusters. *World Journal of English Language, 2*(4), 69–75. https://doi.org/10.5430/wjel.v2n4p69.

Garcia, O., & Wei, L. (2014). *Translanguaging: Language, bilingualism and education*. Palgrave Macmillan.

Gass, S. (1987). The resolution of conflicts among competing systems: A bidirectional perspective. *Applied Psycholinguistics, 8*(4), 329–350. https://doi.org/10.1017/S0142716400000369.

Gass, S., & Selinker, L. (Eds.). (1983). *Language transfer in language learning*. Newbury House.

Gass, S. M., Mackey, A., & Pica, T. (1998). The Role of input and interaction in second language acquisition: Introduction to the special issue. *Modern Language Journal, 82*(3), 299–307.

Good, A. J., Russo, F. A., & Sullivan, J. (2015). The efficacy of singing in foreign-language learning. *Psychology of Music, 43*(5), 627–640.

Guidry, L. (2022). How many Cajun French words do you know? Many fear it's a dying language. *Lafayette Daily Advertiser*. https://www.theadvertiser.com/story/news/2022/03/07/french-language-month-preserves-acadianas-very-precious-commodity-immersion-codofil-louisiana/9361750002/.

Hernandez, E. L., Dietrich, S. L., & Bauman, K. J. (2022). *What languages does the United States speak? A geographic analysis of the languages spoken at home in the United States, 2015–2019*. https://www.census.gov/content/dam/Census/library/visualizations/2022/demo/Poster%20PAA%202022%20Language%20Geographic%20Distribution_20220323.pdf.

Inkpen, D., Frunza, O., & Kondrak, G. (2005). Automatic identification of cognates and false friends in French and English. In *Proceedings of the international conference recent advances in natural language processing* (Vol. 9, pp. 251–257).

Iverson, P., Pinet, M., & Evans, B. G. (2012). Auditory training for experienced and inexperienced second-language learners: Native French speakers learning English vowels. *Appl Psycholing, 33*, 145–160. https://doi.org/10.1017/S0142716411000300.

Jarvis, S., & Pavlenko, A. (2008). *Crosslinguistic influence in language and cognition*. Routledge.

Karim, K., & Nassaji, H. (2013). First language transfer in second language writing: An examination of current research. *Iranian Journal of Language Teaching Research, 1*(1), 117–134.

Koffi, E. (2015). The pronunciation of voiceless TH in seven varieties of L2 Englishes: Focus on intelligibility. *Linguistic Portfolios, 4*(1), 1–23.

Krashen, S. (1989). We acquire vocabulary and spelling by reading: Additional evidence for the input hypothesis. *Modern Language Journal, 73*, 440–464.

Krashen, S. (2003). *Explorations in language acquisition and use: The Taipei lectures.* Heinemann.

Leblanc, R. (1989). Le curriculum multidimensionnel: une approche intégrée pour l'enseignement de la langue seconde. *Études de Linguistique Appliquée, 75*, 78–94.

Lippi-Green, R. (2011). *English with an accent: Language, ideology, and discrimination in the United States* (2nd ed.). Routledge.

Liu, D. (2011). The most frequently used English phrasal verbs in American and British English: A multicorpus examination. *TESOL Quarterly, 45*(4), 661–688.

Lodge, A. (2013). *French: From dialect to standard.* Routledge.

Lorenzi, J., & Batalova, J. (2022). Sub-Saharan African immigrants in the United States. *Migration Policy Institute.* https://www.migrationpolicy.org/article/sub-saharan-african-imammmigrants-united-states-2019.

Nabine, G. (2013). La prononciation des consonnes anglaises chez les apprenants francophones: le cas des élèves de troisième. *ANADISS, 15*, 140–153.

Odlin, T. (1989). *Language transfer: Cross-linguistic influence in language learning.* Cambridge University Press.

Organisation Internationale de la Francophonie. (2022). *La langue française rayonne avec 321 millions de locuteurs dans le monde.* https://www.francophonie.org/la-langue-francaise-rayonne-avec-321-millions-de-locuteurs-dans-le-monde-2140.

Reed, T., & Callie, M. (2014). Teaching for transfer: Insights from theory and practices in primary-level French-Second-Language classrooms. *McGill Journal of Education/Revue Des Sciences de l'Éducation de McGill, 49*(2), 399–416. https://mje.mcgill.ca/article/view/9101.

Ringbom, H., & Jarvis, S. (2009). The importance of crosslinguistic similarity in foreign language learning. In M. H. Long & C. J. Doughty (Eds.), *The handbook of language teaching* (pp. 106–118). Blackwell.

Ruiz Soto, A. G., Hooker, S., & Batalova, J. (2015). *Top languages spoken by English language learners nationally and by state.* Migration Policy Institute.

Storybooks Canada. (n.d.). Retrieved July 9, 2022, from https://www.storybooks-canada.ca/.

Tessonneau, A.-L. (1983). Le continuum intra-linguistique créole et le pouvoir du langage dans la société paysanne haïtienne. *Langage & société, 26*, 51–61.

Thi Diem, H. K., & Eisuke, S. (2014). Challenges confronting teachers of English language learners. *Educational Review, 66*(2), 210–225. https://doi.org/10.1080/00131911.2013.769425.

US Census Bureau. (2020). *2016–2020 American Community survey 5-year estimates.* https://www.census.gov/newsroom/press-releases/2022/acs-5-year-estimates.html.

Wei, L. (2018). Translanguaging as a practical theory of language. *Applied Linguistics, 39*(1), 9–30. https://doi.org/10.1093/applin/amx039.

Yu, L., & Odlin, T. (Eds.). (2016). *New perspectives on transfer in second language learning.* Multilingual Matters.

Chapter 11

American English Language Acquisition among Filipino Learners

Language, Literacy, and Identity

Eric B. Claravall and Maria Selena Protacio

In the 2019 data, around 4.2 million Filipinos, foreign and native-born, lived in the United States (Pew Research Center, 2021). Filipinos are the third-largest Asian origin immigrant group in the United States following Asian origin immigrant groups from China and India. Filipinos make up 18 percent of the Asian population in the United States, and of these 17 percent of the Filipino population are school-aged children. Unfortunately, Filipino children are typically underrepresented in the literature on multilingual learners (Kieffer & Lesaux, 2012).

This chapter grounds its discussion on U.S.-born and immigrant Filipino children's English language learning processes within the sociolinguistic framework. In particular, we highlight the role of history and culture on the linguistic identity of U.S.-born Filipino students and the challenges of learning the dominant variety of American English (i.e., "Standard" American English) as a language of power for immigrant Filipino students. Language forms the structure of our thinking and lays the foundation for literacy development (Bruner, 1986). How we think and the way we articulate our thinking are the products of our early socialization at home (Gee, 2012).

In the case of the Filipino experience, both in the United States and in the Philippines, the colonial thinking around the concept of whiteness and other cultural artifacts associated with whiteness are positioned—consciously or unconsciously—supreme (David & Nadal, 2013). This chapter briefly describes the convoluted colonial history of the Philippines and how this affects the language and cultural identity of Filipino learners in the United States. Ultimately, this chapter offers tangible steps toward decolonizing pedagogies to engage Filipino learners and their families in culturally sustaining literacy practices in the classroom.

SOCIOHISTORICAL CONTEXT

The Philippines has a long and complicated relationship with the United States. After the Spanish-American War in 1898, Spain turned over the Philippine archipelago to the United States as part of the peace agreement stipulated in the Treaty of Paris (Grenville & Berkeley Young, 1966). From then on, the United States colonized the Philippines and developed an American system of public education where English was introduced as a medium of instruction. Under McKinley's presidency, the Philippine Commission, also known as Schurman Commission, was established to advance the American ideals of democracy and civilization in the islands (Hsu, 2012). Around 1,074 American teachers, known as the Thomasites among the locals, fulfilled this mandate of colonizing the minds of Filipinos through education at the beginning of the twentieth century. Hence, the American system of public education, as an "advanced" system of education, was introduced.

The education and language policies played an influential role in the colonization process in the Philippines and the authorization of academic practices based on "the ideology of white racial domination" (Hsu, 2012, p. 49), thereby, delegitimizing the indigenous Filipino ways of being, knowing, and thinking. The American colonial policies on education in the Philippines were instrumental to the subjugation of Filipino minds. American English became the privileged language in school. Students read stories that were remote from their own lived experiences. They read the literary works of Henry Wadsworth Longfellow, Washington Irving, Ralph Waldo Emerson, and other American literary canons (Martin, 2012). This cultural transmission through language and texts led to the adoption of American values, subscription to the ideals of western civilization, and the development of apathy toward nationalism—a miseducation of Filipino youths as Constantino (1970b) intimated in an influential article in the Philippines.

American culture continues to influence the ways of life in the Philippines, particularly the ubiquitous use of English by middle/upper class and educated Filipinos. English as a colonial language has become an intricate part of the linguistic diversity in the Philippines. The 1987 Philippine constitution acknowledged English as an official language alongside Filipino, the national language. Because of their strong English skills and historical ties with the United States, Filipino immigrants have the advantage to thrive living in the United States (Gallardo & Batalova, 2020). Many immigrant Filipino parents use English when speaking with their children at home. Thus, among those ages five years and older, 84 percent are English proficient (Pew Research Center, 2021).

This high level of English proficiency can project a misleading impression that Filipino American children are doing just fine and do not require any additional language support in schools. In fact, Filipino American learners are impacted by the model minority myth (Cunanan et al., 2008). The model minority perpetuates a general idea that Asian Americans are "America's greatest success story" (Wu, 2013, p. 232). According to this myth, Asian Americans' politeness and hard work have led them to achieve academic excellence, entrepreneurial acumen, giftedness in mathematics and science, and exceptional talent in music. However, Asian American success is not monolithic. Because of the model minority myth, some Asian students may not receive the support they need since educators may believe the stereotype that all Asians are high achieving students and do not need any guidance. In the Filipino American context, Filipinos "have lower rates of college completion within subgroups defined by age cohort, sex, region of birth, and the race/ethnicity of their parents" (Ong & Viernes, 2012, p. 33). Unfortunately, there is a paucity of research that addresses the English language needs of Filipino American children (Kieffer & Lesaux, 2012).

A BRIEF HISTORY OF FILIPINO

The Philippines has eight major languages predominantly spoken across the archipelago—Tagalog, Cebuano, Ilokano, Hiligaynon, Bikol, Samar-Leyte, Kapangpangan, and Pangasinan (McFarland, 2008). Given the geographical features of the Philippines and the multicultural aspects of Philippine society that led to the diversity of spoken languages, the Commission on Filipino Language was established in 1991 to institutionalize a lingua franca, as well as to officially standardize a national language for oral and written communication. Filipino became the official national language and lingua franca of the country. Filipino is predominantly based on Tagalog, the language spoken in central and southern Luzon, the largest island in the Philippines and where Manila—the capital of the country—is located. In the United States, the government still uses Tagalog as the language to mark when Filipino immigrants fill out legal forms and census data. This should be changed. All Filipino immigrants speak Filipino, in addition to the other languages spoken in different regions of the country. This makes all Filipinos multilinguals.

The U.S. influence on Filipino ways of speaking is more far-reaching than that of Spain because of the colonial language policies rooted in the Philippine educational system (Leonardo & Matias, 2012). Many Filipinos use American English in their colloquial conversation. The morpho-phonological system of English has been assimilated into the Filipino language (e.g., budget/badyet; correct/korek) since 1945 (Wolff, 1996). Most of these words are used in academic and social discourse. As a remnant of the U.S. colonial policies, English continues to occupy a privileged status in Philippine society.

It is used as one of the official languages in schools in the Philippines along-side the Filipino language. English is typically the medium of instruction in math and science. English is also a separate subject in schools where grammar and literature written in English are taught. In colleges and universities in the Philippines, both Filipino and English are also the official languages of instruction. Even if English is taught in schools in the Philippines, the quality of instruction and levels of English proficiency vary widely.

The development of Filipino, like any language, has gone through many transformations from how Tagalog was used before Spanish colonization to become the basis for developing a lingua franca that is now known as Filipino. Around 20 percent of the Filipino lexicon is derived from Spanish (Quilis & Casado Fresnillo, 2008). The early trading relationships with neighboring Asian countries, the Spanish subjugation of the natives in the archipelago, and the U.S. imposition of the English language in the education system contributed to the richness of Filipino as a national language. However, language and thought intersect. The privileging of English as an intellectual and elite language in the Philippines has created a conceptual dilemma.

English in the Philippines: A Colonial Artifact or a Variety of English?

English has been widely spoken in the Philippines since the American colonial era. When the United States transferred its governance to Filipinos in 1945, the use of English as a language policy in education and government remained unchanged. This policy has been criticized since the American colonial era (Bernardo, 2008). English was seen as an instrument of intellectual subjugation and cultural alienation (Constantino, 1970a). English became the vehicle to teach Filipinos "the moral and civic values of American democracies" (Hsu, 2012, p. 54). This colonial curriculum has continued to influence the contemporary system of education in the Philippines. English brought a caste system into the sociocultural experiences of Filipinos. English has become the language of the Filipino elites and the language of power (Tupas, 2008). Native languages in the Philippines are treated as inferior. When one speaks English, they are perceived as smart and highly educated. The growing Filipino nationalism after World War II led to the establishment of a national language—*Pilipino*, which, in 1987, was renamed *Filipino* to reflect the multilingual context of the Philippines (Martin, 2012). Toward the end of the twentieth century, there was a move to decolonize higher education and embrace the Filipino language as the language of the academy (Enriquez, 1994; Salazar, 1999). Filipino nationalists and scholars advocated for the use of Filipino in the teaching of natural science, social science, and mathematics. Despite this nationalistic move, English remained a dominant language in education, politics, commerce, and entertainment (Canieso-Doronila, 1989; Sibayan & Gonzalez, 1996; Tupas, 2001).

The colonial markings of English in the minds of Filipinos have organically morphed into a variety of English that is uniquely spoken in the Philippines. Gonzalez (1996) described the nuance of Philippine English in terms of pronunciation, grammar, and vocabulary. According to Gonzalez (1996), "educated Filipinos aim at an American English accent but have varying success with the vowel contrasts in *sheep/ship, full/fool*, and *boat/bought*" (p. 89). For example, someone would say "I'm *full na*," where one pronounces full as /fool/. Philippine English grammar is tautological (Gonzalez et al., 2004). In one of the leading newspapers in the Philippines—*The Philippine Daily Inquirer*—an author of an article wrote "If I *will be the one who will talk* and explain, that will be self-serving" (Roque, 2007, para. 9). Lexical innovation has also been observed when Filipinos speak English (Bolton & Butler, 2008). Local languages are inserted in the sentence to create new vocabulary; for example, someone may write, "The storm yesterday destroyed the *nipa hut* that I built." *Nipa hut* is an indigenous house that is made of bamboo, coconut tree, and dried grass. *Nipa hut* is the English translation of the Tagalog word *bahay kubo*. In the American English context, *nipa hut* is called stilt house or thatched house.

Another example of lexical innovation is the colloquial use of the word *salvage* in Philippine English, meaning to kill someone. The etymology of the word, based on corroborated blog posts, can be traced to Marcos's dictatorship in the 1970s. The military men loyal to the former president created a code word for extrajudicial killing of Filipino activists and others who opposed government policies. The word also has visual and auditory similarity with the Spanish loan word *salvaje* (wicked, savage, and abusive). Hence, Filipinos use the word *salvage* differently from its standard English meaning. Finally, there are many English colloquial expressions that are germane to the Philippine context. For example, "I'm getting high-blood" (I am getting angry).

Immigrating to the United States at a school age, many young Filipinos have been exposed to English vocabulary and syntax during their initial schooling in the Philippines. However, social class may influence Filipino students' attitudes toward and dispositions for speaking English (Darvin, 2017). Middle to upper class and highly educated parents tend to favor English when communicating to their offspring at a very young age. This early exposure to the English language provides a head start among many immigrant Filipino children when learning to speak, read, and write English in the United States. However, Filipino immigrant students from lower social classes will not have had much exposure to the English language in Philippine public schools and may need more English language development instruction.

Undoubtedly, Philippine English is an artifact of colonial education and a product of sociolinguistic evolution. Language is a dynamic process that the users continuously adapt and accommodate to enhance communicative intent. In the Philippine context, English is the language of power and prestige. The code-mixing of local languages into English has led to the development of Philippine English as part of world English (Tupas, 2001).

KEY PRINCIPLES RELATED TO
THE FILIPINO LANGUAGE

Filipino belongs to the Austronesian group of languages and is considered a transparent language. Like Spanish, each sound is heard in spoken words. Filipino children learn to read and write using the Tagalog alphabet called the *Abakada*, the foundation of Filipino morphology. It is composed of 5 short vowels and 15 consonants. These letters are articulated phonetically and mapped out in written form using the syllabic system of reading.

The Filipino morphology (i.e., word structure) has affixes, mostly prefixes (e.g., ma-, pa-) and a few suffixes (e.g., -in and -an). However, Filipino is one of those unique languages that uses infixes (e.g., -um), a meaningful string of letters that are attached in the middle of the word (Aronoff & Fudeman, 2005). Some suffixes like -*in* can also function as an infix. Filipino immigrant students who have a heightened awareness of Filipino morphology may be able to transfer their linguistic knowledge to understand English morphology during reading (Kieffer & Lesaux, 2012). Many of these affixes have been added to some English words creating a hybrid lexicon. For example, in this utterance *patext naman sa cell phone mo* (Can I please send a text message to someone on your cell phone?), notice that the word *patext* has a prefix *pa-* and the English word *text*. A morphological characteristic of Filipino words that is absent in English is reduplication (Aronoff & Fudeman, 2005). Consider the base words *tawa* (laugh) and *galing* (excellent). These words are repeated twice to signify superlative or exaggerated action.

This kind of morphological awareness can sometimes transfer to English like in this response made by a former Filipina delegate to Miss Universe: "In my 22 years of existence there is nothing *major major* problem I've done because I'm confident in myself and my family" (*CBS News*, 2010, para. 3).

The mixing of the English lexicon into the Filipino linguistic system demonstrates the long-standing impact of the U.S. colonial policies in the Philippines. As we referenced earlier about the role of language in shaping the mind, the use of English in the Philippines proliferates colonial mentality and can be a factor for social stratification. English has become the preferred language by the elites and the educated Filipinos, which marginalizes the poor and the uneducated speakers of local languages. However, because of the globalized use of English in commerce, tourism, and digital/social media, competency in English can be advantageous to Filipinos. This is mostly true for Filipinos immigrating to the United States.

INFLUENCES OF THE FILIPINO LANGUAGE IN ACQUIRING ENGLISH

While many new immigrant Filipino children come to the United States with basic knowledge of English, the phonological and lexical systems of Filipino could affect students' communicative competence in learning standard American English. As previously discussed, the key principles of the Filipino language may influence how Filipino English learners acquire and master standard American English. The following are some examples of possible influences of the Filipino language.

First, the Filipino language is gender-neutral. Pronouns in the Filipino language are not gendered. Hence, Filipino English learners could initially have a difficult time using gendered pronouns and ignore the use of he/she when speaking. It may also be common for Filipino English learners to interchange *she* and *he* as they are beginning to learn the language.

Second, in Filipino, the word *mga* in front of a word indicates that it is plural and the base word next to it does not change. When learning the inflectional rule in English that -s or -es is added to a word to denote plurality, Filipino English learners may overuse this and add -s or -es to words that have no plural forms. An example may be saying "That is a lot of information*s* I learned today."

Third, there are English phonemes that are uncommon in the Filipino language, causing Filipino English learners to have problems articulating some English words. The most common English phonemes that Filipinos struggle with are /f/, /v/, and /th/. It is common for Filipinos to pronounce words with an /f/ with /p/ such as pronouncing the word *pine* when they actually say *fine* or saying *pour* when they mean to say *four*. They may also struggle with /v/ and substitute /b/. For example, a teacher may think a student is saying *berry* when they are actually saying *very*. Students may also initially struggle with pronouncing the digraph /th/. For instance, when trying to pronounce *three*, the student might say *tree*. At times, this could also sound like /d/ such as the student is saying *dare* when they are saying *there*. For vowels, Filipino has only five vowel sounds. This can influence the way Filipino students articulate English words with short and long vowel sounds. Words like *book, feet, fool, back* are pronounced using the Filipino vowel system. It is important to recognize these pronunciation patterns so that teachers, especially those in the early grades, do not count these as miscues when conducting running records.

Fourth, when initially learning English, Filipino students may have a difficult time with the different tenses of verbs, particularly irregular verbs. As mentioned earlier, Filipino is one of the rare languages that use infixes. In the Filipino language, the past tense is either signified by an infix such as in the word *gawa* or "to do" which becomes *ginawa* or "I did" by inserting the infix *in*. In some cases, the prefix *na* is added to the base word. From the previous example, a person could say *Nagawa ko na* or "I did it." Irregular verbs do not really exist so this may cause confusion for Filipino students who are learning English. In addition, when indicating future events, the Filipino language does not really utilize a future tense. Rather, speakers share specifically when they will do something by saying *mamaya* (later) or *bukas* (tomorrow).

Fifth, Filipinos in the Philippines use a variety of English that is grammatically correct but not typically used in conversation in the United States. For example, Filipinos would say "close the light" (i.e., turn off the lights). A newly arrived student may ask the teacher where the "comfort room" or "CR" is, referring to the bathroom. A Filipino student may ask their teacher for a "Pentel pen"; they are requesting a permanent marker. If someone asks a student if they want a popsicle, some Filipino students may not understand what it means because they might know it by the term "ice drop" instead. As a final example, if someone asks a Filipino student how they are and they reply by saying they are "bad trip," they mean annoyed or frustrated. These examples show that even if Filipino students may be using English words, the meaning of these might not be readily apparent to non-Filipinos.

Finally, pragmatics is an area that could affect how newcomer immigrant students use English in the classroom. For instance, in the Philippines, it is common for students to refer to their teachers, or someone with authority, as Ma'am or Sir rather than Mr, Ms, or Mrs along with the last name. In some schools, students use Teacher plus the teacher's first name (e.g., Teacher Anna or Teacher Ian). The use of these words reflects Filipino values of respect for authority or elders. The use of *po* and *opo*, for example, is commonly heard in a conversation between young children and adults. *Po* is usually attached to the end of the initial sentence, which denotes respect to the receiver of the message. *Opo* means yes in a respectful manner. Thus, new immigrant students may unconsciously include these words when speaking to their teachers.

U.S.-BORN FILIPINOS

As discussed, Filipino families in the United States tend to utilize English in their homes and, as a result, second-generation Filipinos often do not speak the language. Some may have receptive knowledge of Filipino, but they are unable to speak it. Those who learned to speak Filipino at a young age lose it when they enter school (Mendoza Strobel, 2015). In an interview study with ten Filipino families living in a Midwestern state, nine of the families shared that their children could only speak English (Protacio, 2017). Of these nine families, seven of them were being raised in households where both parents were first-generation Filipino immigrants who spoke Filipino as the primary language to one another but used English with their children.

Several of these families initially tried to introduce the Filipino language to their children but were not able to sustain using it for various reasons. One Filipina who was married to a White American initially wanted her firstborn to learn Filipino. For the first 18 months of his life, he was exposed to both English and Tagalog. However, the mother noticed her son was experiencing speech delays, and thus she decided to just use English because she suspected that learning two languages may be related to his speech delays. This, by the way, is not scientifically supported. Empirical studies have shown that learning two languages improves metalinguistic awareness (Bialystok, 2001). Research has unfortunately shown, however, that at times, learning new language results in subtractive bilingualism, that is, learning English can lead to individual's forgetting one's native language (Lightbown & Spada, 2014). The goal would be additive bilingualism where learning a new language can lead to an individual's proficiency in two or more languages.

In another case, a mother started teaching her children Filipino words, but this was not sustained (Protacio, 2017). She shared that she felt guilty for not having the perseverance to teach her children the Filipino language. In another family, a Filipino father shared that his daughter does not identify as Filipino. Even though she knows her heritage is Filipino, she connects more with the American culture. The father also shared they raised her to speak English and not Filipino since they did not want her to feel confused about the language to use.

Colonialism and inferiorization are considered among the many reasons why U.S.-born Filipinos do not speak any of the Philippine languages or lose the language when they enter school. English is viewed as a superior language and a necessity to succeed in mainstream U.S. society (Mendoza Strobel, 2015). This affects the overall identity development of second-generation Filipino Americans and how they may miss the opportunity to learn Filipino as part of their developmental experience as Filipinos in the United States. In defining who they are as Americans, the language is a contentious factor (Tuason et al., 2007).

IMPLICATIONS FOR TEACHERS

When students' home language is Filipino, or one of the Filipino languages (e.g., Cebuano, Ilokano, Ilonggo, or Tagalog), we encourage teachers to view this as additive to Filipino American students' classroom experiences in learning English. Rather than emphasizing only English acquisition, educators can illustrate they value students' native languages and honor students' sociocultural capitals, which is an important aspect of practices that are aligned with decolonizing pedagogy. In this section, we provide recommendations and strategies teachers can use to support Filipino students' language and literacy development.

Leverage Students' Linguistic and Cultural Backgrounds

The legacy of colonialism affects language use and cultural identity among Filipinos (David & Nadal, 2013). To counter this legacy, sharing time (or show-and-tell using cultural artifacts) is an effective way to highlight and leverage multilingual learners' linguistic and cultural backgrounds in the classroom (Synder & Staehr-Fenner, 2021). In one study (Protacio & Edwards, 2015), Aiza, a first-grade Filipina student, selected three artifacts about the Philippines for sharing time. Her father came dressed in a *barong* Tagalog, and she wore a *Maria Clara* dress. Both garments are worn for special occasions in the Philippines. Aiza also shared the Philippine flag and currency. When given more guidance focused on highlighting cultural heritage, Aiza and her family were able to collaboratively plan her second presentation to (1) develop her oral presentation skills, which is one of the main purposes of the sharing time activity, and (2) purposefully choose artifacts that were more significant to Aiza's native culture. This presentation stirred Aiza and her classmates' interest in Philippine culture.

Furthermore, teachers can create a cultural heritage corner in the classroom to showcase artifacts for a period of time. In 1993, the U.S. Congress declared October as Filipino American History Month. To celebrate this in the classroom, teachers can build an exhibition of Filipino artifacts such as crafts, music, photos, and books. They can engage students about the political, social, and cultural importance of these artifacts (Vasquez et al., 2013). The Filipino student, family member, and/or community member can act as a "museum docent" to answer questions or tell some stories about the artifact. As teachers guide students in the discussion of these artifacts, they can emphasize diversity, differences, privilege, and (dis)advantages (Vasquez et al., 2013).

Identify Students' Home Language Backgrounds

Majority of Filipino families in the United States do not teach the Filipino language to their children, in an effort to support assimilation into the dominant culture. Thus, it is important that teachers delve into their students' background to determine what language their students actually speak at home, rather than solely relying on the home language survey, which asks what language is spoken at home. As an example, Selena (second author) was placed in a newcomer ESL class when she was in fifth grade. Her mom noted Tagalog in the home language survey. However, Selena was already fluent and proficient in English at that time, and this limited her opportunities for deeper academic learning. Administering a home language survey is not sufficient. Educators could interview students and probe what language they use at home and to whom they speak this language (Domke & Cárdenas Curiel, 2020). Teachers can also utilize formative assessments and observations. Collectively, all of this information will help educators determine students' need for English language development services.

The inverse is also true. Families may indicate that English is the primary language spoken at home, yet if teachers observe students struggle in learning English, they may discuss with the family why English language development classes may be helpful for the students, while also supporting the students' primary language development at home.

Encourage Families to Maintain the Filipino Language

Teachers should encourage Filipino parents to maintain the Filipino language at home. Studies (e.g., Bialystok, 2010) have shown that bi/multilingualism benefits students' cognitive functioning—higher executive function, more mental flexibility, and attentional control. Bilingual learners also have greater job and business opportunities, and better earnings and occupational mobility (Office of English Language Acquisition, 2020). Wong-Fillmore (1991) argued against *subtractive bilingualism*, students learning a new language at the expense of their first language. Teachers need to promote *additive bilingualism*, students developing their first language while simultaneously learning a new language. Educators need to create a school environment where linguistic diversity is emphasized and appreciated (Martinez et al., 2018). In addition, if teachers can speak another language, they are encouraged to share the experience of learning the language with the students to send a message that bi/multilingualism is honored and valued in the classroom.

Incorporate Diverse Texts in Curriculum

A significant aspect of culturally responsive teaching is to have texts, lessons, and units that reflect the backgrounds and perspectives of all students, not just those from the dominant culture (Lee, 2001). Intentionally include culturally responsive books in the classroom libraries that positively reflect Filipino experiences. Choose stories that highlight Filipino culture and avoid stories that stereotype Filipino families. Select a book—for example, *Hello, Universe*—to read aloud where the main character is Filipino to engage the student's imagination and foster a positive self-concept. Bishop (1990) discusses the importance of having diverse children's literature that would serve as mirrors, windows, and sliding glass doors for students. Texts that reflect the Filipino experiences would serve as mirrors for the Filipino and Filipino American students in the class, and they would also serve as windows for students from other cultural backgrounds. See the textbox below for examples of books that would serve as mirrors for Filipino and Filipino American students that were written by Filipino authors.

ANNOTATED BIBLIOGRAPHY OF BOOKS BY AND ABOUT FILIPINOS

Annotated Bibliography

Entrada Kelley, E. (2017). *Hello, Universe*. Green Willow Books. This Newbery Award-winning fiction book provides multivocal narratives from three middle-school students whose lives intersect in an uncanny event. Virgil Salinas, the central character, is Filipino American and deaf. Kaori Tanaka is Japanese American and a self-proclaimed psychic. Valencia Somerset is also deaf and goes to the same resource class as Virgil. The central themes of the story are friendship, intersectionality, diversity, and cultural identity.

Mabalon, D. B., Romasanta, G., & Sibayan, A. (2018). *Journey for Justice: The Life of Larry Itliong*. Bridge and Delta Publishing. This book introduces the readers to the life of a Filipino immigrant farm worker in California. His desire to improve the life of Filipino farm workers had led to his co-founding of the United Farmworkers Union. This is the first American history book written about the triumph and struggles of Filipino American farmworkers in the twentieth century.

Ribay, R. (2019). *Patron Saints of Nothing*. Penguin Young Readers Group. This National Book Award finalist young adult novel tells the story of Jay Reguero, a 17-year-old Filipino American, who finds out that his cousin in the Philippines was killed in the president's war on drugs. Jay travels to the Philippines to find out more about what really happened to his cousin. This novel addresses compassion, Filipino ways of life, immigrant identity development, family dynamics, and the irony of joy when one returns to their heritage country.

In addition, students should have access to bilingual resources (e.g., Filipino-English dictionaries or online translators). This would allow newcomer Filipino students to have access to their native language to ensure that they are able to use their knowledge of Filipino while they are learning American English. This is particularly important given research showing that an individual's first language facilitates their learning of a second or additional language (Cummins, 1991).

CONCLUSION

We end this chapter with a call for decolonizing pedagogies in language and literacy for Filipino children in the United States. We encourage teachers to provide Filipino students with spaces for sharing their cultural heritage and honoring the linguistic diversity of the Philippines. Language is the soul of culture, and culture is essential to the development of children's identities. When one (un)consciously subscribes to the colonial idea that the dominant variety of English is superior risks being a co-conspirator in perpetuating hierarchical language frames. Decolonizing the ways we think about language choice and use can be made possible by when promoting bilingualism and multilingualism at home and in the classroom (OELA, 2020). Decentering whiteness in the curriculum and highlighting literature that has culturally affirming narratives can potentially develop a robust Filipino American identity.

REFERENCES

Aronoff, M., & Fudeman, K. (2005). *What is morphology?* Blackwell Publishing.

Bernardo, A. B. I. (2008). English in the Philippine education: Solution or problem? In M. L. S. Bautista & K. Bolton (Eds.), *Philippine English: Linguistic and literary perspective* (pp. 29–48). Hong Kong University Press.

Bialystok, E. (2001). *Bilingualism in development: Language, literacy, & cognition.* Cambridge University Press.

Bialystok, E. (2010). Bilingualism. *Cognitive Science, 1*, 559–572. https://doi.org/10.1002/wcs.43.

Bishop, R. S. (1990). Mirrors, windows, and sliding glass doors. *Perspectives: Choosing and Using Books for the Classroom, 6*(3), ix–xi.

Bolton, K., & Butler, S. (2008). Lexicography and the description of Philippine English vocabulary. In M. L. S. Bautista & K. Bolton (Eds.), *Philippine English: Linguistic and literary perspective* (pp. 175–200). Hong Kong University Press.

Bruner, J. (1986). *Actual minds, possible worlds.* Harvard University Press.

Canieso-Doronila, M. L. (1989). *The limits of educational change: National identity formation in a Philippine public elementary school.* University of the Philippines Press.

CBS News. (2010, August 25). *Miss Philippines Venus Raj stumbles on question.* https://www.cbsnews.com/news/miss-philippines-venus-raj-stumbled-on-question/.

Constantino, R. (1970a). *Dissent and counter-consciousness.* Malaya.

Constantino, R. (1970b). The mis-education of the Filipino. *Journal of Contemporary Asia, 1*(1), 20–36.

Cummins, J. (1991). Interdependence of first- and second-language proficiency in bilingual children). In E. Bialystok (Ed.), *Language processing in bilingual children* (pp. 70–89). Cambridge University Press.

Cunanan, V. L., Guerrero, A. P. S., & Minamoto, L.Y. (2008). Filipinos and the myth of model minority in Hawai'i. *Journal of Ethnic and Cultural Diversity in Social Work, 15*, 167–192. https://doi.org/10.1300/J051v15n01_08.

Darvin, R. (2017). Social class and the inequality of English speakers in a globalized world. *Journal of English as a Lingua Franca, 6*, 287–311. https://doi.org/10.1515/jelf-2017-0014.

David, E. J. R., & Nadal, K. L. (2013). The colonial context of Filipino American immigrants' psychological experiences. *Cultural Diversity and Ethnic Minority Psychology, 19*(3), 298–309.

Domke, L. M., & Cárdenas Curiel, L. (2020). There's no one way to be bilingual: Knowing students' language practices. *The Reading Teacher, 74*, 451–455. https://doi.org/10.1002/trtr.1965.

Enriquez, V. G. (1994). *From colonial to liberation psychology: The Philippine experience.* De La Salle University Press.

Gallardo, L. H., & Batalova, J. (2020, July 15). *Filipino immigrants in the United States.* Migration Policy. https://www.migrationpolicy.org/article/filipino-immigrants-united-states-2020#English_Proficiency.

Gee, J. P. (2012). *Social linguistics and literacies: Ideology in discourse* (4th ed.). Routledge.

Gonzalez, A. B. (1996). Philippines English. In M. L. S. Bautista (Ed.), *Readings in Philippine sociolinguistics* (pp. 63–75). De La Salle University Press.

Gonzalez, A. B., Romero, M. C., & Jambalos, T. V. (2004). *Linguistic competence of Filipinos in English across generations.* De La Salle University Press.

Grenville, J. A. S., & Berkeley Young, G. (1966). *Politics, strategy, and American diplomacy: Studies in foreign policy, 1873–1917.* Yale University Press.

Hsu, F. (2012). Colonial lessons: Racial politics of comparison and the development of American education policy in the Philippines. In D. C. Maramba & R. Bonus (Eds.), *The "other students" Filipino Americans, education, and power* (pp. 39–62). Information Age Publishing.

Kieffer, M., & Lesaux, N. (2012). Direct and indirect roles of morphological awareness in the English reading comprehension of native English, Spanish, Filipino, and Vietnamese speakers. *Language Learning, 64*(4), 1170–1204.

Lee, C. D. (2001). Is October Brown Chinese? A cultural modeling activity system for underachieving students. *American Educational Research Journal, 38*(1), 97–141.

Leonardo, Z., & Matias, C. E. (2012). Betwixt and between colonial and postcolonial mentality: The critical education of Filipino Americans. In D. C. Maramba & R. Bonus (Eds.), *The "other students" Filipino Americans, education, and power* (pp. 3–17). Information Age Publishing.

Lightbown, P., & Spada, N. (2014). *How languages are learned* (4th ed.). Oxford University Press.

Martin, I. P. (2012). Diffusion and directions: English language policy in the Philippines. In L. E. Ling & A. Hashim (Eds.), *English in South East Asia: Features, policy, and language in use* (pp. 189–205). Benjamins Publishing Company.

Martinez, D. C., Rojo, J., & Gonzalez, R. A. (2018). Speaking Spanish in White public spaces: Implications for literacy classrooms. *Journal of Adolescent and Adult Literacy*, *62*, 451–454. https://doi.org/10.1002/jaal924.

McFarland, C. D. (2008). Linguistic diversity and English in the Philippines. In M. L. S. Bautista & K. Bolton (Eds.), *Philippine English: Linguistic and literary perspective* (pp. 131–155). Hong Kong University Press.

Mendoza Strobel, L. (2015). *Coming full circle: The process of decolonization among post-1965 Filipino Americans*. The Center for Babaylan Studies.

Office of English Language Acquisition. (OELC, 2020, August 5). *Benefits of multilingualism*. https://ncela.ed.gov/files/announcements/20200805-NCELAInfographic-508.pdf.

Ong, P., & Viernes, K. (2012). Filipino Americans and educational downward mobility. *Asian American Policy Review*, *94*, 21–39.

Pew Research Center. (2021). *Filipinos in the U.S. fact sheet*. https://www.pewresearch.org/social-trends/fact-sheet/asian-americans-filipinos-in-the-u-s/.

Protacio, M. S. (2017, December). *Home language and literacy practices of Filipino parents*. Roundtable presented at the Literacy Research Association Annual Conference, Tampa, FL.

Protacio, M. S., & Edwards, P. A. (2015). Increasing ELLs' parental involvement through sharing time. *The Reading Teacher*, *68*, 413–421. https://doi.org/10.1002/trtr.1327.

Quilis, A., & Casado Fresnillo, C. (2008). *La lengua española en Filipinas: Historia, situación actual, el chabacano, antología de textos*. Consejo Superior de Investigaciones Científicas.

Roque, A. (2007, January 18). *Ecija school faculty bares university exec's mess*. https://web.archive.org/web/20070305032957/http://newsinfo.inquirer.net/inquirerheadlines/regions/view_article.php?article_id=44274.

Salazar, Z. (1991). Ang pantayong pananaw bilang diskursong pangkabihasnan (The pantayo perspective as cultural discourse). In A. Navarro, M. J. Rodriguez, & V. Villan (Eds.), *Pantayong pananaw: Ugat at kabuluhan, pambungad sa pag-aaral ng bagong kasaysayan* (pp. 79–125). Lahi Press.

Sibayan, B., & Gonzalez, A. (1996). Post imperial English in the Philippines: Status change in former British and American colonies, 1940–1990. In A. Fishman, A. W. Conrad, & A. Rubal-Lopez (Eds.), *Bilingual education* (pp. 139–172). Mouton de Gruyter.

Snyder, S., & Staehr-Fenner, D. (2021). *Culturally responsive teaching for multilingual learners: Tools for equity.* Corwin Press.

Tuason, M. T. G., Reyes, A., Rollings, L., Harris, T., & Martin, C. (2007). On both sides of the hyphen: Exploring the Filipino-American identity. *Journal of Counseling Psychology, 54*(4), 362–372.

Tupas, T. R. (2001). Linguistic imperialism in the Philippines: Reflections of an English language teacher of Filipino overseas workers. *The Asia-Pacific Education Researcher, 10*(1), 1–40.

Tupas, T. R. (2008). World Englishes or worlds of English?: Pitfalls of a postcolonial discourse in Philippine English. In M. L. S. Bautista & K. Bolton (Eds.), *Philippine English: Linguistic and literary perspective* (pp. 67–86). Hong Kong University Press.

Vasquez, V. M., Tate, S. L., & Harste, J. C. (2013). *Negotiating critical literacies with teachers: Theoretical foundations and pedagogical resources for pre-service and in-service contexts.* Routledge.

Wolff, J. U. (1996). The character of borrowings from Spanish and English in languages of the Philippines. In M. L. S. Bautista (Ed.), *Readings in Philippine Sociolinguistics* (pp. 63–75). De La Salle University Press.

Wong-Fillmore, L. (1991). When learning a second language means losing the first. *Early Childhood Research Quarterly, 6*, 323–346. https://doi.org/10.1016/S0885-2006(05)80059-6.

Wu, E. D. (2013). *The color of success: Asian Americans and the origins of the model minority.* Princeton University Press.

Chapter 12

Urdu and English

Using the L1 to Influence English Language Learning and Literacy

Rahat Zaidi

Pedagogically, educators might question the role English language learners' (ELLs) primary language can play in their language and literacy learning. Nevertheless, *The Promising Futures Report* (2017) highlights scientific, research-based evidence that disputes the traditional deficit-based learning paradigm for ELLs, proving that their additional language(s) are, in fact, an emotional, cognitive, and academic asset. Acknowledging and using ELLs' primary language within the English and literacy learning process suggest that students have greater confidence in and satisfaction with their learning as well as increased self-esteem, particularly when encouraged to maintain and grow proficiency in their primary language while learning English (Ordona et al., 2017). In addition, there has been some success in North American schools that have used students' existing linguistic knowledge as a resource in authentic learning tasks to effectively prepare students to participate within a global context. However, this linguistically sustaining instruction happens less often than desired, and, currently, educational policies tend to label learners in terms of assets they do not yet possess (i.e., a strong grasp of the English language) (Gonzalez et al., 2009).

In this chapter, I showcase an example of a specific multilingual literacy intervention using dual-language books (DLBs) wherein ELLs whose primary language is Urdu can come to develop critical language awareness skills (Zaidi, 2020) and delve into the comparative features of English and their primary language. I maintain that students can engage with DLBs to develop their language and literacy skills, and use the language in which they are most proficient to support their reading comprehension while developing critical language awareness skills (Edwards et al., 2000).

The Association for Language Awareness (ALA, 2021) defines language awareness as "explicit knowledge about language, and conscious perception and sensitivity in language learning, language teaching, and language use" (para.1). Adding the term *critical* situates the learner within the framework of language awareness but extends it to include abilities and dispositions that can more aptly be linked to the twenty-first century. Using an asset-based approach, such as children's reading materials published in two languages, can help achieve this. The DLB approach permits educators to focus on strengths and culturally relevant teaching styles which can better serve the needs of a culturally diverse student body (Chávez et al., 2016). The approach also builds an understanding and capacity for educators and students alike that enhances language and literacy learning in an innovative and cutting-edge manner and creates an appreciation for diversity and cultural capital (Naqvi et al., 2013). Employing DLBs to this end is a sound strategy; however, their usage should be culturally and linguistically correct to avoid negative stereotypes and fallible assumptions (Semingson et al., 2015), thereby giving the reader the opportunity to build on their cultural knowledge, emotional intelligence, personal identity, and social development (Hojeij et al., 2019).

In this example, using DLBs written in Urdu and English gave the ELLs and the classroom teacher the opportunity to use the strength of the students' primary language to help create confident, lifelong learners (the author considers that not all ELLs are literate, as defined by one's ability to decode written texts, in their primary language and DLBs help to support the development of literacy as well as their own identity as students). In addition, innovative literacy research has suggested language awareness activities that emerge from reading DLBs play a vital and positive role in transforming the literacy acquisition process of multilingual learners (Helot et al., 2018). When incorporated properly into the classroom, DLBs can achieve the objectives of enhanced text engagement and language awareness on the part of the students (Cummins et al., 2012; Swain & Lapkin, 2005).

Approaching language and literacy learning today by incorporating ELLs' primary language and English, as in a DLB, also places everyone squarely in a position to view all students as being multilingual, and constantly being aware of how this comes into play within their classroom (de Jong et al., 2020). This chapter highlights Urdu as the primary language, and, in order to appreciate how this language interplays with the DLBs, I begin with a historical trajectory of the Urdu language.

A BRIEF HISTORY OF THE URDU LANGUAGE

Urdu (/ˈʊərduː/; Urdu: أُردُو, ALA-LC: Urdū) is an Indo-Aryan language spoken chiefly in South Asia (Bhat, 2017) and is the eighth most widely spoken language in the world. Its script was further developed by the invaders of India who came from Central Asia, and who added more letters to the language to make it become the language that would be spoken in Delhi, India (The Editors of Encyclopedia Britannica, 2021).

Urdu under the Colonized Indo-Pak Subcontinent

During the nineteenth century in colonial India, Muslims and Hindus alike spoke the same language (Hindustani) in the United Provinces. British administrators referred to Hindustani as Urdu (Rahman, 2011) and the language was promoted within British policies to counter the previous emphasis on Persian. Both Urdu and Hindustani were learned to exercise power, and the British perceptions of the language were spread widely throughout India, especially in the urban areas. The British also associated the use of Urdu in India with the Muslim population, and the language was officially discarded in favor of Hindi in India after it gained independence (Rahman, 2008).

Urdu in North America

Today, there are over 100 million native speakers of Urdu in India and Pakistan combined. There are also several hundred thousand Urdu speakers in the United Kingdom, Saudi Arabia, Bangladesh, and the United States, represented by over half a million Urdu speakers (The Editors of Encyclopedia Britannica, 2021). Urdu-speaking people initially arrived in North America to work in agriculture and logging. Their numbers increased dramatically in North America after the Immigration and Nationality Act of 1965 that allowed Pakistani immigrants who had professional skills to work in the United States. The largest concentrations of Urdu speakers in the United States are found in New York, Texas, and California. Within these states, they represent a well-educated demographic, having grown into a relatively prosperous community. In fact, by 2017, the number of Urdu speakers in North America had increased to about 22 percent (Camarota & Zeigler, 2017).

Urdu in the Present Day

In modern times, the desire to learn English is inherent and very strong in India. India's Colonial background, combined with the prevailing spoken language trends and practices in India, Pakistan, and Bangladesh, provides strong motivation to be educated in English (Malik & Sarwar, 2016). In fact, even if a South Asian person's English is not very strong, most Urdu speakers have a readily accessible vocabulary of English words and key phrases should they need to use them (Jabeen, 2018). English is perceived as a language of power among Urdu speakers. It is very prevalent in Pakistan, for example, where an Urdu speaker will often switch from Urdu to English to create special effects. This code-switching between English and Urdu is very common among Urdu/English speakers. For those who have immigrated to the United States, in particular, the influence of English is even more prevalent. Unfortunately, unless an Urdu-speaking person lives in a neighborhood with many other Urdu speakers, the second generation tends to lose contact with their native language and culture (Bethany World Prayer Centre, 1997). Therefore in order to avoid this language and cultural loss for Urdu-speaking students and families, educators working in K-12 public schools in the United States would benefit from understanding principled elements of Urdu and how to implement culturally and linguistically sustaining instructional strategies.

PRINCIPLED ELEMENTS OF THE URDU LANGUAGE

The language of Urdu exemplifies a linguistic situation known as digraphia, in which different scripts are used to write the same language (Ahmad, 2020). Urdu's morphological, syntactic, and phonological structure, as well as its basic vocabulary, is shared with Hindi, another Sanskrit language. Of note, and based on religious and cultural affiliations, Urdu vocabulary that represents a higher-level language borrows much from Arabic and Persian. Furthermore, because of its colonial history, Urdu also shares many loanwords (cognates) with English (Dar, 2016).

Urdu's alphabet contains 36 primary letters with additional symbols that are added to modify their sound, and the script is typically read from right to left. Urdu's primary orthographic structure is similar to Arabic and depends on three forms of letters which can be written according to their position in the word: initial, middle, and final. In terms of cross-linguistic relations, Urdu's combination of Arabic–Persian orthography and Sanskrit linguistic roots provides interesting theoretical as well as practical comparisons as demonstrated in table 12.1.

Table 12.1   Urdu Cross-Linguistic Comparisons

Blighty	The Concise Oxford English Dictionary (2011) says "Blighty" (with a capital B) means: "Britain or England, as used by soldiers serving abroad in the first and second World Wars." The origin is "bilayati," a corruption of "wilayati." The Arabic word "wilayat," meaning kingdom or land, is also used with the suffix "" in Persian and Urdu and means "of or concerning foreign land." It was commonly mispronounced among semi-literate natives of the subcontinent as "bilayati" and the British took it as Blighty.
Loot	Lout (لوٹ)
	English adoption as it is used in Urdu is "loot." It is used both as a noun and a verb in English and a derivative is looter.
Chintz	chheent¹ (چھینٹ)
	A colorful cotton fabric with a glazed finish is called "chintz" in English. Its origin is "chheent," meaning speckle, blot, spot, as the fabric is a multicolored printed one.

To Urdu ELLs, English presents certain challenges in grammatical structure. For example, every noun in Urdu carries a gender (masculine or feminine). In Urdu, the biological gender (i.e., person, animal) denoted by a noun usually determines the gender of the noun (e.g., mother: mām; father: bāp). Also true, however, is that in Urdu some words do not carry an obvious gender, per se, and their gender must simply be learned (Schmidt, 2010). For example, the word for "work" (kām) is masculine in Urdu; whereas, in English, natural gender is primarily denoted by pronouns (Jarvis & Pavlenko, 2008) and does not use a similar pattern of gender formation. Words like لحاظ liḥāz (respect, consideration) or نوازش Nawazish (kindness) do not denote gender. In a language like Urdu, there are no fixed universal guidelines with respect to gender identification by way of suffix or prefix of article or adjective. In many cases, it needs to be memorized. Often the biological gender is determined by the noun itself. For example, چڑیا Chiriya (bird), بکری Bakri (goat). Other nouns like گھر ghar (house) do not determine the gender by themselves and require an adjective or an article to do so.

Additionally, some Urdu adjectives agree with the gender of the noun they modify, while others do not. For example, the Urdu adjective خوبصورت khoobsurat, meaning beautiful, is gender-free, as is the word مشکل mushkil, or difficult, which is also used without gender. English adjectives, on the other hand, use different words to describe different genders (e.g., pretty (feminine) vs handsome (masculine)). Furthermore, there are no definite articles in the Urdu language, compared with English where the word "the" represents both singular and plural forms of the definite article. Certain pronunciation patterns prove challenging to Urdu ELLs, including the "w" and "v" sounds, the sound "th," the absence of the trilled "r," and the guttural "g," both being very prevalent in Urdu but not in English (Ahmad, 2002). Probably the most significant difference between English and Urdu is that syntactically, compared to English, Urdu is classified as a subject-object-verb language (Ahmad, 2002; Davidson et al., 2019). English sentences, on the other hand, are based on SVO (subject-verb-object). Urdu shares its vocabulary with Arabic, Farsi, and English, and its vocabulary can be associated with English vocabulary, as illustrated in table 12.2:

Table 12.2   Examples of Urdu Words Used in English

Raj	Raaj راج
Pundit	Pundit (پنڈت)
Bungalow	Bangla (بنگلہ)

Note: Overall, some of the distinctions highlighted above provide an understanding of how educators might better understand how ELL Urdu speakers might capitalize on their L1 while learning English.

Language in Use

The notion that capacities in one language can support or boost the development of another has been affirmed in research on bilingual education (Cummins, 2015; García & Kleifgen, 2010; García & Li, 2014; Wright & Baker, 2017). Research outlines the cruciality of a pedagogical approach that encourages the transfer of intercultural competencies that can be interwoven with the primary language, thereby creating the opportunity to "connect families' home knowledge and practices with the curriculum and instruction to maximize learning" (Alvarez, 2018, p. 98). Cummins's (2007) theories also draw on research that underscores the primary language as a powerful resource for ELLs, particularly for learning and mobilizing bilingual instructional strategies that engage both the home and target languages in the literacy and language learning process. Furthermore, outside of Canada and the United States, various institutions within Europe, including the Council of Europe (2001), also encourage the development of programs in which students learn about other cultures and languages to promote intercultural awareness.

A dual-language approach enables teachers to capitalize on the diverse ethnic and linguistic makeup of classrooms and encourages students to engage with the larger community. It also develops their personal and cultural identities as they learn English (Fort & Stechuk, 2008; Ma, 2008; Sneddon, 2009). The information below was gathered during a study that took place with elementary- and middle-school ELLs from two different school models in Alberta, Canada. The Urdu language was highlighted as it intersected with

English while using a DLB reading approach to English language and literacy learning. Both during and following the reading, facilitated discussions were held, using language awareness activities to spark students' curiosity around the forms of the two languages (e.g., sounds and symbols, word meaning, syntax, and morphology) as the ELLs used language to learn English (Naqvi et al., 2013; Zaidi, 2020).

Sounds and Symbols

The DLBs helped create the opportunity to support typical patterns of primary language (Urdu) use, miscues amendments, and to meaningfully support challenges when speakers of Urdu are learning English. Urdu ELLs were given the opportunity to discuss the unique characteristics of both English and Urdu and to make further comments about the written text:

> In English, if I have to write my name, I will write S-A-I-R-A. But in Urdu, I will have to shorten the letter . . . to give it a small shape and join two or three letters together. Like here I just showed you how to write the word lagar baga in Urdu, the name for hyena. Here I have joined three letters of the alphabet together, . . . and this over here is a symbol. The one that looks like a W is actually a symbol that tells us to pronounce the letter twice. (Saira, guest reader)

Throughout the course of the DLB readings, the student participants noticed that the Urdu alphabet contains 36 letters, is read from right to left, and demands a rolling of the r. This produces the sound of the letter reh, a sound that does not exist in English and is often difficult for speakers of English to replicate, and, additionally, a challenge for ELLs to eliminate when speaking English. Further differentiating from English, Urdu-speaking ELLs noticed that the accent (peish) in Urdu changes the pronunciation of certain words. Conversely, they noticed the distinct absence of accents in the English language.

Student queries also included a curiosity into how Urdu takes parts of a letter and combines it with other parts to make words. For example, students also noticed that English contains vowels, a characteristic shared by both languages (English and Urdu). However, they recognized that there seems to be more vowels in Urdu:

> I noticed that there aren't as many vowels in English as there are in Urdu. I noticed the word sari, and chai. I also noticed the word hijaab appeared several times in the story. Lots of vowels! (Ameena)

Word Meaning

The Urdu-speaking ELLs also reflected personally on their primary language as it appears in the DLB, and how it compared with the English language being presented and learned on the opposite side of the DLB pages. As an example, Maria gave the teacher several examples of English words that had impacted her during the course of the DLB reading, all of which she spelled phonetically while employing the Roman alphabet in her journal:

Egg = Unda
Honey = Shahed
Jingle jangle = Jahan jhankar
Taste = Chakna
Smell = Soughna
Touch = Choona

Maria was trying to comment on the similarities between English and Urdu. The words she chose, however, were not cognates, but they struck her as being interesting, and she remarked that she needed to memorize how to use them, when to use them, and what exactly they meant. In some cases, she relied on the phonetic sound. However, in most cases, she felt the words were very different and she used strategies such as sound/symbol formations and the way the letters appeared on the page.

Syntax and Morphology

Interestingly, the Urdu-speaking ELLs who were normally quiet observers in the class typically became noticeably more engaged through the DLB readings, commenting particularly when they noticed similarities between their primary language (Urdu) and English. They also engaged actively when the stories were projected onto the Smart Board, pointing out relevant aspects of their primary language and sharing their own stories related to the themes and topics outlined in the DLBs. The student participants often responded to queries by the guest reader in their primary language, offering them the opportunity to use their linguistic capital or "funds of knowledge" (Moll et al., 1992, p. 133) to participate in the discussion. Yosso (2005) expanded on this, developing what is known as the Cultural Wealth Model. This model maintains that education can be experienced from a strength-based perspective within a multi-faceted Critical Race Theory design that focuses on students of color who, she iterates, bring talents, strengths, and experiences into the educational environment, much like multilingual students do.

The DLB reading process encourages participants to draw on the familiar and known vis-a-vis their primary language (i.e., in this case, Urdu) and to identify similarities and differences between English and the primary language (Urdu), thereby connecting their growing understanding of historical and geographic influences of both languages to cultural aspects of life, such as food and cultural celebrations. The students' interest in certain aspects of culture, including typical greetings, celebrations, and pastimes, and the design of DLB extension activities enhanced this intercultural and linguistic awareness of both languages. The student participants were encouraged to reflect and compare words in their primary language (in this case, Urdu) with the target language (English) in order to derive conclusions and engage in constructive meaning-making. They were also asked questions about the similarities and differences in words, and the fact that sometimes certain words or concepts exist in one language but not in the other.

Of particular note was the discussion around vocabulary in each language. For example, one reading used the word hippopotamus (for which there is no Urdu word). A guest reader subsequently translated it into Urdu as *water horse*. The ensuing discussion revolved around why such vocabulary would be absent from the Urdu language or, conversely, why English did not just use *"water horse"* to describe this animal. Another example highlighted a word in Urdu to express one's love for someone. Literally translated from Urdu into English, the word involves using the term in Urdu that means *"liver,"* as in the organ. In English, the students felt that this did not make sense because English uses the word *"heart"* to express love, as in *"I love you with all my heart."*

Follow-up activities included students working in groups to employ their knowledge of the Urdu and English texts (including their linguistic, plot, and media analyses) to create an illustrated language journaling and metalinguistic analysis worksheet. The students were asked to write observations they had noticed during the DLB readings and put down any commentary that they felt was relevant. One Urdu student, Sanya, wrote down phonetically what she had heard in English using the Roman alphabet. Her English language skills were such that she was able to take a question from one of the stories that, translated into Urdu, was "How much are they?" and write in the Roman alphabet as she knew it using a phonetic spelling: In ki kya keemat hai? In essence, she was writing in English, but interpreting the question only as she heard it phonetically. She also noticed that, from an English perspective, the comma in Urdu is upside down and the period is represented by a dash. As students were given the opportunity to engage in text-to-self discussions, they made connections between English words in the text and words in the Urdu language.

In essence, the DLBs were used as a meaning-making resource that encouraged individual analysis of words and phrases and provided the students with the opportunity to expand their language and literacy learning and acquisition. The use of DLBs in the ELL classroom enabled heritage language speakers to build capacity and critical language awareness strategies. Furthermore, the DLBs demonstrated the importance of allowing the students to use their entire linguistic repertoire, and the books also showcased the interconnection between student identity and first language. Additional pedagogical strategies, such as scaffolding, allowed teachers to build on their students' first languages. This implies that, by modifying the level of language to fit the needs of their students, teachers were able to give their students a greater level of linguistic understanding. Noticing the differences and similarities between the primary language (in this case, Urdu) and English also enabled the students to foster a sense of confidence and validation in their reading and writing abilities as well as their capacity to read, write, and speak in English.

This was essentially accomplished through students engaging in reflection, guest reader engagement, and teacher-planned extension activities. This process helped lead to the establishment of an emerging awareness of sociocultural relationships that could help build the ELL's language learning capacity in an interesting and relevant manner, effectively developing their English language proficiency and literacy acumen. Using DLBs in an ELL classroom permitted the students to gain positive exposure to the sounds and literary text of the books. The target language (English) was explored on a deeper cognitive level, focusing on how the two languages compare in terms of directionality (how they are written physically), their origins, and their cultural and linguistic relationship to each other. In conclusion, using DLBs was found to be significant for those ELLs who were fluent in their primary language (Urdu), and who experienced challenges with English. These students tended to rely more on the pictures and less on linguistic cues than their peers. DLBs represented an ideal strategy and lead the ELL to feel confident to continue toward a stronger English proficiency.

IMPLICATIONS FOR INSTRUCTION

The current age of transnational mobility, where cultural and linguistic diversity dominates most educational settings, demonstrates the need to highlight the limitations and consequences of monolingual approaches to language and literacy teaching (Prasad, 2018). This chapter examined this issue by seeking what can be learned by using the ELL's primary language (Urdu) in the classroom and how it can have a positive impact. Incorporating DLBs written in Urdu and English enabled the author to showcase the ELLs' primary language as they learn English and become literate in that language. Considering this example, it became evident that ELLs enjoyed experiencing their primary language employed in this manner in the classroom, even if to a limited extent.

Using the DLBs in conjunction with the primary language facilitated and enhanced student learning, helping them to feel more confident and less self-conscious as they witnessed their primary language represented in the classroom. Educators also acknowledged that the judicious use of Urdu in the classroom helped them deliver the English lesson in a more successful manner. Table 12.3 illustrates some examples of the most effective Urdu-English DLBs.

Table 12.3 A List of DLB Examples

	Title	Author and/or Translator	Publisher, Place, Date
1	The Giant Turnip	E: H. Barkow U: Q. Zamini	Mantra Lingua, London, 2007
2	Mei Ling's Hiccups	E: D Mills U: Q. Zamani	Mantra Lingua, London, 2001 & 2000
3	Welcome to the World Baby	E: N. Robert U: Q. Zamani	Mantra Lingua, London, 2005
4	Handa's Hen	E: E. Browne U: Q. Zamini	Walker Books, London 2003 & Mantra Lingua, London, 2005
5	Grandma's Saturday Soup	E: S. Fraser U: Q. Zamini	Mantra Lingua, London, 2005
6	I Took the Moon for a Walk	E: C. Curtis U: A. Jay	Barefoot Books London, 2004 & Mantra Lingua, London, 2008
7	Keeping up with Cheetah	E; L. Camp & J. Newton U: Q. Zamani	Mantra Lingua, London, 2008
8	Buri and the Marrow	E: H. Barkow & L. Finlay U: Q. Zamani	Mantra Lingua, London, 2000 & 2006
9	The Wibbly Wobbly Tooth	E: D. Mills & J. Crouth U: Q. Zamani	Mantra Lingua, London, 2003
10	Augustus and his Smile	E: C. Rayner U: Q. Zamani	Little Tiger Press, London, 2006 & Mantra Lingua, London, 2008

Tang (2002) reiterated that using the primary language in the classroom does not negatively affect students' exposure to English, but rather gains traction in the teaching and learning process. In fact, the pedagogical practices underpinning this type of literacy engagement frame linguistic diversity as an asset as it enriches the shared learning community of the classroom, building literacy and language learning practices that go beyond sound/symbol recognition, and structure a critical language awareness and asset-based mind-set that, it is hoped, will continue throughout the students' schooling. This correlation indicates that bilingual children usually transfer prior linguistic knowledge for acquiring reading skills in an additional language. By engaging ELLs with their primary language and meeting the language learning challenges through an asset-based platform such as DLBs, educators have a better understanding as to how best to educate ELLs who are increasingly entering schools with a proficiency in languages other than English. In so doing, they acknowledge the linguistic and cultural capital their multilingual students bring to the class-room and help to prevent perpetuating the assumption that bilingual children's needs equate those of a monolingual student (Garcia, 2008).

DLB reading stimulates Urdu-speaking ELLs' comprehension of language (English/Urdu) and helps to unearth its multiple dimensions, differences, and commonalities with the English language. It provokes enhanced communi-cative and intercultural competence, and for educators, readers, and Urdu-speaking ELLs, reading a book in English and Urdu gives the opportunity to develop reflective capacity (Beacco et al., 2016). In addition, the strategies employed while reading DLBs position the ELL as being a competent and knowledgeable contributor to their learning (Lewis et al., 2012). In effect, by leveraging their ELLs' funds of knowledge, educators can create, in both practice and in presence, classroom conditions that position students' linguis-tic competencies and their sociocultural histories as valued resources (Alva-rez, 2018; Marshall & Toohey, 2010; Pacheco et al., 2019). Educators can consequently provoke a curiosity among their students as they are given the opportunity to use the classroom and activities as a strategy to examine how each language (English and Urdu) compares to each other structurally, gram-matically, in vocabulary, and in the literacy and language learning process McGuinness's (2005) premise that language awareness, even critical language awareness, is enhanced through bilingualism in that students who are bilingual (or multilingual) require early attention to the forms of different languages.

This type of ELLs' initiative can ignite valuable discussion centering on the specific and unique characteristics shared between the primary language (i.e., Urdu) and English. Therefore, students can demonstrate how they have become aware of differences and similarities in sound, meaning, and script, and using the example of an English/Urdu cross-linguistic reference helps us understand how students engage in thoughtful discussion around comparisons and contrasts with Urdu and English. Consequently, the use of DLBs has the potential for broadening Urdu-speaking ELLs' comprehension of the English language, helping them to acknowledge the multiplicity of languages and cul-tural practices. It provides a clearer picture of how a student's primary language can be used to enhance literacy acquisition and engage students in interesting and creative activities to pursue this objective. As such, the initiative to read

DLBs designates the educator as an agent of change, rather than as simply a deliverer of prepackaged curriculum (Cummins, 2019). This chapter grounded in research furthers our understanding of the cognitive and sociocultural complexities of the ELL classroom and how incorporating primary languages into it has profound implications for English language learners and their teachers.

REFERENCES

Ahmad, I. (2002). Urdu and Madrasa education. *Economic and Political Weekly*, *37*(24), 2285–2287.

Ahmad, Y. (2020, November 23). *Is Urdu really a foreign language?* The Second Angle. https://thesecondangle.com/is-urdu-really-a-foreign-language/.

Alvarez, A. (2018). Drawn and written funds of knowledge: A window into merging bilingual children's experiences and social interpretations through their written narratives and drawings. *Journal of Early Childhood Literacy*, *18*(1), 97–128. https://doi.org/10.1177/1468798417740618.

Association for Language Awareness. (n.d.). *ALA definition*. The Association for Language Awareness. https://lexically.net/ala/la_defined.htm. Retrieved July 11, 2022, from https://www.languageawareness.org/?page_id=231.

Ayres, A. (2009). *Speaking like a state: Language and nationalism in Pakistan*. Cambridge University Press.

Barkow, H., Finlay, L., & Zamani, Q. (2006). *Buri and the marrow*. Mantra Lingua.

Barkow, H., Tolstoy, A. N., Johnson, R., & Zamani, Q. (2007). *The Giant Turnip*. Mantra Lingua.

Beacco, J., Byram, M., Cavalli, M., Coste, D., Cuenat, M. E., Goullier, F., & Panthier, J. (2016). *Guide for the development and implementation of curricula for plurilingual and intercultural education*. Council of Europe Publishing.

Bethany World Prayer Centre. (n.d.). *The Diaspora Urdu*. Retrieved July 11, 2022, from http://www.prayway.com/unreached/clusters/8016.html.

Bhat, A. M. (2017). *The changing language roles and linguistic identities of the Kashmiri speech community*. Cambridge Scholars Publishing.

Browne, E. (2003). *Handa's Hen*. Walker Books.

Camarota, S. A., & Zeigler, K. (2017, October 24). *65.5 million U.S. residents spoke a foreign language at home in 2016*. Center for Immigration Studies. https://cis.org/Report/655-Million-US-Residents-Spoke-Foreign-Language-Home-2016.

Camp, L., Newton, J., & Zamani, Q. (2008). *Keeping up with Cheetah*. Mantra Lingua.

Centre for Applied Linguistics. (September 27, 2021). *Asset-based approaches for educating multilingual learners* [Video]. YouTube. https://www.youtube.com/watch?v=8MIfCHw_ByU.

Council of Europe. (2001). *Common European framework of reference for languages: Learning, teaching, assessment*. Cambridge University Press.

Cummins, J. (2007). Rethinking monolingual instructional strategies in multilingual classrooms. *Canadian Journal of Applied Linguistics*, *10*(2), 221–240.

Cummins J. (2015). Intercultural education and academic achievement: A framework for school-based policies in multilingual schools. *Intercultural Education*, *26*(6), 455–468. https://doi.org/10.1080/14675986.2015.1103539.

Cummins, J. (2019, February 21). *How can teachers maximize engagement among multilingual students?* EdCan Network. https://www.edcan.ca/articles/multilingual -students/.

Cummins, J., Mirza, R., & Stille, S. (2012). English language learners in Canadian schools: Emerging directions for school-based policies. *TESL Canada Journal*, *29*(4), 25. https://doi.org/10.18806/tesl.v29i0.1121.

Curtis, C., & Jay, A. (2008). *I took the Moon for a walk*. Mantra Lingua.

Dar, S. R. (2016). Code switching in English as second language in ESL classroom: Students' identities, attitudes and feelings. *Asian Journal of Multidisciplinary Studies*, *4*, 82–88.

Davidson, D., Vanegas, S. B., Hilvert, E., Rainey, V. R., & Misiunaite, I. (2017). Examination of monolingual (English) and bilingual (English/Spanish; English/ Urdu) children's syntactic awareness. *Journal of Child Language*, *46*(4), 682–706. https://doi.org/10.1017/S0305000919000059.

de Jong, E. J., Yilmaz, T., & Marichal, N. (2020). Multilingualism-as-a-resource orientation in dual language education. In P. C. Ramírez & C. J. Faltis (Eds.), *Dual language education in the U.S.* (pp. 54–71). Routledge.

Edwards, V., Monaghan, F., & Knight, J. (2000). Books, pictures and conversations: Using bilingual multimedia storybooks to develop language awareness. *Language Awareness*, *9*(3), 135–146. https://doi.org/10.1080/09658410008667142.

Fort, P., & Stechuk, R. (2008). The cultural responsiveness and dual language education project. *Zero to Three*, *29*, 24–28.

Fraser, S., Brazell, D., & Zamani, Q. (2005). *Grandma's Saturday soup*. Mantra Lingua.

García, O. (2008). *Bilingual education in the 21st century: A global perspective*. Wiley-Blackwell.

García, O., & Kleifgen, J. A. (2010). *Educating emergent bilinguals: Policies, programs, and practices for English language learners*. Teachers College Press.

Garcia, O., & Wei, L. (2014). *Translanguaging: Language, bilingualism and education*. Palgrave Macmillan.

Godbey, S., Leuzinger, R., Agee, A., Amsberry, D., Baron, C., Heckey, P., Makula, A., Riehle, C., Roberts, L., Ross, L., Sharkey, J., Silva, E., Wolff, N., & Wong, M. (2018). *5 things you should read about asset-based teaching*. ACRL Instruction Section Research and Scholarship Committee. https://acrl.ala.org/IS/wp-content/ uploads/isresearch_5Things_asset-based-teaching.pdf.

González, N., Moll, L. C., & Amanti, C. (2009). *Funds of knowledge: Theorizing practices in households, communities, and classrooms*. Lawrence Erlbaum Associates.

Hélot, C., Frijns, C., Van Gorp, K., & Sierens, S. (Eds.). (2018). *Language awareness in multilingual classrooms in Europe: From theory to practice*. Mouton de Gruyter.

Hojeij, Z., Dillon, A. M., Perkins, A., & Grey, I. (2017). Selecting high quality dual language texts for young children in multicultural contexts: A UAE case. *Issues in Educational Research, 29*(4), 1201.

Jabeen, S. (2018). Code-mixing, code switching and borrowing in Urdu and Pakistani English language in media and daily life conversations. *International Journal of Advanced Research, 6*(11), 805–811. https://doi.org/10.21474/ijar01/8062.

Jarvis, S., & Pavlenko, A. (2008). *Crosslinguistic influence in language and cognition*. Routledge.

Lewis, G., Jones, B., & Baker, C. (2012). Translanguaging: Developing its conceptualisation and contextualisation. *Educational Research and Evaluation, 18*(7), 655–670. https://doi.org/10.1080/13803611.2012.718490.

Ma, J. (2008). "Reading the word and the world": How mind and culture are mediated through the use of dual-language storybooks. *Education, 36*, 237–251. https://doi.org/10.1080/03004270802217686.

Marshall, E., & Toohey, K. (2010). Representing family: Community funds of knowledge, bilingualism, and multimodality. *Harvard Educational Review, 80*(2), 221–242. https://doi.org/10.17763/haer.80.2.h3446j54n608q442.

McGuinness, D. (2005). *Language development and learning to read: The scientific study of how language development affects reading skill*. MIT Press.

Mills, D., Brazell, D., & Zamani, Q. (2000). *Mei Ling's hiccups*. Mantra Lingua.

Mills, D., Crouth, J., & Zamani, Q. (2003). *The wibbly wobbly tooth*. Mantra.

Moll, L., Amanti, C., Neff, D., & Gonzalez, N. (1992). Funds of knowledge for teaching: Using a qualitative approach to connect homes and classrooms. *Theory into Practice, 31*(2), 132–141.

Naqvi, R., Thorne, K. J., Pfitscher, C. M., Nordstokke, D. W., & McKeough, A. (2013). Reading dual language books: Improving early literacy skills in linguistically diverse classrooms. *Journal of Early Childhood Research, 11*(1), 3–15. https://doi.org/10.1177/1476718X12449453.

Ontario Education. (2017, February 16) *Many roots many voices: Supporting English language learners in every classroom*. Government of Ontario. http://www.edu.gov.on.ca/eng/document/manyroots/manyroots.pdf.

Ordona, M., Sandhu, S., & Zhang. N. (2017). *English language learners: Balancing the L1 and the L2 in the classroom* [PowerPoint slides]. The University of British Columbia. http://blogs.ubc.ca/myrnaeducation/files/2017/07/CaseNineResearchPackage.pdf.

Pacheco, M. B., Kang, H.-S., & Hurd, E. (2019). Scaffolds, signs, and bridges: Language ideologies and translanguaging in student-teaching experiences. *Bilingual Research Journal, 42*(2), 194–213. https://doi.org/10.1080/15235882.2019.1596179.

Prasad, G. Z. (2018). "But do monolingual people really exist?" Analysing elementary students' contrasting representations of plurilingualism through sequential reflexive drawing. *Language and Intercultural Communication, 18*(3), 315–334. https://doi.org/10.1080/14708477.2018.1425412.

Promising futures report. ecworkforcemn.org. (2019, May 5). Retrieved August 11, 2022, from https://ecworkforcemn.org/promising-futures-report/.

Rahman, T. (2004, August 23–27). *Language policy and localization in Pakistan: Proposal for a paradigmatic shift crossing the digital divide.* Paper presentation 20th International Conference on Computational Linguistics COLING 2004, Geneva, Switzerland.

Rahman, T. (2008). The British learning of Hindustani. *Pakistan Vision, 8*(2), 19–55.

Rayner, C., & Zamani, Q. (2008). *Augustus and his smile.* Mantra Lingua.

Robert, N. B., Brazell, D., & Zamani, Q. (2005). *Welcome to the world baby.* Mantra Lingua.

Schmidt, R. L. (2010). *Urdu: An essential grammar.* Routledge.

Semingson, P., Pole, K., & Tommerdahl, J. (2015). Using bilingual books to enhance literacy around the world. *European Scientific Journal, 3*(2), 132–139.

Sneddon, R. (2009). *Bilingual books—Biliterate children: Learning to read through dual language books.* Trentham Books.

Stevenson, A., & Waite, M. (2011). *Concise Oxford English dictionary.* Oxford University Press.

Swain, M., & Lapkin, S. (2005). The evolving sociopolitical context of immersion education in Canada: Some implications for program development. *International Journal of Applied Linguistics, 15*(2), 169–186. https://doi.org/10.1111/j.1473 -4192.2005.00086.x.

Tang, J. (2002, January). *Using L1 in the English classroom.* English Teaching Forum. https://americanenglish.state.gov/files/ae/resource_files/02-40-1-h.pdf.

The Editors of Encyclopedia Britannica. (2021, June 4). *Urdu language.* Encyclopedia Britannica. https://www.britannica.com/topic/Urdu-language.

Wright, W. E., & Baker, C. (2017). Key concepts in bilingual education. In *Bilingual and Multilingual Education* (pp. 65–79). https://doi.org/10.1007/978-3-319-02258 -1_2.

Yosso, T. J. (2005). Whose culture has capital? A critical race theory discussion of community cultural wealth. *Race, Ethnicity and Education, 8*(1), 69–91. https://doi .org/10.1080/1361332052000341006.

Zaidi, R. (2020). Dual-language books: Enhancing engagement and language awareness. *Journal of Literacy Research, 52*(3), 269–292. https://doi.org/10.1177 /1086296X20939559.

Chapter 13

The Impact of Portuguese on the Learning of English

Cristiane Carneiro Capristano and Lisley Camargo Oberst

Brazilian Portuguese is the mother tongue, or heritage language, of Brazilians who live in the United States. The United States Census Bureau (2019) estimates that there were, in 2019, 369,981 American citizens with total or partial Brazilian ancestry living in the United States. The Brazilian Ministry of Foreign Affairs (2021) states that there are 1.8 million Brazilians living in different regions of the United States, The ten largest Brazilian communities in the United States can be found in New York, Miami, Boston, Los Angeles, Atlanta, Toronto, Houston, Hartford, San Francisco, and Chicago. Out of these people with total or partial Brazilian ancestry, the American educational system assisted, according to the United States Census Bureau (2019), 157,212 students in 2019: 7.6 percent in preschool, 6.4 percent in kindergarten, 38.6 percent in elementary school, 18.3 percent in high school, and 29.1 percent in college or graduate school. It is paramount for educators in the United States, working with students who speak Brazilian Portuguese as their mother tongue, to know and understand how possible conflicts and confluences in the relationship between the languages may occur in order to best support their students.

This chapter provides key elements of how the Portuguese language impacts English language and literacy development. We analyze the learners' writing production, observing the way students write words in English. The choice for writing materializes the relationship between Portuguese and English making it possible to observe the writer in the practices of language; see Tfouni (2010, 2021). We aim to understand how eventual conflicts and confluences in the relationship between languages are shown in the child's attempts to write words in English. With this knowledge, it will be possible to better understand how the learners' mother tongue influences and intersects with the additional language being learned.

A BRIEF HISTORY OF BRAZILIAN PORTUGUESE

Because of Portuguese colonization, which started in 1532, the Portuguese language originated from the Galician-Portuguese spoken in the Kingdom of Galicia in northern Portugal. Portuguese was transported to Brazil and mixed with languages from other peoples (at first, indigenous languages, then languages of enslaved Africans, and later immigrant languages, such as German, Italian, Japanese, Korean, Dutch, and English)—see Ilari and Basso (2006), Bagno (2017), and Lucchesi (2015). This process made Brazilian Portuguese, in a new space and time, the official and national language of Brazil and the most broadly spoken variety of Portuguese in the United States.

Below we discuss the importance of understanding language and cross-linguistic transfer in order to best support Brazilian Portuguese students in K-12 educational contexts within the United States. Following that, we discuss the syllable, its structure, and function, which will be relevant in understanding the impact of Brazilian Portuguese in the learning process of English. Finally, we provide the instructional implications for the teachers of this cross-linguistic transfer between Brazilian Portuguese and English.

KEY CHARACTERISTICS OF BRAZILIAN PORTUGUESE

It is essential for educators who face the hard task of teaching English to students who speak Brazilian Portuguese to know some characteristics of this language. This knowledge can become a starting point for teachers to recognize the challenges that these learners may face and, at the same time, this knowledge can serve as a guide for effectively teaching in K-12 classrooms.

Brazilian Portuguese is an inflectional romance language. Its phonological archive is composed of 19 consonant phonemes and 7 vowel phonemes. The preferable Brazilian Portuguese syllabic structure is formed by the sequence consonant (C) and vowel (V), even though there are also other important productive structures. All 26 phonemes go through phonotactic constraints, that is, the possible sequence of phonemes in every language, depending on the position they occupy in the syllable, as we will present in the sections below.

Considering the function of each term of a sentence, it is possible to classify, as a general characteristic of Brazilian Portuguese, that pronouns (me, te, se, lhe, o, a, etc.) are not always present or stressed, but when they are, they tend to appear before the verb. Thus, in Brazilian Portuguese, we communicate

"**Me dá** um lápis" instead of "**Dê-me** um lápis." On the other hand, the pronouns in English have an enclitic placement, that is, the pronouns are placed after the verb. Therefore, in English, we would communicate "**Give me** a pencil." Also, in Brazilian Portuguese, the construction of sentences such as "**está** come**ndo**" formed by *be* + gerund is also common. It is common to find Brazilian Portuguese expressions with the preposition "em" (somewhat close to English's *in*), for instance, "Mariana está **na** janela."

Characteristics of the Syllable

Understanding the relationship between mother tongue and additional language can be best understood through children's written language examples. It is through these written examples that we see both the conflicts and confluences that constitute the writer's changeable identity. This changeable identity and the socio-historical influences are revealed through the writer's use of language (Oberst, 2019). Even though we know that additional language contact is always unique, there are tendencies of how children, Brazilian Portuguese speakers, and writers learning English register words in English.

Based on the analysis of a meaningful amount of data in previous papers, we observed two patterns. The first pattern is the one where children, in their initial contact with an additional language, write words in English non-randomly, referring to part or the whole structure of syllables of words in English. The second pattern was observed when students do not do that. There are moments when children don't register such syllabic structures demonstrated by using less frequent or even impossible grapheme sequences in both English and Brazilian Portuguese, which is a pattern that also demonstrates important information about the relationship of the languages for the child. Recognizing these patterns, as well as comprehending the linguistic function for the appearance of such patterns, is important for educators to understand how the learner interacts with another language. By understanding these interactions, educators can better carry out the teaching and learning processes of English as an additional language. In so doing, they are able to look at these orthographically unconventional writings as a source of knowledge and not as mistakes.

Phonology and Orthography

One of the main differences between the phonological-phonetic and orthographic dimensions of both Brazilian Portuguese and English refers to the phonemes belonging to each language. The amount of consonant and vowel phonemes and their characteristics are not the same in both languages. As mentioned before, Brazilian Portuguese has 19 consonant phonemes and 7 vowel phonemes, while English has 24 consonant phonemes and 17 vowel phonemes.

There are significant differences in the phonotactic and syllabic patterns of the two languages. For example, as we will see in the sequence of the chapter, in Brazilian Portuguese, it is not possible to find a syllable formed by a sequence of phonemes as the ones that form the word "spring" (formed by three consonants, one vowel, and one more consonant) or "scrambled" (formed by three consonants, one vowel, and four more consonants) in English.

Understanding the differences between the quantity and quality of phonemes in each language and the possible syllabic patterns in Brazilian Portuguese and English provides educators a better opportunity to support positive transfer for students from Brazilian Portuguese to English. The tendencies found in children's writing through the syllabic structure of the words and through the way the children represent them paint a picture regarding the ways students are able to make sense of their language(s).

According to Selkirk (1984), the syllable is a unit that can be divided into two parts, called onset and rhyme. Both parts can be divided into smaller parts (called branches). The onset can be divided into different numbers of parts, depending on the language. The rhyme can be divided into two parts, called nucleus (or peak) and the coda. As a universal rule—therefore present in most languages—the only indispensable element for the constitution of the syllable is the nucleus. To exemplify, the representation of the internal structural organization of the syllable "flounce" can be seen in Selkirk (1982, p. 338).

The word "flounce" is formed by just one syllable. This syllable is formed, firstly, by the phonemes /f/ and /l/, which occupy the onset. The rhyme is formed by a nucleus and a coda. The nucleus is occupied by a vowel (/a/) and a semivowel (/w/). Finally, the coda is occupied by the consonants (/ns/).

According to Chacon (in press, p. 3, our translation), as the syllable is a unit of the language, it plays an important role both (symbolically) in the structural aspect of the language and (physically) in its effective use and is also relevant for human cognitive and communicative aspects.

Furthermore, understanding how the syllables that form the different words of a language work internally and how these syllables are perceived and written by speakers (and, in the cases analyzed here, by children) is relevant for teachers and educators to be able to observe the impact and relationship of a student's mother tongue in/with the process of learning an additional language and better and more confidently plan their teaching strategies.

To analyze this impact and relationship between languages, we will present the phonemes of Brazilian Portuguese and English based on the descriptions made by Chacon (in press) and Hammond (1999), respectively, summarized in the tables below. In table 13.1, we present the 19 consonants of Brazilian Portuguese and their applications in words that make up the lexicon of this language.

Table 13.1 The Consonants of Brazilian Portuguese

Articulation	Consonant Phonemes	Application in Brazilian Portuguese Words
Plosive	/p, t, k, b, d, g/	**p**ato (*duck*), **t**aça (*cup*), **c**asa (*house*), **b**ola (*ball*), **d**ado (*dice*), **g**ato (*cat*)
Fricative	/f, s, ʃ, v, z, ʒ/	**f**aca (*knife*), **s**apo (*frog*), **ch**oque (*chock*), **v**aso (*vase*), **z**ebra (*zebra*), **j**antar (*dinner*)
Nasal	/m, n, ɲ/	**m**ãe (*mother*), **n**ariz (*nose*), so**nh**o (*dream*)
Lateral and vibrant	/ r, ɾ, l, ʎ /	**r**ato (*rat*), ca**r**o (*expensive*), **l**ama (*mud*), fi**lh**a (*daughter*)

In table 13.2, we present a summary of the seven vowels of Brazilian Portuguese and their applications.

Table 13.2 The Vowels of Brazilian Portuguese

Vowel Phonemes	Application in Brazilian Portuguese Words
/i, e, ɛ, a, ɔ, o, u/	**i**lha (*island*), **e**lefante (*elephant*), **é**gua (*mare*), **a**belha (*bee*), **ó**culos (*glasses*), **o**lho (*eye*), **u**rso (*bear*)

In table 13.3, observe the 24 consonants from the American English phonological inventory and their application in words that make up the lexicon of that language.

Table 13.3 The Consonants of American English

Articulation	Consonant Phonemes	Application in American English Words
Plosive	/p, t, k, b, d, g/	**p**ark (*parque*), **t**ower (*torre*), **c**at (*gato*), **b**ee (*abelha*), **d**og (*cachorro*), **g**ame (*jogo*)
Fricative	/f, θ, s, ʃ, v, ð, z, ʒ/	**f**ace (*rosto*), **th**ink (*pensar*), **s**oup (*sopa*), **sh**op (*comprar*), **v**ase (*vaso*), **th**ey (*eles*), **z**ebra (*zebra*), televi**s**ion (*televisão*)
Affricate	/tʃ, dʒ/	**ch**ocolate (*chocolate*), **g**iraffe (*girafa*)
Nasal	/m, n, ŋ/	**m**other (*mãe*), **n**ose (*nariz*), si**ng** (*cantar*)
Lateral or approximant	/ɹ, l, h, w, y/	**r**at (*rato*), **l**ake (*lago*), **h**at (*chapeu*), **w**ater (*água*), **y**ellow (*amarelo*)

Table 13.4 contains the 11 vowels and 6 diphthongs of English and their applications.

Table 13.4 The Vowels of American English

Type of Phoneme	Phonemes	Application in American English Words
Vowel phonemes	/i, ɪ, e, ɛ, æ, ɑ, ɔ, ʌ, ʊ, u, ə/	bee (*abelha*), fish (*peixe*), pen (*caneta*), bed (*cama*), cat (*gato*), stop (*parar*), urso (*bear*), son (*filho*), good (*bom*), new (*novo*), water (*água*)
Diphthongs	/aw, ay, ey, yu, ɔy, ow/	cow (*vaca*), night (*noite*), say (*dizer*), you (*você*), boy (*menino*), slow (*devagar*)

The phonemes presented above (19 consonants in Brazilian Portuguese and 24 in English; 7 vowels in Brazilian Portuguese and 17 in English) are placed in different and specific positions of the syllable (the ones mentioned above: onset, nucleus, and coda) depending on each language. It is important to notice that each language has its own characteristics and rules which dictate how speakers of that language should produce the phonemes. We call these characteristics "restrictions." These restrictions are, therefore, rules that regulate which phonemes can or cannot appear in each part of the syllable (onset, nucleus, and coda) and the order they do.

In Brazilian Portuguese, all 19 consonants and all 7 vowels can be combined in the two main branches of the syllable, respectively, the onset and the simple rhyme, such as in **ca**sa (*house*), **ge**lo (*ice*), and **bo**la (*ball*), but only a very limited number of phonemes can occupy the other branches. For example, the onset of a syllable may have, at maximum, two consonants. When there are two consonants in the onset, the first position must be occupied by the consonants /p/, /b/, /t/, /d/, /k/, /g/, /f/ e /v/, such as in **p**rato (*plate*), **f**lor (*flower*), **t**rabalho (*work*), **cr**avo (*clove*), and so on. Meanwhile, the second position must be occupied either by the phonemes /l/ or /r/, such as in **pr**ato (*plate*), **pl**uma (*feather*), **br**isa (*breeze*), e **fl**or (flower). On the other hand, in English, the onset can be composed of up to three consonants, which enables a variety of phoneme combinations, such as in **str**aw (*canudo*), **spr**ing (*primavera*), **spl**ash (*respigo*), and **scr**eam (*gritar*).

Finally, there are differences concerning the orthographic structure and function of both languages. Brazilian Portuguese's orthography is considered more transparent than English's, because the number of graphemes that can represent one phoneme in English is generally greater than the possible number of graphemes used to represent the same phoneme in Brazilian Portuguese. An example of this difference is the possibility to represent, in English, the phoneme /i/ by using the graphemes I, EE, E, Y, EY, and others, such as in city (*cidade*), bee (*abelha*), pretty (*bonita*), bicycle (*bicicleta*), and monkey (*macaco*). Meanwhile, in Brazilian Portuguese, the same phoneme is mostly represented by the grapheme I, such as in filho (*son*).

The knowledge of how the phonological inventory, the phonological constraints, and the syllabic patterns of two languages are formed and also the differences and similarities they keep can be an asset for educators who teach students who are learning English as an additional language. The goal of understanding these details is to provide tools so that teachers can observe and comprehend the linguistic processes that are at the base of the orthographically unconventional writings so that they see them as part of the process, and not as mistakes. It is relevant to know the functioning of the languages once we assume that they have an intermingling relationship and can impact on how children write words in what they imagine to be the additional language. Based on the description presented above, the following section contains the analysis of the tendencies observed in the written registrations made by Brazilian children with words in English in order to support students and teachers in K-12 classrooms in the United States.

IMPACT OF BRAZILIAN PORTUGUESE SPEAKING STUDENTS' LEARNING OF ENGLISH

To exemplify the cross-linguistic transfer of students' mother tongue and additional language in the relationship between the languages for Brazilian Portuguese speakers and writers in the context of learning processes of English, we present, in this section, the data on children's writing.

The examples below were made by children, Brazilian Portuguese speakers, and writers, with little or no prior formal knowledge of English. The children were aged between six and seven years. For the textual production, the educator/researcher told a story in Brazilian Portuguese and included keywords in English. At the end of the story, the educator/researcher orally dictated the key words in English that were included in the story so that children could try to write them. The children were not assisted or influenced on how to write the words, unless by the oral dictation made by the educator/researcher.

During the analysis, we aimed to demonstrate tendencies in the way children write words in English considering how many, which ones, and how the selected graphemes were arranged for the graphic representation of the words they heard in the dictation. With this analysis, we sought to discuss how possible conflicts and confluences in the cross-linguistic relationship between languages are shown in these statements and, therefore, allow us to see the impact of children's mother tongue in the process of American English learning. These registrations sometimes refer, in part or in whole, to the structures of the words in English and sometimes they do not.

Representation of the Onset

The first example refers to the representation of the first part of the syllable, the onset. The example presented here is the written registration of the word prince (/pɹɪns/). This word is formed by the syllable pattern CCVCC and the child represented it by writing "PUNSI."

In this case, the child chose the grapheme U to represent the retroflex consonant /ɹ/ (as it appears in words such as porco (*pig*), in Brazilian Portuguese, and car (*carro*), in English), in the second position of the onset. The consonant /ɹ/ is not considered, in Brazilian Portuguese, a phoneme, but a possible form of articulating a sound that happens at the end of words and syllables before consonants. Therefore, it likely won't occur in the onset of words from Brazilian Portuguese speakers. For Portuguese speakers, in varieties where retroflex is produced in speech, there is a tendency for children, during the period of speech acquisition, to replace the consonant with a semivowel, as in the production of the word carta (*letter*) as "caita." This is also a tendency observed in the speech of children who speak English as a mother tongue: it is common to replace the retroflex in the onset of words with the semivowel /w/, like in the production of the word robot (*robô*) as "wobot." This is a similarity that can be explored by educators when dealing with children's unconventional writings.

Due to the impossibility of occurrence of this consonant in the onset of words in Brazilian Portuguese, it is possible that the production of the word during the dictation had a greater duration and lip protrusion, and the tongue was positioned ahead, which are articulatory traits also triggered in the production of the semivowel /w/. This phoneme, although it does not occur in Brazilian Portuguese, is similar to the vowel /u/, whose graphic representation occurs mostly through U, which may have been a motivation for the tendency observed in the written registrations made by the children, as observed in the example mentioned above.

The registration exemplified above may be an indication that children, when faced with the challenge of representing phonemes organized in a way that is not familiar to them, tend to follow similar writing patterns that they follow in their mother tongue. This tendency may be observed by teachers and educators when dealing with students who need to write in their additional language, but still reach for resources they identify from their mother tongue. Using their mother tongue resources is an asset, a form of linguistic capital, that can function as a building block for additional language learning. Knowing the patterns that are shown in the children's writing, as well as the possible phonetic-phonological-orthographic motivations for the emergence of these patterns, is essential so that we can see these unconventional writings not as problems, but as indications of the rich knowledge that children have about the functioning of their mother tongue and the additional language.

Representation of the Nucleus

The following example refers to the representation of the first part of the rhyme, the nucleus. The example chosen is the registration of the word bee (/bi:/). This word is formed by the syllabic pattern CV, and, in the registrations made by the children, it was observed, among other regularities, a tendency in the form of representation of the syllable nucleus. The child represented this word by writing "BI."

In this registration, the child chose grapheme I to represent the nucleus. Because the grapheme/phoneme relation of English is not very direct,[1] it is possible that the representation of words in this language is more challenging for the child (whether with the English as mother tongue or not) than words from Brazilian Portuguese, which has a more (but not totally) transparent grapheme/phoneme relationship. In the registration above, for instance, the syllable of the dictated word is formed by a vowel nucleus predominantly known by children who speak Brazilian Portuguese. However, in English orthography, this phoneme can be represented by a wide variety of graphemes. In the case of bee, the vowel nucleus /i:/ could be represented, in English, by I, EE, E, A, AE, Y, EYE, and others, while, in Brazilian Portuguese, the only conventional orthographic possibility for the representation of the vowel /i/ (vowel phoneme with more phonological features similar to /i:/, being different only by the lengthening feature, a non-distinctive feature for Brazilian Portuguese vowels) is the grapheme I.

Therefore, it is possible to notice a tendency of written registrations made through graphemes that, in the children's mother tongue, would be the only conventional orthographic possibilities for the representation of words that, in additional language, could present other graphemes. That is, when making orthographic registrations of an additional language, in this case English, children regularly look for the possibility of more frequent and familiar representation in their mother tongue. When observing this kind of tendency happening in students' writing, teachers and educators can formulate interventions in order to adapt to orthographic rules by comparing and contrasting the patterns in both students' mother tongue and additional language. We highlight the importance of understanding the possible motivations for the emergence of patterns in children's writing so that we can deal with possible orthography miscues not as problems but as a part of the process of learning an additional language.

Representation of the Coda

The next example refers to the representation of the second part of the rhyme, the coda. The example presented is the registration of the word texts (/tɛksts/).

This word is formed by the syllabic pattern CVCCCC, and, in the written registrations made by the children, it was observed, among other regularities, a tendency in the form of representation of the coda of the syllable. The child represented this word by writing "TETITITI."

In this case, the child correctly chose the graphemes TE to represent the first part of the syllable (the onset). However, they chose the graphemes TITITI to represent the coda, which does not meet the orthographic rules of the word. The syllabic pattern that forms this word, which is not present in Brazilian Portuguese, presents the greatest possible complexity in the coda, a position that, by itself, presents a big challenge for children in both languages due to the lower sound load of the phonemes that occupy their branches. The onset and nucleus of the syllable are occupied by the phonemes /tɛ/, possible and common in Brazilian Portuguese. The coda is occupied by a sequence of four consonants /ksts/, impossible in Brazilian Portuguese.

In the example presented above, the orthographic representation of the onset and the nucleus is made with the same graphemes that could be used in Brazilian Portuguese to represent these phonemes. For the coda, the representation is also made with possible and common graphemes in Brazilian Portuguese for some of the phonemes from the word. However, it is not possible for the sequence of graphemes XTS to represent the phonemes in the same syllable. Thus, the representation was made by the child using a greater number of graphemes than that of the English orthographic convention, so that, in writing, the registration could be interpreted as representing more than one syllable whose patterns are simpler (CV).

Representations such as the one exemplified above indicate a tendency of adaptation of complex and/or non-existent syllabic structures in Brazilian Portuguese, so that the registrations would be written representations that seek an adaptation to the Brazilian Portuguese phonotactic, that is, the possible sequence of phonemes for each language. In other words, when the children need to write words with more complex or even unknown syllables, they regularly look for simpler solutions, known to their mother tongue, in order to make sense of the unknown and/or more complex structure.

Teachers and educators may use the knowledge of the tendency in order to approach complex structures in English in a way that students identify the differences compared to their mother tongue and how to represent them in an accurate way in their writing. One more time, it is relevant to comprehend the process behind children's writing and the possible motivations for the format they chose to represent the words of the additional language so that they are not dealt with as mistakes, but part of the complex relationship of the languages that constitutes the children's learning process.

Idiosyncratic Representations

Different from what we exposed in the sections above, we present in this section a different kind of children's writing. The example we show in this section presents even more unusual and singular characteristics. It is an example of moments in which, only apparently, the child writes the words by using a random sequence of graphemes, for which there would be no motivation. They are what we call idiosyncratic registrations, that is, uncommon forms of written registration. In a superficial observation, this type of children's writing could be considered random, unmotivated, or, even, merely inappropriate written registrations due to lack of attention for the task. However, we do not believe that is the case. For us, these registrations enable us to see what the writer considers to be language. In these examples, it is observed that the child, when trying to write words in English, does not refer, in part or as a whole, to the syllabic structures of the words. That does not mean these writings have no motivations, though. We present, in the sequence, some possible motivations for this type of writing.

In the attempt to write the word crafts (/kræfts/), whose syllabic pattern is CCVCCC (a pattern that does not exist in the child's mother tongue), the child represented the word by writing "HHOHINOIAR." It may seem in a superficial analysis that the child chose a random sequence of graphemes that do not seem to refer to any syllabic or orthographic characteristics of the word in American English.

In this case, it is possible to observe that the sequence of graphemes selected by the child is also impossible in their mother tongue: the graphemes were selected and arranged in disagreement with the syllabic patterns and the phonotactic/orthographic rules of Brazilian Portuguese. In this case, it is possible that the attempt to write words of the English emerges in a dialogic clash characterized by an attempt to establish distance: the additional language is, for the children, something that is not possible or that is strange in their mother tongue.

This explanation becomes even more emphatic if we consider one of the graphemes that is part of this registration: the grapheme H, which was written three times by the child. In Brazilian Portuguese orthography, this grapheme has a very particular functioning, different from other graphemes. It serves, in general, to modify the value of the grapheme that precedes it, forming a digraph with it. In Brazilian Portuguese, the grapheme H can be preceded by C, N, and L, in words such as gan**ch**o (*hook*), gan**nh**o (*gain*), and gal**lh**o (*branch*), in which it represents (along with the preceding grapheme) respectively the phonemes /ʃ/, /ɲ/, and /ʎ/. Furthermore, when it emerges in isolation, at the beginning of a word, it generally does not represent any phoneme, as in the words **h**oje (*today*—[ˈɔʒi]), **h**umilde (*humble*—[uˈmiwdʒi]), and **h**iena (*hyena*—[iˈɛnɐ]). It can also appear in words of foreign origin, incorporated into the Brazilian Portuguese lexicon, representing the phoneme /r/, as with the words **H**onda and Yama**h**a.

In our perspective, it is precisely the characteristics that make this grapheme unique in the orthography of Brazilian Portuguese and, therefore, "strange" for the children, the reasons that led this child to write it three times, two of them in sequence. In their social practices of orality and literacy, children who speak and write Brazilian Portuguese are most likely affected by the functioning of the grapheme H and can, like the child who tried to write crafts in the example mentioned above, refer to this grapheme with unusual functioning to write words in American English. It is, once again, an attempt to find additional language in what is improbable and eccentric in their mother tongue and, therefore, an important asset for teacher and educator to observe when working with students who deal with the complex relationship between languages. One way educators can address this in their classrooms when working with Brazilian Portuguese speaking children learning English is to draw students' attention to the differences and confluences between the languages. It is very helpful for both educators and students to be sensitive to the relationship between languages through discussion about the characteristics of syllables, so that they are aware that languages have similarities and differences. This way, they can work with an intermingled relationship between the languages, and not just with one or the other.

Summarizing the qualitative analysis, we made of the examples presented, we can state that the tendencies in the registration of words in English made by children, speakers, and writers of Brazilian Portuguese, exemplified above, are the conflicts and confluences between Brazilian Portuguese and English. Even when the children seem to seek the most unusual aspects of their mother tongue or the greatest conflicts between it and English, the languages seem to be in a continuum of sometimes approximation and sometimes distancing, which seems to be an indication of the cross-linguistic relationship between these languages.

FINAL CONSIDERATIONS

In this chapter, examining more closely the functioning of written registrations of words in American English made by Portuguese speaking children, we could consider that the contact and insertion of a subject with/in an additional language is consistently heterogeneous and complex process. In the children's writings, we come across facts that point to the cross-linguistic relationship between Brazilian Portuguese and English. The conflicts and confluences between the two are shown in images of distance and approximation that the children maintain with languages as they work to make sense of unfamiliar language patterns drawing from their linguistic capital in their mother tongue. It was possible to observe, in these images, that what is familiar and what is foreign in the languages are intertwined as social voices that, as assumed by Silva (2015), inhabit and constitute the children's possibilities of speaking during their social practices of orality and literacy.

It is still quite common in pedagogical practices focused on additional language teaching to find strict and limiting definitions of what languages are, as pointed out by Coracini (2003). In opposition to this view, in this chapter, we sought to contribute to the strengthening of educational practices in which languages are approached as convergent and in which the heterogeneity and complexity of both the subject and the language(s) are valued.

The reflections proposed in this chapter are also relevant to the field of additional language teaching and learning, especially for American English as an additional language. The analysis of children's written registrations enables us to raise hypotheses that, in our view, contribute to a better understanding of the images constructed by children about the additional language with which they come into contact and the skillful ways students are able to draw on their linguistic resources as they are learning an additional language. Considering this understanding, it was possible to observe which aspects of learning American English are more or less complex for these children. As was pointed out by Coracini (2003, 2007), Revuz (1998), and Uyeno (2003), the contact with an additional language presents uncontrollable conflicts and confluences between the languages, and that intermingled relationship constitutes the way the children will deal with the challenges faced when writing in an additional language. Therefore, it is important to understand the functioning of languages in order to seek ways for educators to deal with such challenges in the classrooms not as problems or mere mistakes, but as part of the process. It is essential to understand the functioning of languages, especially looking at how it happens in the subject's imagination, since, as discussed by Coracini (2003), the image we picture about the foreigner (as well as the foreigner of us) is constitutive of the identity of each subject and, therefore, it is essential for the teaching and learning process. Our analysis allowed us to list at least some of the solutions sought by the child when faced with the challenge of writing an additional language and that can be taken as an asset by educators.

Finally, when the children need to write words in English, they often look for more common solutions for similar situations in their mother tongue. From our perspective, this tendency represents a great knowledge of the children about the functioning of their own mother tongue. As was further discussed by Oberst (2019), the patterns observed in the way children write words in what they imagine to be an additional language are a great source of analysis about the diverse knowledge that children have and access and that can be used as a tool throughout the complex process of learning an additional language. It is essential for the sharing and joint construction of knowledge that teachers and educators are aware of the children's mobilization of different areas of linguistic knowledge. In the process of additional language teaching and learning, understanding how the children circulate across languages, and which aspects of each language are more complex, or even which solutions are sought more frequently, can cooperate with a better way of constructing this process.

NOTE

1. More detailed studies concerning this theme can be found in Kessler and Treiman (2003).

REFERENCES

Bagno, M. (2017). *Dicionário crítico de sociolinguística*. Parábola.

Chacon, L. (in press). Erros ortográficos e características da sílaba na escrita infantil. In M. L. G. Corrêa (Org.), *Pôster acadêmico: é possível ensinar sem modelo? Produção avaliação e crítica.* Mercado de Letras.

Coracini, M. J. (2003). Língua estrangeira e língua materna: uma questão de sujeito e identidade. In M. J. Coracini (Ed.), *Identidade e discurso* (pp. 139–195). Editora da Unicamp.

Coracini, M. J. (2007). Ser/estar entre-línguas-culturas. In M. J. Coracini (Ed.), *A celebração do outro: arquivo, memória e identidade: línguas (materna e estrangeira), plurilinguísmo e tradução* (pp. 116–162). Mercado de Letras.

Hammond, M. (1999). *The phonology of English: A prosodic optimality-theoretic approach*. Oxford University Press.

Ilari, R., & Basso, R. (2006). *O português da gente: a língua que estudamos, a língua que falamos*. Contexto.

Kessler, B., & Treiman, R. (2003) Is English spelling chaotic? Misconceptions concerning its irregularity. *Reading Psychology, 24*(3–4), 267–289.

Lucchesi, D. (2015). *Língua e sociedades partidas: A polarização sociolinguística do Brasil*. Contexto.

Ministério das Relações Exteriores do Brasil. (2021). Retrieved February 23, 2022, from Comunidade brasileira no exterior https://www.gov.br/mre/pt-br/assuntos/portal-consular/arquivos/ComunidadeBrasileira2020.pdf.

Oberst, L. C. (2019). *A escrita de crianças entre línguas* [Master's dissertation, Universidade Estadual de Maringá].

Revuz, C. (1998). A língua estrangeira entre o desejo de um outro lugar e o risco do exílio. In I. Signorini (Ed.), *Língua(gem) e identidade* (pp. 213–230). Mercado de Letras.

Selkirk, E. O. (1982). The syllable. In H. Hulst & N. Smith (Eds.), *The structure of phonological representations 2* (pp. 337–383). Foris.

Selkirk, E. O. (1984). *Phonology and syntax: The relation between sound and structure.* MIT Press.

Silva, A. P. P. D. F. (2015). *BAKHTIN, Mikhail. Teoria do romance I: a estilística* (Paulo Bezerra, Trad., Serguei Botcharov e Vadim Kójinov, Orgs.). Editora 34.

Tfouni, L. V. (2010). *Letramento e alfabetização.* Cortez.

Tfouni, L. V. (2021). Letramento e autoria. *Cadernos de Linguística, 2*, 1–20.

United States Census Bureau. (2019). Retrieved February 23, 2022, from United States Census Bureau https://bit.ly/3tgwEBd.

Uyeno, E. Y. (2003). Determinações identitárias do bilinguismo: a eterna promessa da língua materna. In M. J. Coracini (Org.), *Identidade e discurso* (pp. 37–56). Editora da Unicamp.

Index

About the Contributors

Medha Bhattacharyya is assistant professor of English at Bengal Institute of Technology, Kolkata, India, and Fulbright scholar in residence at Bridgewater State University, Massachusetts, USA. In her book *Rabindranath Tagore's Śāntiniketan Essays: Religion, Spirituality and Philosophy* (2020), she offers critical insight alongside translations of *Śāntiniketan* essays by Asia's first Nobel laureate. Other research interests include Canadian Studies, Translation Studies, Religion, Creative Writing, ESL, and South Asia and Diaspora Studies.

Cristiane Carneiro Capristano is a post-doctorate from the University of São Paulo (USP), doctorate in Applied Linguistics from the State University of Campinas (UNICAMP), master's in Linguistic Studies, and graduation in languages (Portuguese/Italian) from the São Paulo State University Júlio de Mesquita Filho (UNESP). She is currently an associate professor at the State University of Maringá (UEM), part of the Department of Linguistic and Literary Theories and of the Postgraduate Program in Languages (PLE-UEM).

Xia Chao is associate professor of language and literacy education in the School of Education at Duquesne University. Dr Chao's research has been funded by the Spencer Foundation and the National Geographic Society. Her research has appeared in peer-reviewed journals including *Anthropology and Education Quarterly*, *Journal of Early Childhood Literacy*, *Teacher Education Quarterly*, and so on.

Eric B. Claravall is an assistant professor of Literacy and Special at California State University, Sacramento. His research work focuses on the intersection of cognition, instruction, literacy/language development, and decolonizing pedagogy. Dr Claravall is a multilingual speaker. Aside from English, he speaks Filipino, Ilonggo, Spanish, and French. He received his undergraduate and graduate degrees in psychology at the University of the Philippines, Diliman. He went on to study literacy and educational leadership and received his graduate degrees at the University of Massachusetts, Lowell, and San Francisco State University.

Kinji Ito is an assistant professor of Japanese at Appalachian State University. He has published chapters and articles on supporting language learners through oral corrective feedback, translation, and technology. Ito devotes his time to building positive student–teacher relationships to aid his students in pursuing their academic goals. He received a mentor award from the Japan Commerce Association of Washington, D.C., in 2018 and 2021.

Lyudmyla Ivanyuk is an assistant professor in the Education Department at Trinity Christian College, Palos Heights, Illinois, where she teaches courses in literacy education. She has taught English as a second language to Russian and Ukrainian speakers at Kyiv National Linguistic University in Ukraine for four years and to international students at two American universities for four and a half years.

Jieun Kiaer is a professor of Korean Linguistics at the University of Oxford. She publishes widely on lexical interaction between East Asian languages and English. Her recent publications include: *The History of English Loanwords in Korean* (Lincom 2014), *Translingual Words: An East Asian Lexical Encounter with English* (Routledge 2018), and *Delicious Words* (Routledge 2020).

Fanny Macé is an assistant professor at Concordia University in Montreal. She is interested in researching French Applied Linguistics and Assessment, mainly French vocabulary. Her second field of expertise is French sociolinguistics, particularly the issues of minorities' identity. One of her latest research projects dealt with teachers' retention and recruitment in Alberta's FSL and French Immersion Programs.

Hanh thi Nguyen is a professor in the TESOL Program, Department of English and Applied Linguistics, at Hawaii Pacific University. She is the coeditor of *Pragmatics of Vietnamese as Native and Target language* (2013) and has published several papers on Vietnamese phonology, pragmatics, wordplay, and social interaction. Her research interests include Vietnamese applied linguistics, interactional competence development, and classroom discourse.

Hoan Nguyen is an MA candidate in the Department of Second Language Studies at the University of Hawaii at Manoa. She is currently conducting a study on the processing of Vietnamese classifiers using eye-tracking technology. Her research interests include Vietnamese applied linguistics, child second language acquisition, second language processing, and bilingualism.

Lisley Camargo Oberst is a master's in Linguistic Studies from the State University of Maringá (PLE/UEM). She graduated in languages with a single qualification in English from the State University of Maringá (UEM). She researches in the area of language teaching and learning, with emphasis on the relationship between mother tongue and foreign language and writing acquisition. She is currently an English teacher for primary school.

Gabriela Tellez-Osorno is a high-school Spanish teacher who teaches heritage Spanish classes, Spanish as foreign language classes, as well as AVID classes. **Maria José Solis** is a dual language bilingual elementary school teacher who teaches in a second-grade Spanish-English dual language classroom. Both Gabi and Maria José serve as advocates for students and families, scholars invested in supporting Latina/o/x students, and both give back to supporting their fellow bilingual scholars as mentors.

Huy Phung is a PhD candidate in the Department of Second Language Studies at the University of Hawaii at Manoa and will be a lecturer of Vietnamese in the Heritage Language Program in the Department of Linguistics at the University of California San Diego. He has published papers on task-based interaction and multilingual motivation in a second language. His research interests include Vietnamese applied linguistics, project-based language learning, task-based instruction, and second language acquisition.

Kristen L. Pratt is an assistant professor of English for Speakers of Other Languages (ESOL) and bilingual education at Western Oregon University; researches the intersections of language, race, and education with a focus on equitable access to opportunity. Her research has appeared in: *The Journal of Language, Identity and Education; Bilingual Education Research Journal*; and *Linguistics and Education.*

Yvonne Pratt-Johnson, Ed.D., is a professor of Education (TESOL) at St. John's University. She is a four-time recipient of Fulbright-Hays Grants for study abroad programs she directed and developed. Pratt-Johnson has led trips to West Bengal, Bangladesh, and other sites on which teachers acquired knowledge and skills to practice culturally and linguistically informed pedagogy. Other research interests include language acquisition, literacy development, teaching linguistically and culturally diverse students, and equity in education.

Maria Selena Protacio is a professor of Literacy Studies and Teaching English to Speakers of Other Languages (TESOL) at Western Michigan University in Kalamazoo, Michigan. She has conducted qualitative studies in the Philippines and with Filipino American families. Prior to arriving in the United States for her graduate degrees from University of Nebraska-Lincoln and Michigan State University, Dr Protacio was a secondary English and literature teacher in the Philippines.

Sylvie Roy is a professor at Werklund School of Education at the University of Calgary. Her field of study comprises sociolinguistics for change, teaching and learning second and additional languages, ethnography, and discourse analysis. She wrote a book called *French Immersion Ideologies in Canada* from Lexington Books in 2020.

Eliane Rubinstein-Avila is a professor in Teaching, Learning & Sociocultural Studies, College of Education, University of Arizona. Professor Rubinstein-Avila immigrated to the United States in the early 1980s. She completed a doctorate degree in Human Development with an emphasis in language and literacy at Harvard Graduate School of Education (2001). Her research spans several topics, from immigrant/bilingual education to local attitudes toward minoritized languages. She has lived in several geo and sociopolitical contexts—including the middle east. She speaks a few languages, and her main passions are traveling and learning.

Alaa Mohammed M. Shakoori is a lecturer at Umm Al Qura University in Saudi Arabia, where she teaches English courses to Arabic ELLs. She also has some experience as a high-school English teacher. She has a master's degree in TESOL from Seattle University and a doctorate degree in Language, Reading & Culture from University of Arizona. Her research interests focus on ESL teaching and assessment.

Kwangok Song is an associate professor of Literacy Education at the University of Kansas. Her research concerns bilingual and biliteracy practices in immigrant families and communities. Her recent work published in *International Journal of Bilingual Education and Bilingualism* addressed Korean-speaking English learners' reading strategies in online reading.

Bogum Yoon is a professor of literacy education at the State University of New York at Binghamton. Her research areas include cultural and linguistic pluralism and critical global literacies. She brings a critical lens and practical tools to help educators understand social and political contexts of education, as well as to act as agents for change. Dr Yoon's recent book, *Effective Teacher Collaboration for English Language Learners*, promotes collaborative partnerships between ESL and content area teachers for multilingual learners' equitable learning opportunities.

Rahat Zaidi is a Werklund research professor and chair of Language & Literacy at the Werklund School of Education, University of Calgary, Canada. She has published a number of critical works regarding cultural diversity and language pedagogy. Her research expertise focuses on multilingual literacies that clarify intersectional understandings across sociophobia, diversity, immigration, and pluralism. Through her research, she advances social justice and equity and identity positioning in immigrant and transcultural contexts.